KU-546-494

Six Billion Plus

Human Geography in the New Millennium
Issues and Applications

Series Editor
Barney Warf, Florida State University

Human geography is increasingly focused on real-world problems. Applying geographic concepts to current global concerns, this series focuses on the urgent issues confronting us as we move into the new century. Designed for university-level geography and related multidisciplinary courses such as area studies, global issues, and development, these textbooks are richly illustrated and include suggestions for linking to related Internet resources. The series aims to help students to better understand, integrate, and apply common themes and linkages in the social and physical sciences and in the humanities, and, by doing so, to become more effective problem solvers in the challenging world they will face.

Six Billion Plus

Population Issues in the Twenty-first Century

K. Bruce Newbold

ROWMAN & LITTLEFIELD PUBLISHERS, INC.
Lanham • Boulder • New York • Oxford

ROWMAN & LITTLEFIELD PUBLISHERS, INC.

Published in the United States of America
by Rowman & Littlefield Publishers, Inc.
An Imprint of the Rowman & Littlefield Publishing Group
4720 Boston Way, Lanham, Maryland 20706
www.rowmanlittlefield.com

12 Hid's Copse Road, Cumnor Hill, Oxford OX2 9JJ, England

Copyright © 2002 by Rowman & Littlefield Publishers, Inc.

All rights reserved. No part of this publication may be reproduced, stored in a retrieval system,
or transmitted in any form or by any means, electronic, mechanical, photocopying, recording,
or otherwise, without the prior permission of the publisher.

British Library Cataloguing in Publication Information Available

Library of Congress Cataloging-in-Publication Data
Newbold, K. Bruce, 1964–
    Six billion plus : population issues in the twenty-first century / K.
Bruce Newbold.
        p.   cm. — (Human geography in the new millennium)
    Includes bibliographical references and index.
    ISBN 0-7425-1616-4 (cloth : alk. paper) — ISBN 0-7425-1617-2 (pbk. :
alk. paper)
        1. Population forecasting.   2. Population geography.   3.
Population—Environmental aspects.   4. Public health—Forecasting.   5.
Social prediction.   6. Twenty-first century—Forecasts.   I. Title. II.
Series.
HB849.53 .N484   2002
363.9—dc21   2002001947

Printed in the United States of America

⊗ ™ The paper used in this publication meets the minimum requirements of American
National Standard for Information Sciences—Permanence of Paper for Printed Library
Materials, ANSI/NISO Z39.48-1992.

To Blake and James

Contents

Introduction

⟨✦⟩

The World of Child Six Billion

THE LIFE AND DEATH OF
CHILD SIX BILLION

October 1999 saw the birth of child six billion. While some marked the event, it was not necessarily greeted with enthusiasm. After all, the latest billion people had been added to the world's population in just fourteen years, with an additional eighty-three million souls being added each year. Not all agree that population growth is a problem, but there is consensus that the world's population cannot continue to grow indefinitely, as it places increasing pressure on the earth's resources and the ability of states to govern. Little wonder that fears of resource scarcity, environmental degradation, and ethnic, religious, or racial conflicts as an outcome of rapid population growth often dominate discussions of national and international security around the globe.

The world and future that child six billion inherits will likely depend upon where he was born. Although he may have been born in one of the developed countries of North America, Europe, Japan, Australia, or New Zealand, it is more likely that he was born in one of the economically developing countries, which now represent over 80 percent of the world's population and where 98 percent of the world's population growth is now occurring. Put in another perspective, of the eighty-three million children born each year, only one million are born in the developed, industrialized countries, leading the Population Reference Bureau (PRB) to conclude that the twenty-first century will feature a major transformation of the world's population.[1] Child six billion likely faces a rather bleak future if born in the developing world, where health, war, famine, disease, resource scarcity, and environmental degradation are, more often than not, rules rather than exceptions.

In fact, simply surviving infancy and childhood is uncertain. Although large gains in life expectancy and mortality reduction have been made in the past century, there are still widespread disparities. In developed countries[2] the **infant mortality rate**

1

(IMR), which is the number of deaths of infants less than one year of age per one thousand births, was eight, which compares to a world average of fifty-six in 2001. The hardships are scarcely over if child six billion survives his first year of life. Life expectancy at birth, which measures the number of years an individual is expected to live, averaged seventy-five years in developed countries, but only sixty-four in developing countries. In the developing world, 9 percent of children die before they reach age five compared to only 1 percent in the developed world. Some of the poorest indicators are found in sub-Saharan Africa, where the infant mortality rate is ninety-four, individuals can expect to live an average of fifty-one years from birth, and 15 percent of children die before they reach the age of five. But one does not have to travel far to see these conditions: Haiti is the poorest country in the Americas and Caribbean, reflected in an IMR of eighty, a life of expectancy of forty-nine years, and some 12 percent of children dying before the age of five.

To some degree these variations reflect long-term factors, including development and the ability of governments to support health care initiatives. Poverty reinforces poor health by limiting adequate nutritional intake, access to medicines, sanitation, and shelter. War, refugee movements, and simple geographic interaction across space perpetuate poor health and disease. But the high rates of mortality in sub-Saharan Africa and elsewhere also increasingly reflect the rise of infectious diseases, primarily **HIV/AIDS**. The African continent has been particularly hard hit by this epidemic, with an estimated 70 percent of the world's HIV/AIDS population living in sub-Saharan Africa. According to recent reports, the infection rate now approaches one in four among adults.[3] Yet, the epidemic is only a portion of larger health problems and issues in the developing world. Although large improvements in the health of the general population and infant survival rates have been recorded within the past fifty years, infectious and parasitic diseases, including measles, malaria, and cholera, remain the leading causes of death in the developing world. Rapid population growth makes it difficult for governments to keep up with the demand not only for new health care resources, but to maintain what is already present. Poverty, particularly at the household level, has clear implications for health and life expectancy, since it is often associated with illiteracy, poor nutrition, poor sanitation, unsafe drinking water, and crowding, creating an environment that promotes illness.

Health issues aside, the world that child six billion inherits is one that is likely to be scarred by war, resource scarcity, or environmental degradation. Clearly, the collective impact of six billion upon the world's environment and resources is large, and increasing as the population continues to place additional demands on resources, whether for basic survival or advanced consumer durables. Although this appears to be a relatively straightforward comment, there is much disagreement over the association among population, resource, and environmental issues. The reality is that the benefits and costs of population growth occupy some middle ground among these different perspectives. Moreover, it is reasonable to assume that many of the stresses of rapid population growth are closely linked to poverty, educational attainment, health, and the status of women. Rapid population growth will stress forest and agricultural land, potentially leading to the loss of cropland through over-grazing and land degradation, limiting access to safe drinking water, and threatening water resources. This is not to say that population growth is solely responsible for these problems, as they are facilitated by poor conservation practices or lax environmental regulations and pollution. Likewise, environmental degradation is a function not only of the number of people but of how much they consume and how their consumption alters the environment and existing political systems.

It is also reasonable to assume that environmental scarcity will increasingly be reflected in national and international conflicts.[4] While not yet a significant factor in the generation of violence, resource scarcity contributes to political instability. For those living in a developed country, it is easy to forget and dismiss that the well-being of a majority of the world's population remains tied to local natural resources for food, energy, and income. Consequently, conflicts stemming from scarcities of cropland, water, and forests in the developing world may become increasingly common in the near future, affecting the developed world through trade and economic linkages, humanitarian involvement, and migrant or refugee flows.

The importance of this line of argument is to realize the multiple interconnections with population, such as that it underlies many resource or environmental issues. There is, for example, a large potential for violence related to resource scarcity and population issues, with local ethnic conflict or civil strife surrounding access and control of resources a likely outcome of resource scarcity.[5] The reality is that the new face of war will often be a struggle for power and resources within a country or group of countries, often between opposing groups and ideologies. The uprising of Zapatista insurgents in Chiapas, Mexico, in the late 1990s was caused by rapid population growth, inequities in land distribution, and changes in laws governing access to the land. The violence in Chiapas further destabilized Mexico's government and economy, and the resulting devaluation of Mexico's peso caused deep-seated concern within America's financial markets. Conflict in Afghanistan between the Islamic extremist Taliban and the Northern Alliance or recent conflicts in Fiji and Indonesia also represent ethnic and religious tensions between groups. In the former, religious ideology underlies the Taliban's struggle for power, but quickly becomes a conflict that could spread to Pakistan and other neighbors that share similar religious goals.[6] In the latter case, the conflict reflects a history of forced migrations (Indians to Fiji under British rule and Muslim Indonesians out of Java) and the failure of subsequent governments to erase differences between the groups.[7] Alternatively, the new face of war will be one against terrorism in light of the events of September 11, 2001.

Although less likely, violence relating to resource scarcity and population growth may also include large-scale violence created by the growing gap between haves and have-nots, which can be defined at the international, national, and regional scales. Although such conflict might typically be cast as the developed versus developing worlds, conflict between these two groups is less likely than regional conflicts within or between developing nations. The Middle East provides a ready example of the linkage between population, resource scarcity, and the potential for conflict in the form of water rights or other resources including oil, gas, and minerals.[8]

In the past, population pressures could be relieved through voluntary emigration, just as North America and Oceania were settled at a time of rapid population growth within Europe. For child six billion, however, legal immigration options are scarce. Most developed countries tightly control immigration, often restricting entry to those who qualify under specific labor programs, "family preference," or "family reunification" guidelines. Most developed countries also actively promote the entry of individuals who are able to invest in the host country or carry the education or skills that are demanded by developed countries. Yet, there is also a subtle but rising tide of anti-immigrant sentiments, particularly in European countries. Unlike Australia, Canada, New Zealand, or the United States, all of which partially see themselves as "nations of immigrants," European concerns with immigration and national identity have increased, provoking strong right-wing responses. Despite their immigration histories, the United States and Canada are not all that dissimilar, with recent calls to limit **immigrant** intake.

While the movement of legal immigrants is not inconsequential, **illegal immigrants** and refugees dominate the international movement of people. For those seeking a better life elsewhere, illegal immigration may be a desperate, but their only, option. The desperation of some is evidenced by the risky and potentially deadly methods they choose to enter countries, including paying smugglers, traveling through the Channel Tunnel between France and Britain in the undercarriage of trains,[9] or being smuggled aboard ships while living in cargo crates for weeks on end. The smuggling of human cargo, with Chinese "snakeheads" or Mexican "coyotes" assisting individuals in entering a country illegally, has boomed, even though it usually comes with a steep price that indentures the individual for years to come. Some reports indicate that snakeheads are now charging upward of $65,000(U.S.) to smuggle a person into the United States or Canada and provide them with fake identification.[10]

Exemplified by the saga of Mariel Cubans, Indochinese boat people and recent events in Afghanistan, Rwanda, and Kosovo, **refugees** and displaced populations have become an increasingly visible issue. Defined by the United Nations, refugees are persons who are outside their country of nationality and are unable to return owing to fear of persecution for reason of race, religion, nationality, and association in a social or political group.[11] Major refugee producing countries at the turn of the millennium included Rwanda, Iraq, Afghanistan, Somalia, Bosnia-Herzegovina, Kosovo, Liberia, and Sierra Leone. Together, it is estimated that some 7.2 million individuals were displaced from these countries alone.[12] Overall, the United Nations High Commission on Refugees (**UNHCR**) estimated that there were more than fourteen million refugees worldwide in 1997.[13] It is unlikely that child six billion will grow to see these numbers decline, and in fact may become a refugee himself, as ethnic, religious, environmental, or political conflicts increase. Refugees also face a world that increasingly rejects them, as governments fear economic, political, and social instability brought by the arrival of refugees, and Western governments react to the terrorist attacks of September 11, 2001, by tightening refugee admission policies. Instead, those who are displaced are likely to become internally displaced persons (IDPs), individuals who are forced to relocate within their own countries. By the late 1990s, they were estimated to total over twenty-seven million. This group is not protected by international law and has little access to assistance.

TRENDS IN POPULATION GROWTH

How did we get to six billion? How quickly is the population growing? Where or when does population growth end? In order to answer these questions, we must look at historical and current trends associated with population growth. For much of humanity's history, population growth was slow. High birthrates were offset by high death rates from famine, war, and epidemics. It is estimated, for example, that the bubonic plague reduced the populations of Europe and China by one-third in the fourteenth century.[14] Beginning in the 1600s, the world's population started to grow, as life expectancy slowly increased with improvements in commerce, food production, and nutrition. Even by 1800, the world's population was only one billion, but the nineteenth century would bring a surge in population growth, particularly in what we now refer to as the developed countries. From 1800 to 1900, the population of Europe doubled, and North America's population multiplied by twelve, fueled by European immigration.[15] The population of developing countries grew more slowly, but they already held the bulk of the world's population. By 1900, world population was approximately 1.7 billion, increasing to 2 billion by 1930. The mid-twentieth century saw unprecedented population growth, with the world's population reaching three billion by 1960, growing to four billion by 1974. The fifth billion was reached just twelve years later, and by 2000, the total population exceeded six billion.

Accompanying the world's population explosion has been the explosion in the size and number of **urban** areas globally. Currently, approximately 46 percent of the world's population lives in urban areas. While the developing world lags the developed world in the proportion urbanized (40 percent to 75 percent, respectively), the urban population in the developing world is expected to grow rapidly in the coming decades, with upward of 55 percent of the world's population living in urban areas by 2025.[16] Placing urban growth in another perspective, the number of cites in the developing world with populations in excess of one million will jump from 250 in 1995 to 426 by 2015. The number of megacities (cities with populations in excess of ten million) has also grown from eight in 1985 to nineteen by 2000 and is projected to grow to thirty-four by 2015. Most of these new **megacities** will be in the developing world, and megacities will be home to an increasing proportion of the world's population. Indeed, only seven of these megacities (London, Los Angeles, Moscow, New York, Osaka, Paris, and Tokyo) will be in the developed world.[17] The growth of urban areas, driven by natural increase,[18] net rural to urban migration, and urban reclassification provides the raw ingredients for conflict.

The **population explosion** in Western countries during the 1800s marked the beginning of the shift from high to low mortality and high to low fertility, known to demographers as the demographic transition, and formalized by the **demographic transition theory (DTT).** Although the concept of demographic transition can be roughly applied to all countries, with a decline in **mortality rates** followed by an eventual decline in **fertility rates,** the timing, pace, and triggers of the transition will vary. Within the **developed world,** these shifts in mortality and fertility occurred in the later parts of the nineteenth and early twentieth centuries, with major health improvements leading to a decline in infant mortality rates and increased life expectancy. Fertility rates were somewhat slower to change since social and behavioral change defining the desired family size tend to be slower, but fell rapidly after 1900 as more children survived to adulthood, marriage patterns changed, women moved into paid work, and parents placed greater value on the education their children received. In the United States, the **total fertility rate (TFR),** which is the average number of children a woman would have, given prevailing birthrates, dropped from an average of four or five children in 1900 to approximately two children per woman by the 1930s. Canadian and European rates followed a similar pattern.

The most important determinants of population growth are the pretransition fertility rate along with the time lag between the decline in mortality and fertility. Even as mortality and fertility rates in the developed world stabilized and low and stable rates of population growth were realized, much of Africa, Asia, and Latin America was still experiencing relatively high mortality and fertility levels. Since the Second World War, rapid population growth has largely occurred in the developing world when mortality rates were reduced dramatically with the introduction of modern medicines including antibiotics and immunizations. As countries in the **developing world** started their demographic transition, they frequently had higher levels of birth- and death rates than those observed in developed countries a century earlier, with fertility rates in many countries continuing to average more than six children per woman. Fertility reduction in the developing world was also slower than that experienced in the developed world (i.e., the lag between the decline in mortality and fertility was longer). Instead, it varied across countries, defined by differences in social, cultural, and religious expectations; literacy rates; female participation in the workforce; family and economic considerations; and the availability and acceptability of family planning programs. Rates of **natural increase** (the birthrate minus the death rate, indicating the annual rate of population growth) remain high in much of the developing world.

At the dawn of the twenty-first century, there was some evidence that the developing world was finally transitioning from high to low fertility, evidenced by a 2001 TFR of 3.2 (3.6 if China is excluded), a rate that is considerably lower than that observed just a quarter of a century earlier.[19] With the expectation that fertility rates will continue to decline, some analysts have concluded that the risk of population growth has been greatly diminished.[20] While the world's population growth rate peaked in the 1960s and started to decline slowly thereafter as fertility levels started to fall, the population is still rapidly expanding. But the perspective of population decline is a Western-centered one, ignoring growth rates and the potential for growth through **population momentum** in the developing world. The current fertility rate of 3.2 in the developing world translates to a growth rate of 1.6 percent (1.9 percent excluding China). This allows the population in the developing world to double in approximately forty-three years (assuming growth continues at its current rates), or thirty-six years if China is excluded. Even as fertility rates have dropped to 2.7 in Asia and 2.8 in Latin America and the Caribbean, they remain stubbornly high in Africa, with a 2001 TFR of 5.2. Moreover, in countries where fertility rates have dropped quickly, the young age structure of the population will ensure growth for the next two to three decades. Put another way, a huge proportion of the world's population have not started having children. Instead, they *are* children. Consequently, a total world population of 7.5 billion by 2025 cannot be avoided, and most projections place world population between 7.3 and 10.7 billion by 2050, with nearly all of this growth occurring in the developing world (table I.1).

The certainty of continued growth is grounded in three assumptions. First, improvements in **life expectancy** (reduced mortality) will contribute to population growth, as individuals survive longer. Longer life expectancies increase a child's likelihood of surviving infancy and childhood and completing his or her reproductive years. Second, the age structure of a population is key to the expected future growth, with populations having a greater number of individuals in their childbearing years tending to grow faster, irrespective of the fertility rate. Women may have fewer children than in the past, but there are more women having children today. Excluding China, which has seen a shift in its age structure associated with its one-child policy, 36 percent of the population in the developing world is less than fifteen years old. In sub-Saharan Africa, 44 percent of the population is aged less than fifteen years. In comparison, only 18 percent of the population in the developed world is less than fifteen years old, a proportion that continues to decline. The young age profile of the developing world means that this population still has to enter their reproductive years. Even if fertility rates decline, population momentum will ensure sustained population growth. Third, most demographers expect that fertility rates will eventually decline below the replacement level, ending the population explosion. Yet, fertility rates continue to remain above replacement in many regions of the world. Declines have been noted, but it is unknown whether further declines in fertility can be expected, with recent surveys in both Bangladesh and Egypt pointing to the danger in assuming that fertility will continue to drop. Despite early successes in reducing fertility in Bangladesh, with fertility rates dropping from over 6 children per woman in the early 1970s to 3.3 in 2001, fertility rates have remained relatively unchanged through the 1990s. Similarly, Egypt's birthrate has remained at approximately 3.5 since 1993. This trend is far from isolated, with Argentina's birthrate remaining at about three children for nearly 50 years.[21]

Table I.1   Current Population Statistics by Selected World Regions, 2001

	Population Mid-2001 (millions)	Total Fertility Rate	Natural Increase (annual %)	Doubling Time (years)	Projected Population 2025 (millions)
World	6,137	2.8	1.3	51	7,818
North America	316	2.0	0.5	124	382
Central America	138	3.1	2.1	33	190
South America	350	2.6	1.6	42	462
Caribbean	37	2.6	1.3	52	46
Oceania	31	2.5	1.1	65	40
Northern Europe	96	1.6	0.1	653	102
Western Europe	184	1.6	0.1	612	189
Eastern Europe	303	1.2	−0.5	—	287
Southern Europe	145	1.3	0.0	2,121	139
Asia (excludes China)	2,447	3.2	1.7	40	3,283
Asia (includes China)	3,720	2.7	1.4	46	4,714
Western Asia	193	3.9	2.1	33	299
South Central Asia	1,505	3.4	1.8	37	2,061
South East Asia	519	2.8	1.6	41	685
East Asia	1,503	1.8	0.8	85	1,669
Sub-Saharan Africa	673	5.6	2.5	29	1,067
Northern Africa	177	3.6	2.1	34	251
Western Africa	240	5.8	2.7	25	393
Eastern Africa	252	5.7	2.5	29	398
Middle Africa	99	6.6	2.9	23	183
Southern Africa	50	3.1	1.3	52	42

Source: Population Reference Bureau, World Population Data Sheet, 2001.
Note: Present rates of natural increases are likely to change, affecting the doubling time.
(—) indicates data not available or applicable.

As of mid-2001, the world's population was estimated at 6,137 million. With approximately 82,000 births per year, the world's growth rate is currently 1.3 percent per year, meaning it will take just fifty-three years to double the current population, assuming a constant rate of natural increase. **Doubling times** are shorter in much of Africa, averaging just twenty-eight years. Within developed countries and given a growth rate of 0.1 percent, it will take an estimated 809 years for the population to double. Obviously, pronounced differences in population growth and structure separate the developed and developing world, resulting in an unevenly distributed population across the globe. The geographic distribution is becoming more unbalanced. Rapid population growth in the second half of the twentieth century has meant that the share of the world's population residing in the developing world climbed from 68 to 80 percent. Regionally, North America and Europe represent only 17 percent of the current population. According to United Nations projections, the percentage residing in the developing world will grow to 88 percent by 2050 (figure I.1).

Figure I.1.   World Population Distribution by Major Region, 2001.

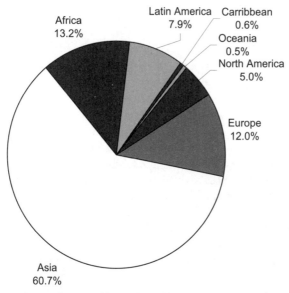

Source: Population Reference Bureau, World Data Sheet, 2001.

These averages tend to hide more local patterns of mortality, fertility, and growth rates. Demographers refer to a TFR of 2.1 as **replacement fertility,** or the number of children needed to exactly replace their parents' generation, accounting for premature death. While many developing countries in Asia still have above-replacement TFRs, China, South Korea, Taiwan, and Thailand have fertility levels lower than replacement. China is, in fact, an important exception. With a population of 1,273.3 million in mid-2001and an annual growth rate of 0.9 percent, China is the world's most populous country. Despite fertility levels that exceeded 7.0 and recorded as recently as the 1950s, its fertility rate has plunged to below replacement level. This low level of population growth has been largely attributed to its restrictive one child policy, which has artificially lowered fertility levels. India, too, has attempted fertility control policies, but has had much less success. Although it has a smaller population (1,033 million), India is growing at a rate of 1.7 percent, meaning it will likely surpass China's population by the middle of the twenty-first century. Progress in fertility reduction is echoed in improved measures of life expectancy and infant mortality. In other parts of Asia, there has been little decrease in fertility in Iraq and Pakistan or a leveling off after a decline in India. In Africa, the transition to a lower fertility regime is just beginning. Fertility rates exceed 6.0 TFR in countries including Congo, Eritrea, Somalia, Burundi, Niger, and Sierra Leone, and there is little evidence that a downward shift in fertility is about to occur. Throughout much of Africa, infant mortality rates remain high (88 per 1,000) and life expectancies are short (fifty-four years). In contrast, most developed countries are experiencing slow growth or even population decline, long life expectancies, and low infant mortality rates.

GEOGRAPHIC PERSPECTIVES
AND DIRECTIONS

Despite attempts to cull some sense of order from population theories, such as the demographic transition theory, the role of space within the study of population has frequently been misplaced. Transition theory, for example, has been soundly criticized for its Western-centered insights into fertility decline. More important, it did not recognize the role of place and culture, with the model providing a weak explanation at best when applied to the different social, political, and economic circumstances of Asia, Africa, or Latin America. By effectively discounting the role of space and place, only modest claims can be made with transition theory to explain demographic processes.[22]

The diversity of population as a subject makes such generalizations difficult. Although the study of population is interdisciplinary in scope, with contributions by sociologists, economists, and anthropologists, the geographic perspective is especially valuable. Geography, by its nature, offers an integrative framework through which to view population (or other) issues. The disciplinary concerns of geography—space, regional variations, diffusion, place, and their role in human and natural processes—provide this unique framework for looking at population issues. Space is not a unique concern to geography, and geographers do not deal exclusively with space, but it is understanding spatial processes, such as the diffusion of ideas associated with small families or birth control techniques, that is of interest. Whether we are interested in population issues related to fertility or immigration, spatial processes are implied as states and their governments alter the demographic makeup of nations through policies related to, for example, immigration or families. Similarly, economic systems will determine fertility behavior, and the mortality of populations and environmental crises related to pollution, deforestation, and water scarcity provide examples of the linkage between regions. These are also dynamic processes, changing over time and across the landscape, and a geographical approach enables the explanation of past, present, and future relationships and patterns.

The geographic literature dealing with population issues has a relatively short, but rich, history. Initially defined in the 1950s, population geography dealt with the geographic character of places.[23] In its infancy, population geography was content to describe the location of a population and its characteristics and to explain the spatial configuration of these numbers. The field of population geography has since grown to draw upon a multiplicity of methods and theoretical approaches. Most writers and researchers now place population within a broader context, recognizing the importance of place and drawing upon the diverse insights provided by geography and related social science disciplines. The diversity of conceptual approaches provided by geography provides a framework through which to view complex phenomena. Economic and cultural geography provide insight into fertility choices, which may reflect the economic needs of the family, including a trade-off between children as labor or "pensions" and the ability to provide an education, or the larger cultural expectations of society. Similarly, political, social, and cultural geography provide insight into the potential for conflict by bridging disparate issues, enabling the recognition of the interrelationships between resources, environment, politics, and policy within the realm of population geography.

CHAPTER STRUCTURE AND AIMS

What does the twenty-first century hold for child six billion and his contemporaries? Will the population explosion result in a scarcity of resources or resource degradation? Why does fertility and mortality vary over time and space? What is responsible for large-scale population movements? While an understanding of demographic issues such as changes in death rates or declines in fertility may simply come from a need-to-know perspective, they cannot be viewed in isolation. Instead, they must be linked to broader issues that shape the economic, political, and cultural environments around us. Nor can they be viewed in geographical isolation. Although it tends to be overlooked, population growth in the developing world directly and indirectly influences the developed world daily through such avenues as immigration policies, trade and economic decisions, and disease patterns.

The primary purpose of this book is to uncover, illustrate, and understand population issues from a geographical perspective. The book relies upon a mix of historical and contemporary perspectives and issues to ground the discussion and illuminate potential problems or issues that are only now emerging, with the intent that it will stimulate the reader to inquire and read further. The book will provide an overview of the themes of fertility, mortality, population movement, HIV/AIDS, and resource conflict within the geographical perspective, revealing the interdependencies inherent within the study of population. In large part, the book represents a synthesis of perspectives, approaches, and the current literature viewed from the geographical perspective. It is also meant to provide an international outlook, rather than relying upon the experiences of the United States alone, which would provide a far too narrow perspective of population issues. Rather than providing a how-to on the mechanics of population research, each chapter identifies and focuses on salient trends and specific issues relevant to each of the themes.[24] Each chapter concludes with a discussion of emergent themes and issues relevant to the theme of the chapter.

Chapter 1 will assess current fertility trends and issues in the developing and developed world. The chapter discusses fertility behavior as it is linked to a broad variety of social, cultural, and economic issues at the micro (individual) level along with broader macro (i.e., nationalism, economic, aging) issues. The other end of our life spectrum is captured in chapter 2, which discusses two major issues in mortality and morbidity. The first issue focuses on the reemergence of infectious and parasitic diseases as challenges to population health in both the developed and developing world. Second, notions of equity, discrimination, and marginalization within modern society are considered by looking at the mortality experiences of African Americans in the United States, Aboriginals in Canada, and males in Russia. Building upon these issues, chapter 3 focuses upon the HIV/AIDS crisis in Africa, the emerging crisis in other world regions, and the demographic, social, and economic implications of this disease. The demographic toll that this epidemic is extracting from countries in Africa endangers their future economic development and national security. As such, it can therefore be seen as a case study of infectious diseases.

Chapters 4 and 5 explore the inherently geographical but complicated issues of immigration and refugee movements. Chapter 4 will provide a brief historical overview of international migration before focusing upon national immigration policies and the conflicting demographic and economic benefits/costs of immigration. Drawn from a largely Western perspective, the discussion will address the emerging anti-immigrant sentiments found within Western countries. Chapter 5 focuses upon refugee movements and the internally displaced population, the processes that generate these movements, and the response by other countries. Both chapters will examine the geographical patterns of movement within these groups, the reasons for movement, and government policies.

Chapters 6 and 7 focus upon the linkages between population growth, resource scarcity, economic development, environmental degradation, and the potential for conflict. Although the linkages between population change and broader issues will be apparent in most chapters, the intent is to draw together ideas from previous chapters and evaluate their relationships with broader socioeconomic and sociopolitical issues. In particular, these chapters are meant to gaze further into the twenty-first century, distilling possible relationships. In particular, chapter 6 focuses on the linkages between population growth, resource scarcity, and economic opportunities, with reference to the conflicting viewpoints. Chapter 7 draws upon current examples of national and international conflict and reveals their linkages to population issues. The chapter will also consider where (and why) it is likely that conflicts will increasingly find their roots in population issues. Finally, the conclusion summarizes this book by distilling the preceding discussion into the five demographic forces that will shape the world.

NOTES

1. *World Population Data Sheet* (Washington, D.C.: Population Reference Bureau, 2001). Unless noted otherwise, population statistics throughout this book are drawn from this source.

2. Following UN classification, the developed world includes Europe, North America, Australia, Japan, and New Zealand. The developing world includes all countries and regions outside the developed world.

3. AIDS Epidemic Update: December 2000, UNAIDS, <http://www.unaids.org/epidemic_update/report_dec00/index_dec.html> (14 Feb. 2001).

4. Thomas F. Homer-Dixon, *Environment, Scarcity, and Violence* (Princeton, N.J.: Princeton University Press, 1999).

5. Homer-Dixon, *Environment*.

6. Roger W. Stump, *Boundaries of Faith* (Lanham, Md.: Rowman & Littlefield, 2000) for a discussion of the Taliban, their religious movement, and implications for the region.

7. Jana Mason, *Shadow Plays: The Crisis of Refugees and IDPs in Indonesia* (Washington, D.C.: U.S. Committee for Refugees, 2001).

8. Hussein Amery and Aaron T. Wolf, eds., *Water in the Middle East: A Geography of Conflict* (Austin: University of Texas Press, 2000).

9. Suzanne Daley, "Channel Tunnel's Risks Defied for a Dream of Life in Britain," *New York Times*, 15 March 2001, 15(A).

10. Tom Fennell, "The Smuggler's Slaves," *Macleans* 113, no. 5 (2000): 14–19.

11. Kathleen Newland, "Refugees: The New International Politics of Displacement," in *Perspectives on Population*, eds. Scott W. Menard and Elizabeth W. Moen (New York: Oxford University Press, 1987), 314–321.

12. *World Population Data Sheet*.

13. See the UN High Commission on Refugees Web site, <http://www.unhcr.ch/un&ref/numbers/numb2000.pdf> (14 Feb. 2001).

14. Alene Gelbard, Carl Haub, and Mary M. Kent, "World Population Beyond Six Billion," *Population Bulletin* 54, no. 1 (March 1999).

15. Gelbard, Haub, and Kent, "World Population."

16. United Nations, *World Urbanization Prospects: The 1999 Revision* (New York: United Nations, 2000).

17. United Nations, *World Urbanization Prospects*.

18. Fertility rates tend, on average, to be lower in urban areas in the developing world, but remain greater than replacement in many cases.

19. China is frequently excluded from population indicators because its one-child policy has dramatically altered its demographic future and sets it apart from other developing nations.

20. See, for example Barbara Crossett, "How to Fix a Crowded World: Add People," *Sunday New York Times*, Week in Review, 2 November 1997, 1; Ben Wattenberg, "The Population Explosion Is Over," *New York Times Magazine*, 23 November 1997, 60–63; Lori Ashford, "New Population Policies: Advancing Women's Health and Rights," *Population Bulletin* 56, no. 1 (March 2001).

21. Carl Haub, "Flat Birth Rates in Bangladesh and Egypt Challenge Demographers' Projections," *Population Today* 28, no. 7 (October 2000): 4.

22. Michael S. Teitelbaum, "Relevance of Demographic Transition Theory for Developing Countries," in *Perspectives on Population*, ed. Scott W. Menard and Elizabeth W. Moen (New York: Oxford University Press, 1987), 29–37.

23. Population geography first rose to prominence as a field of study in geography with Glenn T. Trewartha's call for its increased study at the 1953 Association of American Geogra-

phers annual meeting. The text is reprinted in Glen T. Trewartha, "A Case for Population Geography," *Annals of the Association of American Geographers* 43 (1953): 71–97. See also Wilbur Zelinsky, *A Prologue to Population Geography* (Englewood Cliffs, N.J.: Prentice Hall, 1966).

24. The book cannot hope to cover all aspects of each theme. Indeed, entire books can and are written pertaining to refugees, immigrants, HIV/AIDS, and so forth. Undoubtedly, it will neglect issues that some readers will interpret as important. Hopefully, the references and other lateral insights will be sufficient to direct the reader to appropriate resources. For instance, John Weeks's text, *Population: An Introduction to Concepts and Issues*, 7th edition (Belmont, Calif.: Wadsworth, 1999), provides excellent coverage of measurement and data sources for a range of population issues.

1

❦

Fertility and State Policy

"THE STATE HAS NO PLACE IN THE NATION'S BEDROOMS"

The demographic transition is frequently used as a template to mark the shift from high to low mortality and fertility, along with the consequent population explosion as life expectancy and mortality rates are improved. This shift in fertility regimes occurred throughout much of North America and Europe in the nineteenth and early twentieth centuries. In North America, the transition to modern fertility patterns, marked by stable and slow population growth, was essentially completed by the 1930s. In Canada, the French-speaking province of Quebec was an exception, with a TFR in excess of 4.0 during this time and a slower decline in fertility levels than elsewhere in the country. In other countries, the transition occurred much later, with many developing countries not experiencing mortality declines until the 1950s and still waiting for TFR to decline.

Over the past century, worldwide improvements to mortality have been striking. Despite remaining variations in the mortality experience across space, its reduction has been achieved through improvements to sanitation, nutrition, and health care. Understanding and controlling fertility have been more problematic, reflecting its biological and social components. Worldwide, large variations in fertility rates are observed, ranging from a high of 7.5 in Niger to a low of just 1.2 in Bulgaria and Latvia, two countries that are now faced with a population decline (see figure 1.1).[1] Several other European countries, including Russia, Germany, Italy, and Spain, also have fertility rates that are well below the "replacement" level of 2.1 children, which is the number of children needed to exactly replace the current generation. Clearly, there is a large variation in fertility behavior.

Fertility behavior is generally perceived to be a personal, private affair, with the United Nations affirming the right of couples to determine the number and spacing of children. As minister of justice in Prime Minister Lester B. Pearson's cabinet,

15

Figure 1.1.   World Variations in Total Fertility Rates, 2001.

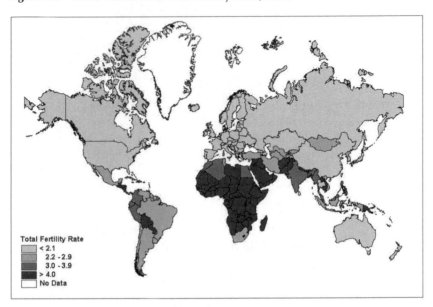

Total Fertility Rate
< 2.1
2.2 - 2.9
3.0 - 3.9
> 4.0
No Data

Source: Population Reference Bureau, World Data Sheet, 2001.

Pierre Elliott Trudeau made his now famous statement that "the State has no place in the nation's bedrooms" in reference to changes to Canada's criminal code.[2] Despite his claims, most governments, including Canada's, have either an explicit or implicit presence within the bedroom, feeling that *it is* legitimate to intervene in individual fertility decisions. In countries where governments deem fertility too high, programs encourage lower fertility rates through family planning programs that educate men and women on the benefits of smaller families and increase accessibility to and use of contraceptive devices. More stringent fertility programs, including China's one-child policy, have also been implemented in order to reduce fertility. At the opposite end of the spectrum, governments, including many West European governments, may view fertility as being too low. Anxiety over an expanding elderly population and a smaller labor force that is able to support the elderly has prompted concerns regarding the survival of social programs and a loss of economic and/or political power. In both cases, other policies such as access to legal abortion, child tax credits, or day care services indirectly influence fertility behavior.

Although the demographic transition theory has been widely applied, it has also been extensively criticized because of its Western-centric biases and its failure to account for myriad variations such as higher fertility levels, alternative forces associated with the decline in mortality, or social and cultural issues.[3] The failure of the demographic transition theory to explain differences across countries in demographic events has meant that its two key components (mortality and fertility) are typically focused upon individually. This chapter focuses upon fertility, its determinants, and its ability to be influenced through policy. Complicating matters, however, is the fact that there is little agreement on what constitutes a desirable rate of population growth. Is it sufficient to simply replace the current generation? Can societies with below-replacement fertility, such as Europe, survive and grow? What are the political, economic, and social implications of below-replacement fertility? In such countries, governments may actively promote fertility through **pro-natalist** policies, typically by providing financial incentives to couples. Yet, how can governments speak of needing to increase fertility, when there is an abundance of it elsewhere that could be used to augment growth in the developed world through immigration? Elsewhere, countries with rapid population growth will attempt to reduce fertility and slow population growth, with China's experiment at fertility control being the most widely known. Using both historical and current examples from the developed and developing world, the potential and shortcomings of fertility policy are illustrated. The outcome of either pro- or **anti-natalist** policies are difficult to assess, since fertility policies are also often confounded by the unanticipated outcomes or effect of other policies. Every aspect of society influences fertility behavior. In turn, fertility and childbearing impact all of society. The interconnections are both minute and large: straddling political, economic, and social ideologies, meaning that control of fertility behavior and the design and implementation of fertility policies are difficult tasks. Of interest too is the apparent paradox of concurrent fertility promotion and reduction.

WHAT DETERMINES FERTILITY?

Characteristic of pre-industrial societies, survival in pre-revolutionary Russia was difficult. Life expectancy was just over thirty years. Infant death rates might have reached upward of 30 percent of all live births, and 50 percent of all children died by the age of five. In response to such high death rates, families were large, with family structure reinforced by cultural practices including early marriage before the age of twenty, and any form of birth control was a criminal offense.[4] To remain single was a disgrace, and divorce was a sin. Within forty years of the revolution, fertility rates had declined to levels comparable with most Western societies.

While social, economic, and environmental considerations demanded large families in pre-revolutionary Russia, the Hutterites, a devoutly religious group found in the United States and Canada, value large families, with an average size of eleven children recorded in the early 1900s.[5] Even at its peak, the fertility of this group fell far below the biological maximum, defined by **fecundity,** or the physiological ability of individuals to have children. What is less evident are the social dimensions that work to keep fertility below its maximum level, including the role of economic issues, the government, and other institutions in altering fertility behavior. Similarly, cultural values regarding family size and the social roles of men and women alter fertility and the timing of fertility reduction. In many African states, for example, women enter into sexual unions at younger ages, and contraceptive use remains low, but families average six or seven children, far below the maximum. Cultural practices, including breastfeeding or abstinence from intercourse after birth, and indigenous birth control techniques help to keep fertility below its maximum.

We can look at the experiences of Russia, the Hutterites, and other countries in order to generalize the determinants of fertility. At an abstract level, demographer John Bongaarts identified four variables that explained nearly all the variation in fertility levels across populations.[6] These include the proportion married or in a sexual union; the proportion using contraceptives; the proportion of women who are infertile; and the incidence of abortion. First, in all societies, marriage has clearly been an institution that has promoted fertility. The longer a woman waits to enter a sexual union, the lower the fertility rate. Conversely, where women marry at a young age, fertility rates tend to be higher due to the increased exposure to risk of pregnancy. Cultural values and practices relating to sexual activity, childbearing outside of marriage or union, and contraceptive use will have an impact upon fertility decisions as well. In the past, the age at entry into marriage and the age at entry into a sexual union were the same, but the increasing availability of modern birth control techniques and acceptance of premarital intercourse has meant that this is no longer the case. Celibacy, abstinence (either voluntary or involuntary [i.e., through impotence]), along with frequency of intercourse within a union will either eliminate or alter the risk of pregnancy.

Second, contraceptive use and abortion are the key determinants of fertility in most developed countries. The "reproductive revolution," signaled by the availability and development of modern and effective family planning methods such as the birth control pill, made it easier to avoid pregnancy. Increased access to methods of birth control and the desire to limit family size helped fertility reductions and, when used in developing countries, fertility decline has been much more rapid than developed countries experienced during their **fertility transition.** Despite the reproductive revolution, contraceptive use varies dramatically over space and echoes variations in fertility levels. Among women who are in sexual unions and of reproductive age that use modern contraceptives in the United States and Canada, for example, the rate of modern contraceptive usage exceeds 65 percent.[7] Somewhat lower levels of use are observed in Europe, particularly in Eastern Europe where contraceptive use rates are approximately 40 percent.

In the developing world, contraceptive use lags usage rates found elsewhere, but family planning programs have had a strong influence on fertility by raising the awareness of means or the need for contraception and control. Contraceptive use is lower in Asia, Latin America, and Africa as well, with less than 10 percent in the latter using modern birth control methods in some areas. Instead, the regulation of fertility largely lies with traditional methods (i.e., withdrawal), and the low incidence of contraceptive use is attributed to religious beliefs or societal values. Various governments have also decried the use of birth control methods as an unwanted intrusion of lax Western morals, even in the face of the HIV/AIDS epidemic, a risk that can be reduced through condom use.[8] When and how birth control is practiced also varies. Women in developed countries tend to start using birth control in their late teens or early twenties to delay childbearing and, following the birth of a child, to achieve desired spacing. In the developing world, contraception use frequently starts *after* the desired family size is achieved.

Third, abortion is one of the most common forms of modern birth control in the world and is assumed to be an important reason for low birthrates in much of the developed world.[9] Legal in much of the world, including Canada, the United States, most of Europe (except Ireland), China, India, and Russia, abortion rates are highest in China and Russia (approximately 55 and 31 per 100 in 1990, respectively),[10] and access to abortion is easier than to contraception devices in Russia.[11]

Finally, the inability to conceive is associated with voluntary or involuntary fecundity. Breastfeeding, for instance, reduces (but does not eliminate) the likelihood of pregnancy for as long as twenty-one months.[12] With modernization, breastfeeding has tended to decline, which may be of particular concern within the developing world where, in the absence of other birth control techniques, fertility may increase. Sterilization also provides a method for lowering fertility, although this is a more popular procedure in developed countries where it is generally used to prevent further pregnancies after a desired family size has been achieved.

Together, these four variables explain nearly all variations in fertility, with the importance of each determinant depending on the cultural, economic, health, and social factors within a population. In many African societies, babies are breastfed until age two or three, and women may be expected to abstain from intercourse for up to two years after birth, both of which increase the spacing between births. Although Bongaarts provides insight into the key determinants of fertility, the question remains as to what determines social forces that mold fertility choices. Why, for instance, would marriage be delayed? Why would contraceptive use increase? How do the cultural values attached to children change?

To answer these questions, we must turn to theories of fertility transition over time and space.[13] These may be roughly distinguished by microeconomic interpretations, characterized by Easterlin's[14] "supply and demand" framework along with the "diffusion-innovation" perspective, proposed by a number of authors.[15] Both frameworks find their roots within the demographic transition theory, which ascribed declines in fertility to societal changes related to industrialization and urbanization. In the face of declining mortality and improved economic opportunities, the demographic transition theory implies that people will eventually realize that more children will survive into their reproductive years than can be afforded, resulting in a decline in fertility that preceded modern birth control methods. Urbanization and industrialization, therefore, set the stage for declines in fertility such as in pre-twenti-eth-century Europe and North America, creating a way of life that made it more expensive to raise children.[16] Rather than using children to augment household income, children were to be "invested" in through such means as educational opportunities.

The linkages among urbanization, industrialization, and fertility within the demographic transition theory were, however, criticized, especially within the context of the developing world where the correlation between development and fertility is weak. Several countries in Asia (i.e., Bangladesh) and Latin America (i.e., Haiti) remain poor, underdeveloped, and have low levels of urbanization, but are also experiencing fertility decline. In other words, development and economic security is not a sufficient condition to cause fertility to decrease. Building upon the demographic transition theory are the neo-classical theories of fertility decline. Easterlin's classic supply-demand framework defines fertility choice as the outcome of a rational calculation of the costs and benefits associated with fertility behavior, contextualized relative to cultural and household expectations. Families try to maintain a balance between the potential supply of children and the demand for surviving children. Where death rates are high, high fertility ensures the survival of children to an economically active age, and there is no incentive to control fertility. The response to high mortality reflects children as a source of security and labor, a preference for a son, or a desire to "replenish" the population. In effect, children may be likened to pension plans, contributing to production and income within the household or the care of elders, making large families a necessity and an investment in future security.

If, on the other hand, supply exceeds demand, fertility regulation becomes important. The decision to control fertility is then based upon the financial and social costs of raising a child, as more children are being produced and surviving into their reproductive years. Casting fertility behavior as an economic choice means that children are, in many ways, seen as luxury items and subject to both time and investment. Investment is represented by the *direct costs* of education, clothing, food, and so forth, as well as *opportunity costs,* representing forgone investments and purchases of other consumer goods. Parents are then faced with a trade-off between quality and quantity. In the developed world, quality is emphasized, with resources concentrated on a relatively small number of children. Children in the developed world are not expected to contribute to the economic well-being of the household or to support parents in their old age. Instead, they represent large direct costs associated with education, clothing, and food, along with indirect or opportunity costs of having children at a time when the same dollar value could be spent on other consumer goods and demands for leisure time.

Criticism of neo-classical determinants of fertility behavior has lead social scientists to link changes in fertility behavior to the diffusion of ideas across space.[17] As with any process, diffusion of social norms or new ideas varies spatially, with the timing of the fertility transition hinging upon the diffusion of social norms and new ideas including birth control techniques. In the past, the preference for small families diffused out of urban areas and from high- to low-income groups. Although important, diffusion is not a spatially smooth process. For instance, poor or inadequate transportation or communication infrastructure, especially evident in rural, agricultural, and poor regions of the world, creates barriers that alter the diffusion of new ideas or norms. Religious ideology remains a persuasive force limiting the success of family planning programs and the promotion of birth control methods. Cultural practices may likewise preclude the use of contraceptive devices, such as the condom, which is viewed as an interference during sexual intercourse.

The uptake of new ideas or norms also depends upon the individual. If new ideas such as birth control are to be accepted, individuals must feel that they exert some power or control over life events. In societies where women lack control and power, fertility rates tend to remain high. The key, therefore, is to produce greater equity between males and females, which is accomplished vis-à-vis improvements in educational attainment, occupational status, or income opportunities. Improved education status and paid employment have reduced fertility, with a near universal relationship between improved educational levels among women and decreased fertility. Women with better levels of education also tend to have a higher uptake of family planning, tend to wait longer between pregnancies, and stop childbearing at an earlier age than those who are less educated. There is an even stronger relationship between women's education and child health, with higher educational attainment linked to healthier and better-nourished children, which in itself promotes a reduction in fertility. Although the exact relationship is unclear, completion of education may delay entry into marriage and expands employment options, suggesting that women delay fertility in order to earn an income. Employment also exposes women to new ideas, behaviors, and influences outside the family. However, gender equity in employment is vital: if employment does not translate to power and does not enable women to make decisions regarding health care, contraception, the timing of children, and so forth, then declines in fertility are unlikely to occur.[18]

THE ROLE OF THE STATE: FERTILITY REDUCTION

There has been growing recognition since the 1980s of the need to control population growth within developing countries. Despite its complexity, governments have not stopped attempting to influence fertility behavior. Many governments currently view their population growth rate as being too high, including Sri Lanka, Pakistan, Niger, and Peru. In response, programs to reduce population growth rates by controlling fertility behavior have been enacted, although most have met with varying levels of success. Two long-term and well-known examples are discussed below, both of which provide insights into the abilities and shortcomings of fertility policy.

China

Identified as one of the most successful, albeit controversial fertility control programs, China's one-child policy has received considerable lay and academic attention.[19] Initially, China's government viewed family planning and fertility reduction programs as suspect, assuming instead that socialism would ensure the equitable distribution of resources across society. By the late 1960s, however, China's leadership recognized the limits to growth and the need for population control. With TFR in excess of 7.0, rapid growth was acknowledged to hinder attempts to improve the economy and raise the standard of living. Beginning in 1979, the Chinese government advocated its one-child program, with the goal of stabilizing the population at 1.2 billion, accomplished through a combination of social pressures including propaganda and local political activism and coercion, increased availability of contraception and family planning resources, and a series of economic incentives and disincentives. For those committing to the program, cash bonuses where paid, with one-child families given preference in school admission, housing, and job applications in urban areas. In rural areas, the program was altered slightly, so that families would receive the same food rations as a two-child family and the same-sized plot for private cultivation as a two-child family. Disincentives to large families were also employed, requiring families having more than one child to repay all benefits received.

By the late 1990s, China's total fertility rate had dropped below replacement and is currently 1.8. The apparent "success" of the program seemingly follows from the ability of the Chinese government to exert control over the population to limit births, a recognized feature of China's communist society. The program's success could also be attributed to the promotion of personal and national economic benefits and the program's link to broader health issues, which together engendered the desire for smaller families within the Chinese population. Yet, even as fertility rates declined and population growth slowed, the program has not been without its critics. Internally, a significant proportion of the Chinese population resisted the one-child policy, reflecting deeper cultural issues or economic necessity and the importance placed on the birth of male children. Although higher financial incentives were also attached to the birth of daughters among couples who endorsed the one-child policy and the government's allowance of more than one-child in some rural areas, the prospect of a one-child family meant that approximately 50 percent of families would not have a son. Poverty further reinforced the importance and contribution of male children to family welfare, and couples frequently opted to disregard the one-child policy in their efforts to have a son. More disturbing, reports of female infanticide and abuse of women who give birth to girls were not uncommon,[20] and it was suggested that the set of disincentives deterred women from seeking appropriate prenatal and pregnancy-related care, increasing the risk of death for mother and child.[21]

The true success of the program has also been questioned since declines in fertility can be traced to the 1960s. Fertility decline was furthered in the 1970s with government policies of delayed marriage, longer spacing between births, and fewer children, so that by the early 1980s the TFR had already dropped below 3.0.[22] In other words, the decline in fertility levels would appear to have been well established by the mid-1970s. Far from inducing fertility decline, the one-child program may therefore have simply enhanced the motivation for smaller families, codifying family size as a national goal through the provision of a set of incentives and disincentives.

Continued economic liberalization will likely promote small families in the coming years as the direct and opportunity costs of children are realized, particularly in urban areas. Conversely, economic liberalization may also *promote* fertility among the poor as a means of ensuring their economic success in an economy that is increasingly separated by the rich and poor, leading observers to question whether the low rates of fertility can be maintained over the longer term. Even with an estimated population of 1.27 billion in 2001, the target population of 1.2 billion has been exceeded, owing to demographic momentum and the young age of the population. The government has already loosened its restrictions on early marriages and has relaxed its one-child policy, permitting two children in certain circumstances, suggesting that a substantial demand for larger families may remain within the population, particularly in rural areas where economic liberalization has increased pressure for children as a means of family support and production. Chinese planners are also recognizing that the rapid reduction in fertility levels in just twenty-five years has resulted in a young population (aged fifteen years and less) that is substantially smaller than previous generations, creating a heavy burden of old-age dependency. Like many countries in the developed world, the Chinese government is trying to cope with an **aging** population and a shrinking labor force that supports the elderly. Moreover, the erosion of traditional family structures means that children no longer care for their elderly parents, posing additional problems, making a further relaxation of the one-child policy to meet the problem of an aging population possible.

India

In a country where the total population exceeded one billion in 2000, India's attempts and success at fertility control contrast markedly with those of China and remain a key issue. Although the recognition of the need to control population growth emerged much earlier within India than it did in China, the government was primarily committed to rapid economic development as a means of fertility reduction. In other words, family planning was, at first, seen as a long-term objective: government policy emphasized economic development with the expectation that reductions in fertility would naturally follow as income prospects improved. With little progress in reducing fertility apparent and the population continuing to grow, its control was increasingly seen as crucial to India's economic success. That is, rather than fertility reductions stemming from economic improvement, fertility reduction was targeted as a means of improving economic performance, making the

Indian government the first to initiate a national program to slow population growth in 1953.[23] Providing support mainly through family planning clinics, progress was slow and the impact on fertility was minimal, with the TFR remaining near 6.0 by the early 1960s. In response, the Indian government reorganized family planning programs on multiple occasions throughout the decade, pursuing reductions in fertility along a number of fronts by investing in family planning programs that were meant to educate and provide the means for birth control, legalizing abortion, and financial incentives to make sterilization more acceptable to the poor. The government also initiated disincentives, including the denial of maternity benefits to women after the birth of the third child. However, the emphasis upon family planning programs tended to divert funds from needed general health programs, including maternity and child health services, both of which are crucial to the success of any program promoting fertility reduction. Therefore, the government's own policies worked counter to the intended results.

Not surprisingly, fertility failed to respond even as mortality rates continued to decline, meaning the population was growing at an ever-faster rate. With mounting frustration over the failure of family planning programs and economic development policies to bring about a decline in fertility, the Indian government instituted an enforced sterilization program in 1976. Officially, there was no coercion to participate in the program, but the fact that government employees needed to produce two candidates for sterilization, wide-scale bribery, and a series of disincentives including the denial of licenses essentially meant that sterilization was indeed forced upon the population. Although some twenty-two million individuals were sterilized, most were older males who had already achieved their desired family size, once again the program was ineffective in reducing total fertility. The forced sterilization program also carried a heavy political price tag with the defeat of Prime Minister Indira Gandhi in the 1977 general election. Her defeat sent a clear message that population control policies that fail to recognize the rights of the population and broader relationships can bring about the fall of the government. Although much less aggressive, subsequent governments continued to recognize the need for family planning programs, combining abstinence with monetary rewards and improvements in the scope of family planning services. Interestingly, TFR had decreased to 4.75 by the early 1980s; declines that may better be attributed to increased literacy programs for women and an increase in the average age of marriage, rather than family planning programs per se. Although still high, rates have continued to decline, even among the poor, as radio, television, and other forms of communication help popularize the idea that small families are better.

With a current TFR of 3.2, still well above the replacement level, and a population that has exceeded one billion, India's National Population Policy 2000 marks its most recent attempt to reduce fertility, with the hope of reducing fertility to 2.1 by 2010 and to stabilize the population by 2045.[24] Emphasizing quality of life issues associated with smaller families, the program targets improvements in public health, immunization rates, women's education opportunities, and reproductive health. It is questionable, however, whether the policy can be implemented. Large-scale funding would be required, and it is not clear whether this will be made available. Even if the money were available, other administrative problems, including a slow moving bureaucracy and corruption, may scuttle the program. Even as the central government has backed off sterilization programs, individual states continue to promote it through a variety of methods, including coercion, with enticements of loans, housing, and land to those who are sterilized after two or more children.[25]

The failure of family planning within India proposes a number of issues. Critics have charged that Indian programs have been inconsistent and typically lacked direction, with demographic targets tied to oscillating rewards and disincentives. The program has also failed to offer more flexible birth control methods such as the pill or IUD (intrauterine device). Instead, it focused upon sterilization in a country that has historically low use of contraception. Other contraceptive techniques still represent only a small proportion of contraceptive use within India. India's lack of success runs deeper than inconsistent or narrow policy objectives, failing to account for the broader social context within which reproduction occurs, including the role of women, the interrelationship among classes, and the political consequences of fertility policies. Like China, sons are preferred over daughters, providing economic security or additional labor, especially in rural areas, while the role of women within Indian society is typically marginalized and relegated to one of motherhood.

Class within Indian society is particularly important as a determinant of fertility. Unlike China, with its supposedly classless society, totalitarian government, and tight control over the actions of its population, India's democratically elected government represents a fractious population divided along caste, religious, and ethnic lines. Mazumdar notes, for instance, that the desire for small families came from India's middle class, where low fertility fit with their own beliefs and aspirations.[26] Elsewhere, high child mortality, illiteracy, the marginalized role of women, and traditional extended family structures dominate fertility options, meaning that fertility is unlikely to decline quickly. In effect, a minimum of two economic and demographic realities can be observed, with fertility policies representative of the middle class imposed upon the lower class, but failing to recognize the household economies of this group.

The middle-class outlook was not completely accidental. In order to succeed, fertility policy would need to depend upon improvements in employment, health, and gender equity among the lower class. But this would also threaten the current political and economic power structure. Internal political interests have also played an important role, with some Indian states failing to curb population growth while others have succeeded. Fertility reduction has been greatest in the more literate and prosperous southern states. The democratic implication is that any reallocation of seats within the Indian government would lead to a loss of political power for those states were population controls were more successful and an increase in political power elsewhere, hardly an incentive to promote fertility reduction.[27] The reality of the demographic, political, and class relationships within India weakens any national attempts to reduce fertility.

India's population has not yet realized the benefits of smaller families, and family planning programs have not been able to generate the social revolution needed to make small families the norm. The failure of family programs is hardly surprising given the complexity and multidimensionality of fertility behavior. Empirically, it may be difficult to distinguish the impact of family planning programs from the effect of other societal changes, including improving economic conditions. More generally, India's failed attempts to encourage lower fertility are not representative of all fertility programs, but it does reflect the difficulty of implementing these sorts of policies. Indeed, family planning programs have succeeded in altering fertility behavior when properly instituted, increasing the use of contraceptive methods and contributing to declines in fertility. Successful programs have explicitly recognized that a decline in fertility is as dependent upon individual and societal motivations as it is upon technology and the government. Government policies alone are insufficient to promote change, and the mere provision of a family planning program is inadequate to reduce fertility in the absence of a social environment that encourages changes in fertility behavior. Most family planning programs fall short of their goals because they fail to understand how to influence desired family size. As in the case of India, if birth control and smaller families contradict the interests of many and individuals fail to see the benefit of smaller family sizes, declines in fertility are unlikely to occur. It is increasingly recognized that for family planning programs to succeed, they must work to change the context of the social and cultural environment to encourage smaller families. This means that population policy will need to extend beyond family planning to encompass a variety of segments within society, including the provision of health care, the removal of socioeconomic barriers to contraceptive use, the involvement of religious leaders, the involvement of males (as husbands and fathers), and a synergy between development initiatives such as literacy and communications infrastructure.[28]

THE ROLE OF THE STATE: FERTILITY PROMOTION

From the perspective of the developed world, one of the most important demographic events in recent history was the **baby boom,** which presented a departure from the long-term trend of declining fertility. Generally referring to those born between 1946 and 1964, it affected the United States, Canada, and other nations involved in the Second World War, although the demographic impacts tended to be greatest in North America. In the United States, TFR peaked at 3.58 in 1957, up from 2.19 immediately after the war. In Canada, TFR reached a slightly higher level (3.9) and peaked slightly later (1959). In both countries, the rise in fertility was an expression of the pent-up demand for children following the war and Great Depression, along with rising incomes and expectations. By the mid-1960s, fertility rates had once again dropped to levels similar to those observed prior to the baby boom. In Canada, TFR dropped below the replacement level of 2.1 by 1972. Surprisingly, the decline was led by Quebec, an issue that is discussed later in this section. Although the baby boom was demographically important, with their numbers impacting upon the provision of education in the 1950s and 1960s, careers and leisure pursuits, and retirement, social welfare programs, and health care as the baby boom generation ages into retirement within the next decade,[29] it was a short-term phenomenon. Instead of representing a sea change in fertility behavior, it only temporarily boosted fertility. Over the longer term, fertility rates continued a decline that was first noticed decades earlier.

While many countries are faced with overpopulation and rapid population growth, a handful of Western industrialized or former Soviet bloc countries are faced with the opposite problem—too few births, an implication of the long-term trend toward lower fertility rates. Beginning in the 1970s, TFR fell below replacement levels (2.1) in many industrialized countries, particularly in Europe. Already, fourteen European countries including Sweden, Italy, Ukraine, Russia, Germany, Hungary, and the Czech Republic have negative population growth, meaning that deaths outnumber births. Other countries, including Japan and Canada, are also faced with low fertility rates and slowing population growth. Even in China, where the government has long been concerned with rapid population growth, concerns have turned to an aging population and its support.

Within most Western nations, the decline in birthrates to below replacement levels has been linked to deep societal and economic changes.[30] Promotion of gender equity has meant that women have become increasingly educated. Increased employment and career aspirations have provided greater financial autonomy, contributing to declines in fertility as women seek careers outside their homes. Rising consumer aspirations further reinforce the opportunity costs of children, even as fears of unemployment, downsizing, and the uncertain future of the welfare state temper future economic prospects. Together, these effects have prompted many to either delay childbirth or to reduce the desired family size, challenging many long-held assumptions about the timing of marriage and children.

Seemingly paradoxical, low birthrates and a slowing or decreasing population growth rate have their own set of problems. Although the anticipated consequences of an aging society are still unclear, the Canadian *Review of Demography* concluded that low fertility is a serious problem, having more disadvantages than advantages.[31] From a demographic perspective, low fertility results in an increasing proportion of elderly. In Canada, the elderly population (aged sixty-five plus) represented just 7.8 percent of the population in 1951, growing to 13 percent in 2001 (figure 1.2a). Current projections place it at approximately 20 percent by 2025, altering the age distribution of the population from its typical pyramidal shape dominated by a young population to a rectangular one, characterized by a proportionately larger elderly population (figure 1.2b).[32] The United States has seen similar increases in its share of the elderly population, representing just 4.1 percent of the population in 1900, 13 percent in 2001, and is projected to grow to over 20 percent by 2030.[33] In Europe, the elderly already represent greater than 15 percent of the population in several countries, including Sweden (17 percent), the United Kingdom (16 percent), and Belgium (17 percent), with continued growth ensured.

Not surprisingly, economists have tended to assume that the marketplace will be able to react to population change. If children are scarce, they will become more valuable and the system will correct itself, either by finding substitutes for children (unlikely!) or by placing greater value on children, achieved through various incentive programs. Yet, it is unclear what the economic effects of low or negative population growth would be. Ester Boserup, a Danish economist, promoted the idea that population growth triggered economic development.[34] Over the long run, countries with growing populations would be more likely to post strong economic growth than a stationary or declining population. It has generally been assumed, for example, that population growth provides an economic stimulus; while declining population growth rates imply slower economic growth. Overall, the main economic impacts are expected to be minimal, with an aging population associated with higher savings rates, greater expertise, less unemployment, and higher innovation, although educational costs for retraining and continuing education of an older labor force are likely to increase. Likewise, low or negative population growth should not influence rates of technological change, consumption, or investment, although the distribution of these impacts across regions or age groups are unlikely to be equal, as is the case with the consumption of medical care.[35]

The negative economic impacts associated with low or negative population growth may be associated with greater inequalities within society. There is little doubt that countries with an aging population will face an increased burden of supporting the elderly, placing pressure on social welfare programs. Countries with low fertility rates will have a smaller labor force with which to support the elderly population and may face severe labor shortages that threaten the economic livelihood or stability of the country.[36] The changing age structure of the population therefore raises questions regarding the provision of income security for the aged, housing, transportation, and other services, highlighted by recent debates regarding the crisis of Social Security in the United States. Health care provision is of particular concern, since the elderly, and particularly those older than seventy-five, consume a disproportionate share of medical services. Concurrently, the welfare of children may suffer as funds are diverted to meet the needs of the elderly population.

The largest negative consequences of low or negative population growth may, in fact, be political rather than economic.[37] Internally, countries may face a "graying of politics," as political and economic concerns increasingly represent those of older generations at the expense of the young. Internationally, a shrinking population has been associated with demographic marginalization. A "population implosion" may infringe upon the very essence of nationality, with governments fearing that a declining population will threaten the ability of a country to defend itself. Even

Figure 1.2a.   Population Pyramids for the United States, Canada, and Mexico, 2000.

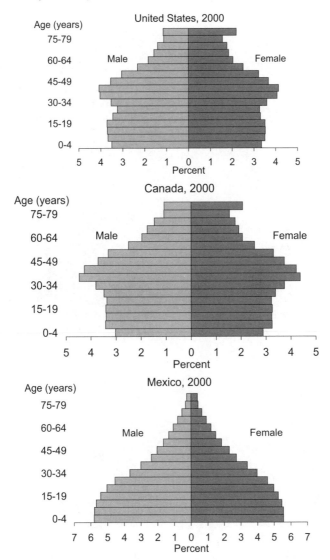

The age profiles of countries with rapid population growth, such as Mexico, resemble a pyramid because each age group (cohort) is larger than the one born before it (greater than replacement fertility). Populations that are growing slowly, such as Canada and the United States in 2000, show less of a pyramidal structure in response to changes in fertility and mortality. By 2025, the **age pyramids** of Canada and the United States are projected to be "rectangular," signifying the impact of an aging population and slower growth. The baby boom (ages 30–49) is visible in both Canada and the United States. The lower rates of mortality and longer life expectancies for females are also observable within the pyramids.

Source: U.S. Census Bureau, 2001, International Database.

Chapter 1

Figure 1.2b. Population Pyramids for the United States, Canada, and Mexico, 2025.

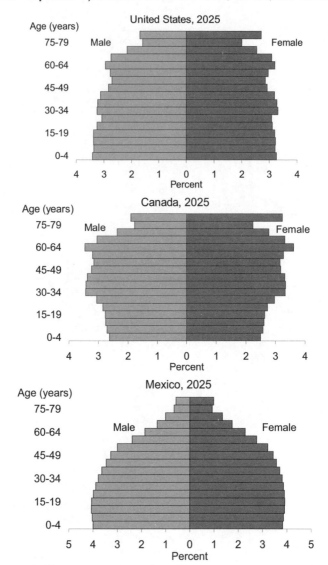

By 2025, the age pyramids of Canada and the United States are projected to be "rectangular," signifying the impact of an aging population and slower growth, while Mexico's age structure largely retains its pyramidal shape, although the effects of reduced fertility are apparent.

Source: U.S. Census Bureau, 2001, International Database.

national identity is at stake, with national influence dependent upon the vitality and size of a population.

Fearful of "demographic suicide" and the economic implications of an aging population, many countries have adopted pro-natalist policies intended to either promote fertility directly or ease the opportunity costs of children, with the expectation that fertility rates will increase. Faced with slowing or declining population growth rates since the 1970s, Eastern European countries have the longest history of pro-natalist policies.[38] Policies typically addressed the issue through a combination of financial incentives or restriction to contraception and abortion services. Meant to ease the opportunity costs of children, financial benefits commonly include paid maternity and paternity leave, free or reduced cost childcare, and tax breaks for large families. Most of these programs are not advertised as fertility policy by explicitly targeting a desired number of children. Instead, policies are presented as antipoverty, pro-woman, or pro-family measures, and are meant to influence socioeconomic conditions related to fertility decisions.

Countries and national governments are not alone in their concern with declining fertility rates and slowing population growth. In Northern Ireland, the Protestant majority has expressed concerns that the Irish Catholic population, with its higher fertility rates, will eventually tip the demographic (and therefore democratic) balance in its favor. Likewise, the Israeli government is fearful of the demographic implications of low fertility among the Jewish population and high rates among Palestinians. Despite high levels of education, Palestinian women in the Gaza Strip and West Bank have fertility rates of 7.4 and 5.4, respectively, rates that will allow the Palestinian population to double in twenty years under current fertility conditions.[39] Although Israel's population has benefited from immigration, the Jewish fertility rate is just 2.67 (higher among ultra-Orthodox Jews). Arabs and other non-Jews already make up approximately one-fifth of the population, sufficient for Israeli's to worry about the future viability of a Jewish democratic state.

Quebec, Canada's French-speaking province, provides yet a third example of regional concerns associated with fertility and population size. Historically, birthrates within the province were higher than the Canadian average, as Quebecers resisted the adoption of contraception and fertility changes. Even in the late 1950s at the peak of the baby boom, Quebec's TFR was in excess of 4.0 children, giving the province one of the highest fertility rates in the industrialized world. The delayed uptake of newer fertility norms and contraceptive techniques reflected the control of the Roman Catholic Church and its traditional stance against contraception. In Quebec's case, the Church also encouraged large families as a "demographic investment" that ensured the survival of French Canada within the Canadian Confederation.[40]

Quebec's demographic advantage was lost in the 1960s. The liberalization of the Church and rapid emancipation of women contributed to declining fertility rates, enabling them to drop below the Canadian average. By the mid-1980s, Quebec had one of the lowest rates of fertility in the world at that time (1.37),[41] and its share of the Canadian population had dropped from 32.3 percent at the time of Confederation in 1867 to 24 percent in 2000. Responding to this apparent crisis, Quebec's Commission de la Culture reported in 1985 that the province needed to take action to counter demographic trends that threatened the province's existence as a "distinct society," an issue that has dominated provincial politics since its foundation. The commission and other commentators pointed out that the demographic situation threatened the political strength of the province and its cultural sovereignty, in addition to the problems of providing for an aging population. Robert Bourassa, then premier of Quebec, echoed the concerns of the commission by declaring that increasing birthrates was the most important challenge for Quebec.[42] In response, Quebec initiated a series of pro-fertility programs, including more generous tax deductions for children, higher family allowances, longer parental work leaves, and more day care opportunities. Beginning in 1988, the Quebec government also offered baby bonuses based upon family size, with $500 for the first child, $1,000 for the second, and $6,000 for the third and subsequent children. Revisions to this policy in subsequent years raised the bonuses slightly.[43]

Evidence from Eastern Europe and Quebec indicates that the effects of pro-natalist policies are short-lived and only moderately successful. Over the short term, fertility rates frequently increase, but the longer-term impact is less successful. Statistics Canada, for example, identified a slight recovery in fertility rates in the years following the introduction of pro-natalist policies, with TFR reaching 1.6 in 1996, but dropping again to 1.5 in 1997, remaining below the Canadian average in 2000.[44] If anything, most observers believe that incentives merely accelerate or alter the timing of the first birth, rather than changing the desired family size by increasing the number of "higher order births" (i.e., second, third, or higher born children). Over the longer term, the relationship between financial incentives and other attitudinal factors related to fertility are difficult to measure and unknown. Demographic factors, such as fewer women in their childbearing years, means that birthrates are likely to remain low. Restrictions on access to abortion services also have a short-term effect on fertility, as couples quickly adjust their own practices or resort to illegal abortions.

Countries have also explored alternatives to fertility promotion by looking at other policy alternatives such as delayed retirement to keep individuals within the labor force, or delaying the start of welfare programs as the United States has done. Immigration offers an alternate to pro-natalist policies, although it is a problematic one. Traditional immigration countries such as Canada, Australia, New Zealand, and the United States can still expect significant long-term population growth through immigration and a younger age structure, even though their fertility rates are at (U.S. = 2.1) or have dropped below replacement level.[45] In Europe, governments may also choose to increase immigration, but do so with great risk. Europe has not been seen in the past as a major destination for immigrants (although short-term work programs are the exception), and current immigration numbers are insufficient to reverse population decline, while further increases in immigration levels may result in ethnic confrontation.[46] Most European countries have imposed strict immigration policies, and some have actively encouraged their foreign-born populations to leave.

THE ROLE OF THE INTERNATIONAL
COMMUNITY: CONFLICTING MESSAGES

Although we like to think that reproductive choices are personal, the previous discussion indicates that states and their governments will often take either an active or accidental role in promoting fertility. Growing concern within developed countries with rapid population growth in the post–Second World War era prompted international institutions and governments to influence fertility policies.[47] At first, the developing world was slow to respond to programs promoting fertility reduction, arguing instead that economic development was the best contraceptive. Population policies were also viewed as an infringement upon state sovereignty from former colonial or imperial powers. With stagnating economies, high child mortality, and an increasing realization that women wanted to limit their own fertility, governments in the developing world increasingly warmed to the idea that population growth should be slowed. The United Nations became the driving force through its sponsorship of the first meeting on global population in 1954. Other UN organizations, including the World Health Organization **(WHO)** and **UNICEF** (United Nations Children's Fund), have incorporated reproductive health into their programs and under the auspices of the United Nations Population Fund (UNFPA).

The U.S. government has taken a more independent approach, preferring to direct its money through its own Agency for International Development **(USAID)**, reflecting its own concerns and policy goals.[48] Largely driven by security concerns that saw rapid population growth as a threat to U.S. security via trade, political conflict, immigration, or damage to the environment, USAID has been the largest single donor to family planning programs. Initially, programs emphasized family planning practices or specific demographic targets, but grew to provide contraceptive information and related health services to support child and maternal health by the 1970s. Critics have long argued that the programs were too narrowly focused, failing to respect religious beliefs or making insufficient investments in social and economic opportunities. Most notably, abortion opponents criticized U.S. involvement in family planning programs because of their belief that family planning programs promote abortion. In fact, U.S. law has prohibited the use of such funds to pay for abortion services since the 1970s.

The 1980s saw a significant shift in U.S. population policy under the Reagan administration. Supported by **economic optimists** including Julian Simon, who argued that world population growth was "good," the administration declared at the 1984 International Conference on Population in Mexico City that population growth actually had a *neutral* effect on economic development. Reflecting its connections with the religious right, the Reagan administration also opposed the use of funds for abortion services, withdrawing all financial support from any organization that provided such services even when it used its own money to provide legal abortions. At the same time as the United States was reversing its position on population growth, developing countries had largely stepped back from their earlier opposition to family planning programs. Instead, the benefits of small families and the need to slow population growth were promoted. Despite U.S. opposition, the 1984 conference ultimately supported family planning initiatives and urged governments to make such services available.

After taking office in 1993, the Clinton administration waived funding restrictions set in place by the previous Republican administrations and increased funding to family planning programs. Eight years later, the Bush-Cheney administration reinstated restrictions to family planning programs within days of taking office,[49] returning to restrictions imposed at the time of the Mexico City conference. The so-called global gag rule denies U.S. funding to private overseas organizations if they use other (non-U.S.) monies to provide abortion services or if they lobby for changes to the abortion law in their own country. Unfortunately, such restrictions actually undermine the success of family planning programs. Broadly speaking, the number of family planning providers is likely to be reduced as funding disappears. Ultimately, the global gag rule will undermine family planning's objective of preventing unwanted pregnancies and improving maternal and child health. In fact, the ubiquity of abortion suggests that there is a large unmet need for family planning programs that can prevent the use of abortion services by providing counseling or other options.[50] In cases where legal abortion is not an alternative, women may choose illegal abortions, increasing the risk of death or injury when faced with an unwanted pregnancy. Family planning programs can also reduce fertility levels by helping with birth spacing, improving the odds of survival of mother and child, preventing unsafe abortions, and reducing the incidence of sexually transmitted diseases including HIV. Studies have clearly shown that as use of family planning methods increase, abortion rates decrease, and that increased funding of family planning programs reduces abortion.[51]

Leading up to the fifth UN conference on population held in Cairo in 1994, discussions once again centered on the relationship between population growth and development. Despite the success of family planning programs in the developing world, critics of these programs viewed them as an invasion of personal liberties. Instead, it was argued that family planning programs should be better integrated into a broader view of health, and that women's well-being should be of paramount importance. Responding to the critics, the conference redefined views of population growth and how to address it, linking population growth to **sustainable development.** Rather than focusing primarily on national interests, the conference promoted investment in human development, particularly the status of women. Family planning was to be integrated into a broader health agenda, including pre- and post-natal care, sexually transmitted diseases, and cancer screening. Infant, child, and maternal mortality and the alleviation of poverty were to be targeted, and universal access to family planning services, primary school education, and increased access by girls and women to higher education were promoted. However, abortion was not promoted as a method of family planning, clearly recognizing the legal, moral, and religious viewpoints of abortion within different countries.

Although the success of the 1994 conference is still being evaluated, early reviews give mixed results. Many countries had articulated and implemented new population policies along with reproductive health programs. However, funding shortfalls by donor countries, including the United States and other developed countries, will limit the reach and effectiveness of programs. The success of the Cairo conference must also be evaluated within the context of broader health reforms and economic liberalization. Many developing countries had already started to change their policies and institutions, promoting a broader health agenda that incorporated reproductive health and gender equity. For example, the World Health Organization's Health for All by 2000 (HFA 2000) program was an early promoter of societal health.[52] Initiated in 1977, HFA 2000 emphasized the promotion and protection of health, realized through the provision of primary health care, which stressed comprehensive basic services for all rather than sophisticated curative medical care for a few. Primary health care thus became WHO's basic strategy for health improvement, notably for its concern with factors supporting health, including water supplies, sanitation, education, food supply, along with programs promoting child and maternal health and family planning. A particular emphasis has been placed upon the health and education of children, adolescents, and women within the developing world. Among children, there is increasing recognition that childhood health is linked to health in later life. Consequently, improving early childhood nutrition, greater access to immunizations, better hygiene, improved education opportunities, and safe water supplies have been promoted. Among women, where gender differences are often reinforced by societal or cultural norms, programs have targeted equity issues, working to narrow gaps in literacy, education, and income opportunities.

EMERGENT THEMES AND ISSUES

The low fertility rates that now characterize much of the developed world and the perceived social, economic, and political consequences will likely influence demographic decisions in the coming years, including programs and calls to increase TFR levels. Despite this rather paradoxical situation, in light of concerns with high fertility elsewhere, steps to reduce global fertility levels are likely to be the dominant issue. Since the 1950s and the beginning of the population explosion in the developing world, demographers and governments alike have searched for indications that the characteristic high fertility levels found in the developing world would decrease. While fertility rates have declined as expected in some instances, population growth will continue for the next few decades, fueled by population momentum associated with the young age structure, increased life expectancies, and above replacement fertility. The multidimensional factors associated with fertility decline, which are further complicated by national and international policies, make it difficult to ascertain whether all countries will eventually move through some form of fertility transition. Pressure within segments of China's population to have more than the allotted one child shows a continuing desire to have larger families, and the problems associated with a rapidly aging population may force the government to relax its fertility policy. However, it is also a misconception that China has its population under control. Large-scale population movements from rural to urban areas have lead to growing regional inequities, insufficient urban infrastructure, degradation of resources, and the potential for urban conflict. In India, despite a half century of promoting fertility reductions, fertility rates remain relatively high, with TFR greater than 3.0. Fertility rates continue to remain above replacement in many other regions. Despite early successes in reducing fertility in Bangladesh, which saw fertility rates drop from over 6.0 children per woman in the early 1970s to 3.3 in 2001, fertility rates have remained relatively unchanged through the 1990s. Similarly, Egypt's birthrate has remained at approximately 3.5 since 1993, and it is uncertain whether it will be further reduced.[53]

After observing fertility transitions in Asia and Latin America, all eyes have focused on Africa, where fertility rates remain stubbornly high, and most African nations (notably sub-Saharan Africa) have made little progress toward fertility transition.[54] In short, much of Africa is still waiting for the fertility transition. Africa is arguably faced with the most pressing fertility concerns: some fifty years after mortality levels were dramatically reduced in the developing world, Africa's TFR remains at 5.2, while sub-Saharan Africa still has fertility rates in excess of 5.6. Fertility rates this high, corresponding to an annual increase of 2.5 percent, enable the population to grow at a rate of 2.6 percent and double in just twenty-seven years. While population growth is expected to slow and there is emerging evidence that fertility rates will ultimately decline, the population of Africa will, under current conditions, double by 2050. In sub-Saharan Africa, only South Africa, Zimbabwe, Kenya, and Namibia would appear to have entered a period of transition in fertility behavior, which could be characterized by high contraceptive use, longer life expectancies, and a declining fertility rate. Fertility reduction remains a distant goal among the majority of sub-Saharan countries.

Why has fertility remained so high in much of Africa? Given that fertility behavior is complex, it is not surprising that a combination of factors mediated through culture and society continue to promote high fertility within Africa. In general, the lack of economic development, subsistence agricultural practices, and low incomes maintain historically high fertility regimes, with many societies continuing to desire large families for the security they provide. Strong lineage associations, where children are expected to help the extended family, mean that children provide both security and labor. In Africa, children are vital in the production of agricultural crops and are therefore a form of inexpensive labor.[55] Children may also provide additional income to the household by working outside the home or migrating elsewhere and remitting income to the parents. The lack of high-quality transportation and communications systems, gender inequities in access to education, occupation opportunities and power, and the continued absence of a strong family planning program reinforce high fertility. In some instances, small families or attempts to limit family size are discouraged.

Although most observers expect fertility rates to decline in African states, the question remains as to when large-scale reductions will occur, how far rates will drop, and how long it will take to achieve significant reductions. Like explanations for fertility decline, the answers to these questions are also multidimensional. First, although contraceptive use is increasing, it is used more for control of the spacing of children or after desired family size is achieved, rather than as a form of fertility control to limit family size. Less than 20 percent of married women use some form of modern birth control in many African nations, which compares with 65 percent or greater in North America. Second, mortality remains high in many African nations. As we have already noted, mortality rates have decreased within Africa, but perhaps not sufficiently to initiate fertility decline. The general rule is that life expectancy at birth must be greater than fifty years for fertility to decrease. This has only been recently achieved in some African states, while in others (particularly sub-Saharan states), life expectancy hovers near or remains below the fifty-year mark. Third, the HIV/AIDS crisis may reverse gains in life expectancy. Although there is no evidence that fertility choices will be affected, declines in life expectancy have already been noted. It has been estimated that life expectancies in Zimbabwe are now twenty-one years lower than they would have been without AIDS.[56] Fourth, gender equity is a distant goal in many societies. Women remain marginalized, literacy rates remain low, and rapid population growth and economic crises in the 1980s and 1990s prevented many countries from expanding educational opportunities to meet the growing population. Health care systems are also casualties of high rates of population growth and stagnant economies that have limited development, modernization, and investment in basic health care services. Many systems are poorly funded or in ruin, preventing access to the most basic of health services at a time when both mother and child are in need.

In the past, policy options have offered little hope of reducing fertility levels in Africa,[57] evidenced by the experiences of the United Nations and other international groups that have worked since the 1950s to address population growth issues. This is not to imply that progress in reducing fertility has not been (or is not) possible, merely that the implementation of successful family planning programs is challenging. African governments have recognized the intimate link between population and development and have promoted programs that would reduce fertility levels, but have frequently lacked the financial ability to fully implement programs. Alternatively, they have not sufficiently involved all stakeholders, including religious leaders and men that would work to ensure success by altering social, political, and economic forces influencing fertility choices that prove slow to change. Ensuring that fertility rates are reduced in Africa will provide an ongoing challenge.

NOTES

1. For example, the Population Reference Bureau projects Latvia's current population of 2.4 million to decline to 1.8 million by 2025. Germany's population, currently 82.2 million, is projected to decline to 70.3 by 2025. Two other European countries, the Czech Republic and Ukraine, had a TFR of just 1.1 in 2001.

2. This comment was made to the media during an interview on 22 December 1967, when Trudeau was the justice minister in Prime Minister Pearson's cabinet.

3. John C. Caldwell, "Toward a Restatement of Demographic Transition Theory," in *Perspectives on Population*, eds. Scott W. Menard and Elizabeth W. Moen (New York: Oxford University Press, 1987), 42–69.

4. Sergi Maksudov, "Some Causes of Rising Mortality in the USSR," in *Perspectives on Population*, eds. Scott W. Menard and Elizabeth W. Moen (New York: Oxford University Press, 1987), 156–174.

5. John R. Weeks, *Population: An Introduction to Concepts and Issues*, 7th edition (Belmont, Calif.: Wadsworth, 1999).

6. John Bongaarts, "A Framework for Analyzing the Proximate Determinants of Fertility," *Economic Development and Cultural Change* 4 (1978): 211–235.

7. *World Population Data Sheet* (Washington, D.C.: Population Reference Bureau, 2001). Unless noted otherwise, population statistics throughout this book are drawn from this source.

8. Peter Gould, *The Slow Plague: A Geography of the AIDS Pandemic* (Oxford, U.K.: Blackwell, 1993).

9. Weeks, *Population*.

10. Weeks, *Population*.

11. Stanley Henshaw, "Induced Abortions: A World Review, 1990," *Family Planning Perspectives* 22, no. 2 (1990): 76–89.

12. Weeks, *Population*.

13. Karen Oppenheim Mason, "Explaining Fertility Transitions," *Demography* 34, no. 4 (November 1997): 443–454.

14. Richard A. Easterlin, "An Economic Framework for Fertility Analysis," *Studies in Family Planning* 6 (1975): 54–63; Richard A. Easterlin and Eileen M. Crimmins, *The Fertility Revolution: A Supply-Demand Analysis* (Chicago: University of Chicago Press, 1985).

15. Weeks, *Population*.

16. Although discussed later one, fertility was already starting to decline (predominately in the upper classes) in Europe at the time of Malthus's writings. Had he foreseen that fertility decline was to occur across all classes, his writings may not have been so dark.

17. John Cleland and Christopher Wilson, "Demand Theories of the Fertility Transition: An Iconoclastic View," *Population Studies* 41 (1987): 5–30.

18. Alene Gelbard, Carl Haub, and Mary M. Kent, "World Population Beyond Six Billion," *Population Bulletin* 54, no. 1 (March 1999).

19. For additional information on China's one-child policy, see Jim P. Doherty, Edward

C. Norton, and James E. Veney, "China's One-Child Policy: The Economic Choices and Consequences Faced by Pregnant Women," *Social Science and Medicine* 52 (2001): 745–761; Johns Hopkins University Population Information Program, "Population and Birth Planning in the People's Republic of China," *Population Reports* 1, no. 25 (1982); Jeffrey Wasserstrom, "Resistance to the One-Child Family," in *Perspectives on Population*, eds. Scott W. Menard and Elizabeth W. Moen (New York: Oxford University Press, 1987), 269–276.

20. Wasserstrom, "Resistance to the One-Child Family," 269.

21. Doherty, Norton, and Veney, "China's One-Child Policy," 745.

22. Weeks, *Population.*

23. Vina Mazumdar, "Fertility Policy in India," in *Perspectives on Population*, eds. Scott W. Menard and Elizabeth W. Moen (New York: Oxford University Press, 1987), 259–268.

24. O. P. Sharma, "India Proposes Retooled Population Policy," *Population Today* 28, no. 3 (April 2000): 6.

25. Celia W. Dugger, "Relying on Hard and Soft Sells, India Pushes Sterilization," *New York Times*, 22 June 2001, 3(A).

26. Mazumdar, "Fertility Policy in India," 259.

27. Sharma, "India Proposes," 6.

28. Iran has been very successful in promoting family planning and contraceptive use, with the use of modern contraceptives rising from 24 percent in 1976 to 56 in 1997. See Farzeneh Roudi, "Iran's Revolutionary Approach to Family Planning," *Population Today* 27, no. 7 (July/August 1999): 4–5.

29. See, for example, David Foot, *Boom, Bust and Echo* (Toronto: McFarlane, Walters, and Ross, 1996); Doug Owram, *Born at the Right Time: A History of the Baby Boom Generation* (Toronto: University of Toronto Press, 1996).

30. Jean-Claude Chesnais, "The Demographic Sunset of the West," *Population Today* 25, no. 1 (January 1997): 4–5.

31. Review of Demography, *Charting Canada's Future* (Ottawa: Health and Welfare, 1989).

32. Eric G. Moore and Mark W. Rosenberg, *Growing Old in Canada* (Ottawa: Statistics Canada Cat. No. 96-321-MPE, 1997).

33. <http://www.prb.org/pubs/usds2000/> (March 2001). See also Judith Treas, "Older Americans in the 1990s and Beyond," *Population Bulletin* 50, no. 2 (May 1995).

34. Ester Boserup, *Population and Technological Change: A Study of Long-Term Trends* (Chicago: University of Chicago Press, 1981); Ester Boserup, *The Conditions of Agricultural Growth* (Chicago: Aldine, 1965).

35. Review of Demography, *Charting Canada's Future.*

36. See, for example, Moore and Rosenberg, *Growing Old*; Victor W. Marshall, *Aging in Canada*, 2nd edition (Markham, Ont.: Fitzhenry & Whiteside, 1987); Treas, "Older Americans."

37. Geoffrey McNicoll, "Economic Growth with Below-Replacement Fertility," *Population and Development Review* 12 (1986): 217–237; Kingsley Davis, "Low Fertility in Evolutionary Perspective," *Population and Development Review* 12 (1986): 397–417.

38. Henry P. David, "Eastern Europe: Pronatalist Policies and Private Behavior," in *Perspectives on Population*, eds. Scott W. Menard and Elizabeth W. Moen (New York: Oxford University Press, 1987), 250–258.

39. Philippe Fargues, "Protracted National Conflict and Fertility Change among Palestinians and Israelis," *Population and Development Review* 26, no. 3 (September 2000): 441–487.

40. Gary Caldwell and Daniel Fournier, "The Quebec Question: A Matter of Population," *Canadian Journal of Sociology* 12, no. 1–2 (1987): 16–41; Roderic Beaujot, *Population Change in Canada* (Toronto: McClelland & Stewart, 1991).

41. Caldwell and Fournier, "The Quebec Question," 16.

42. Beaujot, *Population Change.*

43. Jean Dumas, *Report on the Demographic Situation in Canada 1990* (Ottawa: Statistics Canada Cat. No. 91-209).

44. Alain Belanger, *Report on the Demographic Situation in Canada 1998–99* (Ottawa: Statistics Canada, Cat. No. 919-209-XPE).

45. Mary Mederios Kent, "Shrinking Societies Favor Procreation," *Population Today* 27, no. 12 (December 1999): 4–5.

46. See the discussions by James F. Hollifield, Phillip L. Martin, Rogers Brubaker, and Elmar Honekopp, and Marcelo M. Suarex-Orozco, in *Controlling Immigration: A Global Perspective*, eds. Wayne A. Cornelius, Philip L. Martin, and James F. Hollifield (Stanford, Calif.: Stanford University Press, 1992).

47. Gelbard, Haub, and Kent, "World Population."

48. Gelbard, Haub, and Kent, "World Population."

49. Peter H. Kostmayer, "Bush 'Gags' the World on Family Planning," *Chicago Tribune*, 25 January 2001, 2(A). Note that Kostmayer is the president of Zero Population Growth (ZPG). Additional references can be found on the ZPG Web site, <http://www.zpg.org/ Reports_Publications/Reports/report188.html> (11 April 2001). See also Liz Creel and Lori Ashford, "Bush Reinstates Policy Restricting Support for International Family Planning Programs," <http://www.prb.org/press/bushreinstates.html> (2 February 2001).

50. Timothy King, *Population Policies and Economic Development* (Baltimore: Johns Hopkins University Press, 1974).

51. Barbara Shane, "Family Planning Saves Lives, Prevents Abortion," *Population Today* 25, no. 3 (March 1997): 1.

52. Sarah Curtis and Ann Taket, *Health and Societies: Changing Perspectives* (London: Arnold, 1996).

53. Carl Haub, "Flat Birth Rates in Bangladesh and Egypt Challenge Demographers' Projections," *Population Today* 28, no. 7 (October 2000): 4.

54. Thomas J. Goliber, "Population and Reproductive Health in Sub-Saharan Africa," *Population Bulletin* 52, no. 4 (December 1997).

55. Goliber, "Population."

56. Up-to-date statistics on the HIV/AIDS epidemic are available at <http://www.unaids-.org/epidemic_update/report_dec00/index_dec.html#f ull> (3 March 2001).

57. Goliber, "Population."

2

‒⊃✴✵⊂‒

The (Un?)Certainty of
Death and Disease

As the counterpoint to fertility, the decline in mortality rates from their historically high levels initiated the demographic transition. In much of Europe and
North America, improvements to human survival and longer **life spans** resulted in
rapid population growth, aided by modernization and advances in sanitation and
nutrition. Declines in mortality were apparent shortly after the onset of the Industrial Revolution, with Europe's population more than doubling between 1800 and
1900.[1] By the first half of the twentieth century, developed countries had completed
their mortality transition, characterized by long life expectancies, low infant death
rates, and slow population growth rates. In the developing world, the second half of
the twentieth century brought rapid population growth, with the initiation of mortality declines in the postwar era. Here, the pace of mortality decline tended to be
much more rapid than that experienced in the developed world, assisted by the
importation of modern medicines, health care, and immunizations.

The past one hundred years have seen remarkable improvements in life expectancy, yet in the end we all still die. Typically expressed as the number of deaths per
one thousand persons, death does not happen equally. Instead, it varies by age, sex,
socioeconomic status, race, ethnicity, and location, with the developed world characterized by lower death rates than elsewhere (figure 2.1). Graphing the age-specific
death rates of American and Mexican males and females (figure 2.2), the J-shaped
function is a characteristic that is found in all countries and populations. The standard age pattern is characterized by differences between males and females and by
death rates that are comparatively high in the first year of life, decline through childhood and adolescence, and then increase into old age. Among women, lower death
rates are shown from birth onward, with female life expectancies averaging seventy-
nine years in the developed world, or an average of seven more years of life than
men. This sex differential is actually greatest for young adults, with the death rates

41

of fifteen- to twenty-four-year-old males approximately three times that of females in the same age group, a difference that is largely attributed to the increased risk of HIV/AIDS, suicide, accidents, or homicides among young males. Moreover, despite overall gains in life expectancy over the past thirty years, fifteen- to twenty-four-year-old males have actually experienced increasing mortality,[2] even though most deaths in this group are preventable. Higher socioeconomic status, whether measured by education, income, or occupation, also confers greater life expectancy.

While death rates quickly portray the risk of dying, demographers typically prefer the complementary measures of life expectancy (the average duration of life beyond age *x*) or the infant mortality rate (the number of deaths to infants less than one year of age divided by the number of live births). Both measures provide descriptions of the mortality experiences of a population and a society's quality of life (figures 2.3, 2.4). As of 2001, global life expectancy at birth averaged sixty-seven years. Averaging seventy-five years, Western (developed) countries enjoy some of the longest life spans and lowest infant mortality rates (eight per one thousand). Conversely, with an average life expectancy of just fifty-one years, sub-Saharan Africa has one of the shortest average life expectancies and one of the highest infant mortality rates (ninety-four per one thousand). The two measures are obviously closely linked, with reductions in infant mortality rates historically extending life expectancy. More

Figure 2.1.   World Variations in Mortality Rates, 2001.

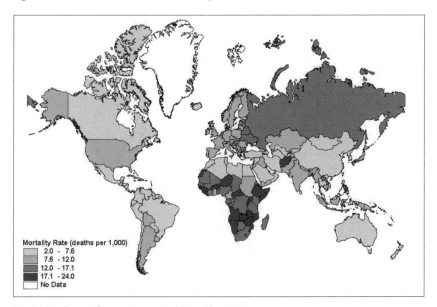

Source: Population Reference Bureau, World Data Sheet, 2001.

Figure 2.2.   U.S. and Mexican Age-Specific Death Rates by Sex, 1995.

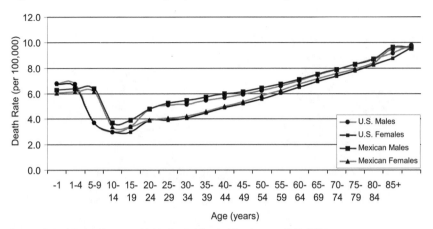

Source: United Nations Demographic Yearbook, Historical Supplement, 1948–1997.

recently, Western nations have seen life expectancies increase through enhanced medical intervention and breakthroughs that can extend life among the elderly.

What is of particular concern are threats to longevity and health from new diseases, along with inequalities in health within and among societies. Consequently, rather than focusing on the mortality process and its mechanics, as most population texts do, the intent of this chapter is to highlight two major themes. The first theme, the reemergence of infectious and parasitic diseases, challenges population health in both the developed and developing world. With the advent and widespread use of powerful antibiotics in the mid-twentieth century, science thought that infectious and parasitic diseases were controllable and ultimately could be eliminated as serious causes of death. The control of measles, mumps, polio, and other common childhood diseases, along with the complete eradication of smallpox further solidified the impression that modern medicine would be able to overcome diseases that had been a scourge to humans for centuries. Yet, in the past two decades, infectious and parasitic diseases have reemerged as threats to societal health. Drug-resistant strains of malaria and tuberculosis and the emergence of new diseases such as HIV/AIDS and ebola have further shaken scientific complacency.

The second theme, inequities in the mortality experience, engages notions of equity, discrimination, and marginalization within modern society by contrasting the mortality experiences in the United States, Canada, and Russia. Race in particular has clear implications for mortality experiences, with African Americans or Canadian Aboriginal infant mortality rates and other health indicators rivaling rates observed in the developing world. Minority groups such as African Americans or indigenous populations are doubly disadvantaged, with shorter life expectancies and

Figure 2.3.   World Variations in Life Expectancy at Birth (years), 2001.

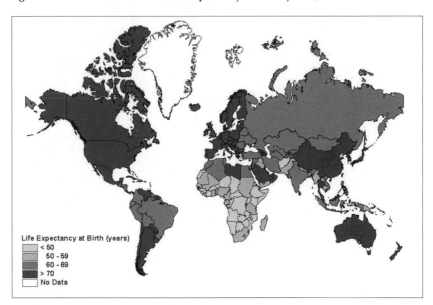

Source: Population Reference Bureau, World Data Sheet, 2001.

higher infant mortality rates on average than their white counterparts. In contrast, Asian Americans reflect the other end of the health and socioeconomic spectrum, with a female life expectancy of eighty years.[3] Russia, on the other hand, which at one time proudly displayed its health system as a triumph of a state-controlled medical system, has experienced increases in mortality over the past three decades as economic conditions deteriorated and its health care system was neglected.

THE (RE)EMERGENCE OF INFECTIOUS AND PARASITIC DISEASES (IPDs)

For much of human history, the average person could probably expect to live only twenty to thirty years. Infant mortality rates were high, and approximately half of all deaths occurred before age five, usually associated with poor nutrition or infanticide. With advances in agriculture and the domestication of animals, humans were able to establish year-round settlements. Infectious diseases such as bubonic plague found a new home in human settlements and became the prevalent cause of death, as denser populations and relatively poor sanitation allowed infectious diseases to thrive. Trade between settlements transported illness and disease across space.[4] The

Figure 2.4.   World Variations in Infant Mortality Rates, 2001.

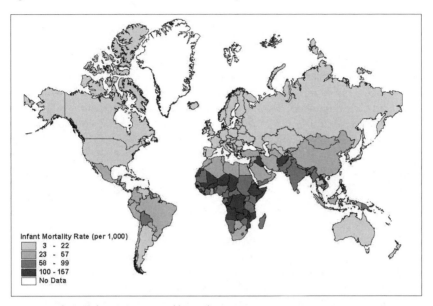

Infant Mortality Rate (per 1,000)
- 3 - 22
- 23 - 57
- 58 - 99
- 100 - 157
- No Data

Source: Population Reference Bureau, World Data Sheet, 2001.

nineteenth and twentieth centuries saw improvements in housing, sanitation, and nutrition, allowing life expectancy in Europe and North America to increase to forty years. The poor health standards and living conditions observed in American, Canadian, and British cities during the Industrial Revolution gave rise to new public health initiatives. This intervention was spearheaded by the elite not out of goodness but out of fear that their own health and perhaps more important, their profits, hinged upon the conditions of the working poor.[5] Although infectious diseases, including tuberculosis, bronchitis, pneumonia, influenza, and measles remained the main cause of death, their incidence declined with environmental improvements, occurring long before medical intervention was widely available.[6] Some diseases such as diphtheria, however, did not respond to societal improvements, declining only when large-scale immunization programs began. In fact, it wasn't until the 1950s that a decline in mortality, particularly among the older population, could be associated with the application of low cost public health programs. Since then, improvements to life expectancy within developed countries have generally been attributed to advances in medical and biological sciences, as opposed to general economic improvements or public health. The mortality transition also results in a shift in the ages when the majority of deaths occur. In countries at the beginning of the transition, younger age groups are at greater risk of dying since children are particularly susceptible to many infectious diseases. Even now, approximately 40 percent of deaths in the developing world occur among children less than five years old. In the developed world, most deaths occur among the elderly, with less than 2 percent of deaths occurring among those less than twenty years old.

Omran's **epidemiological transition**[7] provides a useful framework for looking at these temporal trends in mortality, echoing the decline in mortality set out in the demographic transition theory. However, Omran's theory asserts that modernization not only brings about reductions in overall mortality levels and the timing of death, but also results in a shift in the major causes of death from infectious and contagious diseases to chronic, degenerative disorders. As recently as the mid-eighteenth century, tuberculosis, cholera, diarrhea, and pneumonia/influenza were the leading causes of death throughout the world. Through much of the later half of the twentieth century, resources were marshaled to control infectious and parasitic diseases. By the late 1990s, only pneumonia and influenza remained among the top ten causes of premature death within the developed world. Instead, chronic noncommunicable and degenerative diseases, such as cancer; diabetes; liver, cardiovascular, or neurological diseases, have replaced infectious diseases as the leading cause of death in the developed world. As the incidences of disease and premature death were reduced, individuals were able to enjoy longer life expectancies.

Countries occupy different stages in this transition and progress through it at different rates (table 2.1). Unlike the developed world, where socioeconomic improvements resulted in declining mortality over a span of decades, most developing countries have moved quickly through the epidemiological transition, directly benefiting from the transfer of public health knowledge and medical technology from the developed world. This has meant that the developing world has experienced a much more rapid decline in mortality levels than that experienced in the developed world. International campaigns have inoculated children against many common diseases, the most successful of which was the eradication of smallpox in 1977. Still, many children remain at risk, and IPDs remain the leading cause of death in the developing world. Each year, UNICEF estimates that over 900,000 children die of measles, which alone accounts for over one-half of preventable deaths among children.[8] In Africa, IPDs represent upward of 50 percent of all deaths, especially among the young and very old. One reason that infectious diseases cause a larger percentage of deaths in these areas is purely demographic. The proportion of the population surviving into older ages, where the risk of death from chronic degenerative diseases is greater, is small in many parts of the developing world. Instead, young populations, widespread poverty, malnutrition, and inadequate public health care systems contribute to the high death toll, even though a majority of existing IPDs can be prevented through immunization, safe drinking water, proper food storage, safe sex practices, and personal hygiene.

In the postwar era, huge financial resources were committed to the eradication of infectious diseases. Most notable among these programs was the eradication of

Table 2.1 Leading Causes of Death in the United States and Mexico

	United States (1998)		Mexico (1999)	
Rank	Cause of Death[a]	Percent	Cause of Death[b]	Percent
—	All Causes	100.0	All causes	100.0
1	Heart diseases	31.0	Heart diseases	15.6
2	Malignant neoplasms	23.2	Malignant neoplasms	12.1
3	Cerebrovascular diseases	6.8	Diabetes mellitus	10.3
4	Chronic obstructive pulmonary diseases	4.8	Accidents	8.0
5	Accidents and adverse effects	4.2	Liver diseases	6.1
6	Pneumonia and influenza	3.9	Cerebrovascular diseases	5.8
7	Diabetes mellitus	2.8	Prenatal conditions	4.3
8	Suicide	1.3	Pneumonia and influenza	3.2
9	Nephritis, nephrotic syndrome, and nephrosis	1.1	Assault	2.8
10	Chronic liver disease and cirrhosis	1.1	Chronic obstructive pulmonary diseases	2.5
11	Septicemia	1.0	Malnutrition and other nutritional deficiencies	2.2
12	Alzheimer's disease	1.0	Congenital malformation, deformations and chromosomal abnormalities	2.2
13	Homicide and legal intervention	0.8	Bronchitis, emphysema, and asthma	1.8
14	Arteriosclerosis	0.7	Renal insufficiency	1.8
15	Hypertension with or without renal disease	0.6	Intestinal infectious diseases	1.3
—	All other causes	15.8	All other causes	14.0

Source: United States, National Vital Statistics Report 48, no. 11 (2000). National Institutes of Statistics, Geography and Informatics, 2000.
[a]Based on International Classification of Diseases, 9th rev.
[b]Based on International Classification of Diseases, 10th rev.

smallpox. Its successful defeat in the 1970s seemed to confirm that infectious diseases could greatly be controlled through large-scale public health initiatives. Another major program targeted malaria, a health problem that has plagued humanity throughout history. The drainage of swamps and the control of mosquitoes, the "vectors" that carry malaria, through the application of the pesticide DDT resulted in dramatic reductions in the number of new cases. But the gains were only temporary. After 1963, commitment to the programs waned and the disease returned, worse than before. Long-term use of DDT had given birth to DDT-resistant mosquitoes. Concurrently, inadequate treatment regimes, poor drug supplies, or the misuse of drugs contributed to the rise of drug-resistant malaria.[9] Despite worldwide attempts to control malaria, the disease is as prevalent today as it was at the start of the campaign. The reemergence of malaria should have served as a warning that complacency in the fight against infectious diseases was not an option. The experience with malaria and other microbes indicated that diseases could emerge or reemerge as the causal microbe evolved into a more infectious form, or as new pathways to infection appear. The rise of new IPDs, including the fearsome ebola, a usually deadly disease for which there is no known cure, multidrug resistant tuberculosis, malaria, and meningitis, and new forms of cholera have further shaken our complacency in science's ability to control infectious disease.

A variety of factors have been responsible for the reemergence of IPDs, including change to the natural environment. Human-induced changes can cause genetic changes in organisms or the vectors that transmit diseases (e.g., as in the case of DDT-resistant mosquitoes). Further, the misuse of antibiotics contributes to the rise of drug-resistant forms of malaria and tuberculosis, and HIV/AIDS has resulted in an increase in tuberculosis and pneumonia. Agricultural practices affect the environment within which microbes live and spread, and social, economic, and political conditions have facilitated their return and spread. Population movement has long been an important avenue for the spread of disease. Historically, the bubonic plague was brought to Europe from Asia, and European explorers brought smallpox to North America and Oceania, decimating the indigenous populations who had no resistance to the disease. Settlement and urbanization have concentrated populations and allowed the sustained presence of diseases that were formally epidemic in small areas or for short periods. Cholera, nearly nonexistent in rural areas, quickly rose to epidemic proportions with urbanization, as people were brought together and the risk of contagion was escalated in crowded and unsanitary conditions. Today, rapid urbanization in the developing world repeats this process, as migrants settle in crowded and inadequate conditions. More recently, the surge in IPDs has been due to a breakdown in the provision of public health, with civil strife a prime cause as it disrupts the distribution of needed drugs and food, and refugees fleeing conflict frequently find themselves living in poor and unsanitary conditions that promote the spread of disease. In 1994, more than half a million refugees fled fighting in the

Congo and settled in refugee camps in neighboring countries. Within thirty days, some 50,000 people died as cholera moved through the camps.[10] Similar numbers were reported among Rwandans fleeing the genocide in Rwanda.

The twenty-first century brings with it new challenges in the control of IPDs. Rapid population growth and urbanization has meant that governments have not been able to provide adequate or basic health care or infrastructure such as clean water. Perhaps more worrisome is the speed and ease of transference of disease. The rapidity of movement across countries through jet travel poses additional challenges. Airplanes offer a highly effective means of transportation for disease, with the potential to spread illness and disease across the world in a matter of hours. The arrival of a Congolese woman in Hamilton, Ontario, with symptoms similar to ebola and who had just left the Congo hours earlier, prompted North America's first ebola scare in February 2001.[11] Although ebola was ultimately ruled out, it is only a matter of time before a real case arrives in North America.

WORLDS APART: VARIATIONS ON MORBIDITY, MORTALITY, AND LIFE EXPECTANCY

Since the 1950s, most countries have seen an increase in life expectancy and a reduction in infant mortality. Reductions were particularly dramatic in developing countries with the ability to treat or eradicate infectious diseases such as malaria, smallpox, and yellow fever, where improvements in basic health status had immediate effects. Despite improvements in indicators such as life expectancy or infant mortality within the past fifty years, widespread variations remain. As of 2001, life expectancy in the developed world averaged seventy-five years, being slightly longer for women (seventy-nine) than men (seventy-two). In the developing world (excluding China), life expectancies are lower, averaging sixty-four and sixty-one years from birth among women and men, respectively.[12] Improvements have been slower in sub-Saharan Africa than any other region,[13] with life expectancies in sub-Saharan Africa just fifty-one years, compared to seventy-seven years in North America, seventy-one years in Latin America, and sixty-seven years in Asia. At ninety-four deaths per one thousand births, infant mortality rates are similarly higher in sub-Saharan Africa. In comparison, infant mortality rates are only 7 per 1,000 in North America, 9.0 in Europe, and 55 in Asia.

In summarizing worldwide variations in life expectancy and infant mortality, it is apparent that we tend to make two assumptions. First, it is assumed that health indicators will consistently improve. We have come to expect improvements with life expectancy as medical science continues to make discoveries and as the population is increasingly taught to make lifestyle choices (i.e., smoking) that will extend or protect life. Second, it is generally assumed that poor indicators of health are found only in the developing world. In other words, we are assuming that the Western, developed world has the advantage of an accessible and developed health care system that ensures population health. Yet, neither of these assumptions is correct, as is seen by recent declines in life expectancy and increases in infant mortality in Russia. Even within the developed world, with access to cutting-edge medical systems, it is readily apparent that we do not have everything right. Health and mortality differentials in the developed world are particularly problematic, not because they represent populations that require large-scale intervention and have little access to health care, but for the exact opposite reasons. That is, in the presence of a large health care infrastructure, poor mortality experiences within segments of the population seem to be a paradox, yet are common throughout much of the developed world. Rather than focusing on the triumphs of the medical system, the following sections look at its failures and shortcomings.[14]

Russia

As recently as 1900, Russian life expectancy was only slightly greater than thirty years, reduced by infant mortality rates that most likely reached three hundred per one thousand and a child mortality rate of up to 50 percent.[15] Within a relatively short period of time, the former Soviet Union had successfully reduced mortality and increased life expectancy within its population, with rates in the early 1960s comparable to those found in the United States and elsewhere in the developed world. Despite these dramatic improvements in health in the post-revolutionary period, the Soviet Union could not keep pace with the West with respect to basic health outcomes from the 1960s onward. As life expectancy and infant mortality continued to improve in the West, they deteriorated in the former Soviet Union. By the 1990s, observers of Russia's demographic system noted that male life expectancy had dropped from sixty-five years in 1987 to fifty-seven in 1994. Similarly, female life expectancy dropped by more than three years to an average of seventy-one years.[16] Although there is some disagreement about what caused the declines in mortality, most placed this decline within the context of the breakup of the Soviet Union in 1989 and its corresponding economic and social turmoil, along with inadequate health services, lack of prescription medicine, alcohol abuse, and smoking behavior.

Russia's mortality experiences run counter to typical expectations, demonstrating that mortality decline and the epidemiological transition are not unidirectional. While the exact causes of the deterioration of health outcomes are unknown and debated, they reflect a much longer process dating back over thirty years to the Soviet era. Infant mortality in the Soviet Union was always relatively high, but research in the 1970s by Davis and Feshbach[17] notes infant mortality rates started to diverge from Western experiences. While infant mortality rates continued to decline in the West, rates in the former Soviet Union stabilized at approximately twenty-five and then increased to over thirty by the mid-1970s. At about the same time, the Soviet Union stopped publishing detailed mortality statistics, a point that speaks for itself.[18] Davis and Feshbach attribute the increase in the infant mortality rate to social, economic, and medical reasons, including increased smoking and drinking among mothers, poor maternal nutrition and health, inadequate health care during pregnancy, and unsanitary conditions in hospitals. They also noticed strong regional differences in mortality, with the rise in infant mortality lead by Central Asian republics including Uzbekistan and Kazakhstan, along with the Caucasian Republics of Georgia and Armenia.

The declining life expectancy among Russian men in the 1990s was not new either, but instead reflected longer-term trends, with Soviet indices worsening relative to the West as early as the 1970s. After a temporary improvement in life expectancies in the 1980s, which was attributed to an aggressive anti-alcohol campaign under President Mikhail Gorbachev, the gap between the Soviet Union and the West continued to grow into the 1990s. As with infant mortality, a portion of the widening gap was the result of increasing life expectancy in the West. But the gap also reflected deeper institutional problems within the Soviet Union itself, including inadequate health services and the general neglect of the Soviet and Russian health care system. Alcohol abuse and high rates of cardiovascular disease and injury also contributed to declining life expectancy.

Although male life expectancy had rebounded to sixty-six years by 2001, and Russia's infant mortality rate had dropped to sixteen in 2001, it remains to be seen whether these measures will continue to improve in the near future. The democratically nascent Russia continues to grapple with economic and social reform, and its health care system remains in a state of crisis. Russia must first catch up to the levels of infant mortality and life expectancy that were observed in the 1960s before approaching Western levels. In the meantime, political uncertainty and stalled economic reforms mean that its health institutions remain underfunded, and social and economic conditions remain poor, neither of which are conducive for improvements to life expectancy.

African Americans

The poor health outcomes of Russia and the neglect of its health care system contrast markedly with American trends and health experiences. Americans have access to some of the best health care in the world, and their health care system consumes a significantly higher proportion of the **gross domestic product (GDP)** than other developed countries.[19] A casual observer might, therefore, expect the United States to have the lowest infant mortality rate or the highest life expectancy. In fact, with an infant mortality rate of 7.1 and a life expectancy of seventy-seven years, health indicators within the United States are rather poor by Western standards. Instead, the honors of lowest infant mortality rate and longest life expectancy go to Sweden (3.4) and Japan (eighty-one years), respectively. In fact, one hardly needs to travel far within the United States to observe health indicators that are more akin to those found in the developing world than the developed world, placing American indicators closer to the bottom of the developed world's list than the top.

In large part, the poor performance of American mortality indicators reflects the poor health status and mortality conditions of its minority populations. Health disparities are particularly noticeable among African Americans. Despite dramatic improvements in life expectancies since 1900 (from approximately 33 years to 71.3 years in 1998), they remain shorter than white Americans, who average 77.3 years of life. In Washington D.C., male life expectancy among African Americans is only fifty-nine years, the shortest in the nation. African American mortality rates are nearly double those observed within the white population at every age except the very oldest, having higher rates of death from almost every major cause relative to whites, especially for heart disease, cancer, HIV/AIDS, and homicide. The increased risk of death is magnified among young African American males, where homicide is the leading cause of death, while white men are more likely to die in accidents[20] (table 2.2). Blacks are also several times more likely to die from AIDS than whites.[21] Smaller geographic scales show these same disparities. Across the United States, infant mortality rates are highly variable, with many of the Southern states having above average rates, including Mississippi (10.5), Louisiana (9.8), and South Carolina (9.6). The District of Columbia had a 1998 IMR of 16.2, the highest in the nation.[22] Within the state of Illinois, which is one of the richest states in the United States, the 1998 IMR (8.2) was worse than the national average (7.0). This value, however, reflects a white IMR of just 6.3, and an IMR of 16.8 among African Americans, rates that are comparable to Sri Lanka (16.8) and Russia (16.5)! At an even smaller scale, the 1993–1997 average IMR within the city of Chicago was 18.3 among African Americans, but just 7.4 among whites.

While the disparities in mortality experiences of black and white Americans are startling, they are hardly surprising, reflecting the continued marginalization of blacks within American society, measured by inequalities in education, economic status, or occupation. Despite improvements in their overall economic and social status from the 1930s onward, blacks continue to be marginalized within U.S. society. Although legislation has reduced the social and economic gulf between blacks and whites, it remains substantial. For instance, median overall household income in 1999 was $40,816, yet for blacks, the median household income was only $27,910. Similarly, blacks experience lower educational attainment, with only 13.5 percent completing four or more years of college, compared to 21.9 percent in the total population.[23] Minority children suffer disproportionately from economic deprivation, with child poverty among black children running three times that of white children.[24] The prevalence of poor mortality outcomes is also an indicator of social problems within the African American community that encompass socioenvironmental risks, personal risks, and inadequate service provision. Poor health outcomes among African Americans are also linked to broader health concerns, including housing conditions, access to public health, and poor infrastructure. Latent racism and ongoing economic inequalities will perpetuate the differences for the foreseeable

Table 2.2 Leading Causes of Death for Black and White Males Aged 25–44 in the United States, 1998

	Black Males			White Males		
Rank	Cause of Death[a]	Number	Rate	Cause of Death	Number	Rate
—	All causes	19,732	384.0	All causes	63,954	187.3
1	Accidents and adverse effects	3,091	60.1	Accidents and adverse effects	16,479	48.3
	Motor vehicle and adverse effects	1,575	30.6	Motor vehicle and adverse effects	8,036	23.5
	All other accidents and effects	1,516	29.5	All other accidents and effects	8,444	24.7
2	HIV infection	3,052	59.4	Diseases of the heart	8,693	25.5
3	Homicide and legal intervention	3,031	59.0	Suicide	8,594	25.2
4	Diseases of the heart	3,783	54.2	Malignant neoplasms	7,690	22.5
5	Malignant neoplasms	1,630	31.7	HIV infection	3,381	9.9
6	Suicide	781	15.2	Homicide and legal intervention	2,982	8.7
7	Cerebrovascular diseases	498	9.7	Chronic liver disease and cirrhosis	2,214	6.5
8	Diabetes mellitus	397	7.7	Cerebrovascular diseases	1,137	3.3
9	Pneumonia and influenza	354	6.9	Diabetes mellitus	1,071	3.1
—	All other causes	3,769	73.3	All other causes	10,991	32.2

Source: United States, *National Vital Statistics Report,* 48, no. 11, 2000.
[a]Based on *International Classification of Diseases, 9th rev.*

future. The marginalization of African Americans also extends to the health care system, a system that provides fewer services and clinics in poor areas, and where blacks are less likely to be insured and less likely to use health care facilities than their white counterparts. [25] Moreover, differences in mortality by race remain even after comparing individuals with similar levels of income and education.

The fact that the United States trails other developed countries on key population indicators reflects its patchwork health care system that is dominated by user-pay or private health insurance, as opposed to state-funded, universal health care programs seen in countries such as the United Kingdom or Canada. The situation is magnified among African Americans, where their lower socioeconomic position within American society makes the affordability of private medical plans less likely, meaning that those who are in greatest need for care can least afford it. In 1998, for instance, black children were three times more likely than whites to be covered by Medicaid (39 percent versus 13 percent), and 20 percent of black children had no health care insurance. In comparison, less than 11 percent of white, non-Hispanic children lack some form of health insurance.[26] While public health programs such as Medicare or Medicaid are available for the poor or elderly, these programs are limited and means-tested. For the remainder, it has become too expensive to pay for private health insurance, and an estimated forty million Americans have no insurance, meaning they forgo medical treatment, rely upon social service agencies for assistance, or utilize emergency room services where the cost of medical attention is significantly greater. The structure of the American health care system extends to the location of service providers. Physicians, clinics, and institutions locate in areas with higher financial returns, and inner-city areas have fewer services. Over the past two decades, the number of public hospitals that provide care for the poor has declined from 1,778 in 1980 to 1,197 in 1999, victims of hospital closures, acquisitions, or mergers.[27] Inner-city areas have difficulty in recruiting doctors and frequently depend upon federal programs such as the National Health Services Corp., created in 1970 to provide basic care to inner-city neighborhoods. These structural barriers to care mean that poor, inner-city areas are frequently underserviced, a situation that may be worsened under the new Bush administration, which has proposed cuts to a variety of health programs for people without health insurance.[28]

Canadian Aboriginals

The United States does not monopolize poor health among its subpopulations. Comprising approximately 4 percent of the Canadian population, Aboriginal peoples (the indigenous Canadian population including North American Indians, Inuit, and Metis) bear a disproportionate burden of illness regardless of the indicator used,[29] despite the existence of generous government health programs.[30] For example, the life expectancy of Aboriginal males is only sixty-four years, compared to approximately seventy-three years for Canadian males. For females, life expectancy is approximately seventy-one years, eight years less than the Canadian average of seventy-nine years. High infant mortality rates (16.3 among Inuit, 13.8 among Native American Indians) exceed the Canadian average of 7.3, with disparities heightened in more remote locations or on reservations.

Responsibility for Aboriginal health care lies within the federal government's domain and is administered through provincial or territorial plans. Status Indians (individuals registered under the Indian Act of 1876, which formally recognized their Aboriginal heritage and brought Aboriginals under the control of the federal government) and the Inuit also receive nonmedical services such as drug, eye, and dental care through the Medical Services Branch of Health and Welfare Canada. Like the United States, the poor health outcomes of Canadian Aboriginals are linked to their economic and social conditions as well as a history of oppression and marginalization, reinforced by racism and discrimination. The impacts of colonialism, both pre- and post-1867, have had widespread and long-term impacts on the health of the population. Early on, epidemics of smallpox, measles, and tuberculosis destroyed large parts of the population. Under federal control, Aboriginals were often forced into residential schools that removed children from their parents and replaced their traditional culture and way of life with a European one. The stress associated with cultural dispossession and **assimilation** into Western society has weakened traditional cultural structures and values by removing traditional sources of support and identification. It is likely that such factors negatively influence Aboriginal health by promoting the disintegration of the community, hindrance of good health care practices, and participation in risky health behavior.

Marginalization and discrimination cannot account for all health disparities. Environmental conditions such as inadequate housing, lack of running water or unsafe water, poverty, poor housing conditions, and low self-esteem reinforce high rates of alcohol and substance abuse, themselves partly responsible for the observed disparities in health. Geographic remoteness and physical access to health care play a role in the health status of the Aboriginal population. While residents of urban areas may have access to a greater variety of services, they may not be utilized to their full benefit. In remote, rural areas, on-reservation service provision may only be in the form of a resident community health representative and a doctor who fills in on a semiregular basis.

EMERGENT THEMES AND ISSUES

Changes to the mortality experiences of populations were one of the most significant events of the twentieth century. Unlike the previous century, the twenty-first century will likely see less dramatic changes to life expectancy within the developed world. Similarly, the developing world will likely see some change, although the degree of change and direction is unclear. It is, in fact, equally likely that life expectancy will *decrease* in parts of the developing world as infectious diseases including HIV/AIDS continue to take their toll. As we look ahead over the coming decades, four nonexclusive issues relating to the mortality and **morbidity** experiences of populations can be raised, including the implication associated with aging societies, the threats to mortality gains posed by urbanization, the renewed threat of infectious and parasitic diseases, and the provision of health services and other programs to improve population health.

First, the twentieth century has witnessed remarkable improvements in life expectancy, with a concurrent increase in life expectancy after age sixty-five. Advances in medical technology have meant that an increasing number are surviving into old age, but it is among the "old-elderly," variously referred to as those greater than seventy-five, eighty, or even eighty-five years that the largest increases in morbidity (sickness) are observed. Therefore, are improvements to life expectancy a double-edged sword? For example, what are the implications of aging Western societies in terms of increased morbidity, service provision, and support of a growing elderly population? Has this increase come at the expense of an increasing number of years of morbidity?

Answering these questions is not simple, as they imply a quality versus quantity question. The extension of the quantity of life may come at the expense of quality, defined by deteriorating and chronic health conditions, increased reliance on others such as family or service providers for support, and expensive medical intervention. The increasing disability among the elderly further devolves into value-laden questions of the need for medical intervention to save or prolong a life at all costs and may require a shift in thinking and resources to improve the quality of life or "years of health." The incidence of death from heart disease within America has, for example, declined in the past three decades. It has also meant, however, that people tend to live longer with heart disease. In large part, this is due to better medical treatment and the advent of new drugs that have increased survival rates.[31] Since, however, such diseases cause only half of the reported disability and loss of functioning, improvements in health do not necessarily lead to increases in life expectancy. Most individuals will now experience some period of disease and disability before death, with health status among the elderly increasingly associated with nonfatal conditions, including arthritis, vision loss, and Alzheimer's. These conditions, and others, will become increasingly important causes of disability and functioning loss in old age.

A larger elderly population and numbers of disabled elderly imply greater need for support. It is generally expected that as life expectancy increases, the number of disabled people, particularly among the old-elderly, will increase, placing ever-greater strains on the health care system. Institutional support, in the form of nursing homes or chronic care facilities for an increasingly old and disabled elderly population will require policy attention. As noted by Eric Moore and Mark Rosenberg, keeping up with the demand for space within institutions will be a crucial issue.[32] Market-driven systems will create service-rich and service-poor areas if the use and provision of services reflects an ability to pay. While this may be given and acceptable in the U.S. health care environment, countries with socialized medicine programs, including Canada and England, may be faced with a service provision crisis, and/or large variations in the type, quality, and quantity of resources available for the elderly.

Second, although urbanization has not been specifically addressed within this chapter, it poses additional, specific challenges to mortality and morbidity experiences. Currently, 40 percent of the developing world's population resides in urban areas, and it is projected that a majority of the developing world's population will live in urban areas by 2020. Historically, urban areas have lead fertility decline, creating a reason for optimism if this urbanization pattern continues. In the nineteenth century, urban residents in Europe and North America were among the first to widely practice family planning techniques, helping to spread the idea of smaller families to rural areas. Fertility is also lower in cities in the developing world where the costs of childbearing are higher and family planning services are more available. Historically, mortality and disease rates have also been lower in urban areas relative to rural areas.[33]

While urban areas may confer health benefits, significant emerging health concerns may place urban residents at a disadvantage with respect to mortality experiences in the near future. Urban health advantages hide the huge disparity between the urban poor and their wealthy counterparts, particularly in the developing world where mortality experiences are frequently far worse in poor urban than rural areas.[34] In one study in Bangladesh, for example, infant death rates varied from 95 to 152 per 1,000 in urban areas, higher than both middle-class urban areas (32) and rural Bangladesh.[35] Continued in-migration from rural areas and increasing population density may push mortality and morbidity higher in urban areas. Many cities in the developing world have grown faster than their infrastructure, leaving large proportions of their populations without adequate and safe water or sanitation, allowing diseases associated with poverty to increase in urban areas. It is important to realize, however, that while the poor may bear a greater burden of disease, they alone do not experience increased mortality and health deprivation in urban areas. Cities in the developing world have high levels of air and water pollution, with air pollution in parts of Asia having a marked impact upon health. Children are at the greatest risk. Third, infectious diseases, including HIV/AIDS, also pose a larger risk in urban areas. Poor living conditions is a key factor in the transmission of disease, while more permissive sexual norms than in rural settings and the presence of male migrant workers who frequent prostitutes promote the HIV infection.[36] One United Nations estimate found HIV infection rates up to four times higher in urban areas. Given these trends, the traditional advantage of urban areas is likely to be diminished in the future.

Third, infectious and parasitic diseases remain a threat to health. In the developed world, there is a need for action to avoid epidemics associated with the importation of disease. Despite safety nets that are designed to prevent diseases from entry, such as the health screening of immigrants, the system is not foolproof. Systems and procedures must be in place if epidemics are to be avoided. The developing world faces its own set of problems. Among these, the poor living conditions associated with rapid urbanization and poverty in many cities of the developing world create an ideal breeding ground for disease. Clearly, steps must be taken to rectify these problems, whether by controlling internal migration or by providing appropriate infrastructure. Controlling internal migration is difficult and only possible in authoritarian regimes such as China. Even there, where internal migration is supposedly controlled, the illegal migration of Chinese peasants to cities in search of new opportunities remains a problem for authorities. Provision of appropriate nutrition and sanitation or infrastructure is no less problematic given the huge price and political implications in a world were economic and food assistance is frequently tied to the political agendas of the developed world. Yet, less than half the population have access to clean water in some developing countries, and more than one-third of the world's population under the age of five are underweight and undernourished, compromising their current ability to survive along with their future ability.

Finally, improvements in life expectancy and infant mortality can hardly be removed from the provision of health care and related services. While some authors[37] have called for a medically driven response to the problems of IPDs and other health threats via the development of new vaccines, antibiotics, and improved laboratories, these methods carry a high price and may be years in research and development. Frequently, their applicability in the developing world is limited, as demonstrated by the reluctance of drug companies to provide drugs to combat HIV/AIDS in these locations. As discussed in the following chapter, the HIV/AIDS epidemic poses a particular challenge in parts of Africa, Asia, and the Caribbean. In sub-Saharan Africa, life expectancy has only recently exceeded fifty years, but currently averages just thirty-seven years in Zambia, and thirty-nine years in Malawi and Rwanda. Moreover, life expectancies in some of these sub-Saharan countries have already fallen due to AIDS.[38] The economic and social impact of HIV/AIDS and its demographic implications—orphans and a shrinking labor force—are staggering, creating the potential for civil unrest and war. The monies and resources to deal with HIV/AIDS are limited, and Western drug companies may be disinterested in finding an inexpensive cure—their fortunes await in the developed world.

If expensive medical programs and intervention cannot provide the assurance of basic population health, other directions must instead be pursued. As a starting point, improvements to life expectancy must be achieved through a renewed commitment to public health programs and basic health care, providing a frontline defense against IPDs, maternal health, and other health concerns. The idea of providing basic health care is, of course, not new, since the World Health Organization and other groups have been promoting basic health care for some time. Unfortunately, the provision of basic health care has fallen off the radar screens of many countries and agencies, as they wrongly believe that this goal has been met. With less than half the population in the developing world having access to health care, the numbers tell the true story. In China, huge numbers of rural residents are without primary health care, as the system of rural-based health care (China's highly regarded "barefoot doctors") and free rural clinics has disintegrated over the past decade. In its place, new market-driven health care, with its higher costs and profit orientation, has taken hold. Poor rural residents are unable to afford even basic medical care in local, private clinics, and the cost of basic medicines is beyond the reach of most people's income. Recent Chinese health statistics are also telling of the decline of health care, with a quadrupling of tuberculosis cases in the past fifteen years, declining immunization rates, increasing maternal mortality, and increasing infant mortality in rural areas.[39] Unfortunately, China's declining basic health care system is more the rule in the developing world than the exception. Elsewhere, public health care has been diminished in the face of civil strife, ethnic rivalries, and overburdened governments that lack the financial ability to implement health programs.

The provision of basic health care to meet the needs of the population is only one piece of the health puzzle, being insufficient on their own to ameliorate or remove inequalities in morbidity or mortality. Instead, it is increasingly realized that the broader determinants of health, including education, sanitation, and nutrition, lifestyle options (i.e., smoking, drinking, and drug use behavior), housing conditions, and personal power, impact directly upon health and mortality experiences.[40] Despite the importance of these factors and their contribution to health, governments have been relatively slow to address disparities. The Canadian government, for example, has attempted to address health disparities within the Aboriginal population, although past attempts to improve their health status have tended to focus upon a rather narrow, biomedical definition of health that can be addressed simply by the importation of Western medicine. Consequently, health policy has typically reacted to *departures* from health, neglecting the broader determinants of health. More generally, governments have focused their resources on the delivery of health care within their domestic populations. Addressing the broader determinants of health also means that governments and other institutions must focus upon reducing economic and social disparities at both the international and national levels, with the goal of equalizing health indicators between advantaged and disadvantaged groups such as African Americans or Aboriginals. In large part, the gap in mortality and morbidity rates between Aboriginals and the Canadian population could be closed through a combination of improved living standards, lifestyles, social control, access to health care resources, and equity between groups.[41]

Clearly, however, investments in public infrastructure to provide clean drinking water, sanitation, appropriate housing, public education, or other programs, let alone the provision of basic health care services within the developing world, are limited. While needed, such a broad response to health conditions and mortality experiences is likely to be constrained by budgets and inadequate resources, as previously noted in chapter 1. Attempts to do so are further constraining population growth and political agendas that shape economic assistance, with growth frequently slowing the attainment of these goals in low-income countries and creating a young population that places large demands upon costly educational, social, and health services. Solutions will not come easily or inexpensively.

NOTES

1. Alene Gelbard, Carl Haub, and Mary M. Kent, *World Population Beyond Six Billion*, *Population Bulletin* 54, no. 1 (March 1999).

2. Joseph A. McFalls, Jr., "Population: A Lively Introduction," *Population Bulletin* 53, no. 3 (September 1998).

3. John R. Weeks, *Population: An Introduction to Concepts and Issues*, 7th edition (Belmont, Calif.: Wadsworth, 1999).

4. For a discussion of the geographical diffusion of illness, see Andrew Cliff and Peter Haggett, "Spatial Aspects of Epidemic Control," *Progress in Human Geography* 13 (1989): 315–347; Andrew Cliff and Peter Haggett, *Atlas of Disease Distributions: Analytical Approaches to Disease Data* (Oxford: Blackwell, 1988); Peter Gould, *The Slow Plague: A Geography of the AIDS Pandemic* (Oxford: Blackwell, 1993).

5. Michael Bliss, *A Living Profit* (Toronto: McClelland & Stewart, 1974); Terry Copp, *The Anatomy of Poverty* (Toronto: McClelland & Stewart, 1974).

6. Thomas McKeown, *The Role of Medicine: Dream, Mirage, or Nemesis* (Princeton, N.J.: Princeton University Press, 1979).

7. Abdel Omran, "The Epidemiological Transition: A Theory of the Epidemiology of Population Change," *Milbank Memorial Fund Quarterly* 49 (1971): 509–538.

8. <http://www.unicef.org/gavi> (12 April 2001).

9. S. Jay Olsahansky, Bruce Carnes, Richard G. Rogers, and Len Smith, "Infectious Diseases—New and Ancient Threats to World Health," *Population Bulletin* 52, no. 2 (July 1997).

10. Olsahansky, Carnes, Rogers, and Smith, "Infectious Diseases."

11. Joanna Frketich, "Anatomy of Ebola Scare in Hamilton," *Hamilton Spectator*, 17 February 2001, 1(A).

12. *World Population Data Sheet*, Population Reference Bureau (Washington, D.C.: Population Reference Bureau, 2001). Unless noted otherwise, population statistics throughout this book are drawn from this source.

13. Thomas J. Goliber, "Population and Reproductive Health in Sub-Saharan Africa," *Population Bulletin* 52, no. 4 (December 1997).

14. From a theoretical standpoint, the biomedical model and body as machine, two dominant themes in Western medicine, have been criticized. For reviews of this literature, see Sarah Curtis and Ann Taket, *Health and Societies* (London: Arnold, 1996); Kelvyn Jones and Graham Moon, *Health, Disease and Society* (London: Routledge, 1992).

15. Sergei Maksudov, "Some Causes of Rising Mortality in the USSR," in *Perspectives on Population*, eds. Scott W. Menard and Elizabeth W. Moen (New York: Oxford University Press, 1987), 156–174.

16. John Haaga, "High Death Rate among Russian Men Predates Soviet Union's Demise," *Population Today* 28, no. 3 (April 2000): 1.

17. Christopher Davis and Murray Feshbach, *Rising Infant Mortality in the USSR in the 1970s* (Washington, D.C.: U.S. Bureau of the Census, Series P-95, no. 74, September 1980).

18. Maksudov, "Some Causes," 156.

19. In 1991, for example, the United States spent 13.0 percent of its GDP on health care. In Canada, it was 9.9 percent.

20. McFalls, "Population."

21. <http://www.ameristat.org/mortality/Racial_Ethnic_Differences.html> (10 March 2001).

22. Population Reference Bureau, *Kids Count Data Sheet* (Washington, D.C.: Population Reference Bureau, 2000).

23. United States Bureau of the Census. <http://www.census.gov/population/www/soc-demo/educ-attn.html> (10 March 2001).

24. U.S. Bureau of the Census, *Current Population Survey*, Series P-60 (Washington, D.C.: Bureau of the Census, 1998).

25. Norman J. Waitzman and Ken R. Smith, "Separate but Lethal: The Effects of Economic Segregation on Mortality in Metropolitan America," *Milbank Quarterly* 76, no 3. (1998): 341–373.

26. <http://www.ameristat.org/children/HealthInsuranceCoverageChildren.html> (10 March 2001).

27. Sheryl Gay Stolberg, "After Two Centuries, Washington Is Losing Its Only Public Hospital," *New York Times*, 7 May 2001, 1(A).

28. Robert Pear, "Bush Budget on Health Care Would Cut Aid to Uninsured," *New York Times*, 4 April 2001, 3(B).

29. The indigenous populations in the United States, Australia, and New Zealand show similar discrepancies in morbidity and mortality statistics, representing a common history of oppression, racism, and discrimination that has created a population that remains marginalized.

30. Numerous authors have written on the health of the Aboriginal population. See the works by T. Kue Young, *Health Care and Cultural Change: The Indian Experience in the Central Artic* (Toronto: University of Toronto Press, 1988); Peter H. Stephensen and Susan J. Elliott, *A Persistent Spirit: Towards an Understanding of Aboriginal Health in British Columbia* (Vancouver: UBC Press, 1995); Health and Welfare Canada, *Aboriginal Health Care in Canada* (Ottawa: Minister of Supply and Services, 1992).

31. Judith Treas, "Older Americans in the 1990s and Beyond," *Population Bulletin* 50, no. 2 (May 1995).

32. Eric G. Moore and Mark W. Rosenberg, *Growing Old in Canada* (Ottawa: Statistics Canada Cat. No. 96-321-MPE, 1997).

33. See the broader discussion of urban issues, including the perspectives from the developing and developed worlds in Martin P. Brockerhoff, "An Urbanizing World," *Population Bulletin* 55, no. 3 (September 2000).

34. Trudy Harpham and Carolyn Stephens, "Urbanization and Health in Developing Countries," *World Health Statistics Quarterly* 44, no. 2 (1991): 62–69.

35. Referenced from Brockerhoff, "An Urbanizing World," 23.

36. United Nations, *AIDS and the Demography of Africa* (New York: United Nations, 1994).

37. Olsahansky, Carnes, Rogers, and Smith, "Infectious Diseases."

38. Up-to-date statistics on the HIV/AIDS epidemic are available at: <http://www.unaids.org/ /epidemic_update/report_dec00/index_dec.html> (April 2001).

39. Elisabeth Rosenthal, "Without 'Barefoot Doctors,' China's Rural Families Suffer," *New York Times*, 14 March 2001, 2(A).

40. Robert G. Evans and Gregory L. Stoddart, "Producing Health, Consuming Health Care," *Social Science and Medicine* 31, no. 12 (1990): 1247–1363.

41. See K. Bruce Newbold, "Problems in Search of Solutions: Health and Canadian Aboriginals," *Journal of Community Health* 23, no. 1 (1998): 59–73.

3

⸎

The Impact of HIV and AIDS

While the previous chapter introduced mortality experiences and briefly discussed the HIV/AIDS epidemic, it is useful to take a more detailed look at this disease, along with its web of interrelated demographic, social, and economic effects. After all, the human immunodeficiency virus (HIV), the virus that causes AIDS (acquired immunodeficiency syndrome) has resulted in an epidemic that is far more extensive than was forecasted just a decade ago. By December 2000, 21.8 million people worldwide had died of AIDS since the beginning of the epidemic in the early 1980s, including 4.3 million children. Worse, the toll is expected to double within the next decade. Another 36.1 million people were living with HIV/AIDS at the dawn of the millennium, a number that can only be assumed to increase or represent a portion of the true number of infected, given the difficulties of reporting or screening in many countries. Most HIV cases (95 percent) are found in the developing world, where the scale of the epidemic has profound economic, social, demographic, and political implications.

HIV most likely entered North America sometime in the 1970s; the world was introduced to HIV and AIDS in 1981 when it was identified among gay men in the United States. Globally, it was likely around for much longer. A reexamination of a blood sample taken in 1959 confirmed the presence of HIV/AIDS at that time.[1] Commonly thought to have emerged somewhere in Central Africa and present-day Congo, the scientific community is still at a loss to explain exactly where it came from, although the most plausible theory is that the virus somehow moved from monkeys across the species barrier into humans, perhaps through hunting, religious, or cultural ceremonies, with recent evidence all but cementing this theory.[2] With little interaction and population mobility, it had potentially survived for decades within the human population, albeit at very low levels and within a spatially confined area. Civil war in the Congo in the early 1960s likely facilitated its movement into the larger population, carried by soldiers and aided by refugee movements and famine. It would emerge as a major public health concern and a leading cause of death throughout the world within a generation.

Technically, AIDS is not a single disease, but a complex of diseases and symptoms that lead to a degenerative and disabling death. Nearly 100 percent fatal, HIV kills by destroying the bodies' immune system, increasing susceptibility to infections and other malignancies. Frequently, opportunistic infections such as tuberculosis or once rare forms of pneumonia or cancers (i.e., Kaposi's sarcoma) are the direct causes of death, but all are facilitated by the initial HIV virus. The disease follows a slow progression for the first five to ten years after infection with few outward signs of its progression and presence. Yet, this slow progression makes it so deadly, giving infected persons years to spread it. Eventually, HIV infection leads to full-blown AIDS, a transition that occurs when an HIV infected person has at least one of the following: opportunistic infection, malignancy, dementia, weight loss of 15 percent of body weight, or a T-helper count below two hundred.[3]

Carried by blood or other body fluids, transmission of the virus occurs through a number of pathways. In the North American and European context, homosexual activity carries the greatest risk of infection, with men having sex with men (MSM) accounting for 49 percent of infections in the United States.[4] Risk of infection is increased through unsafe sexual practices or the number of sexual partners. Injecting drug use and the sharing of contaminated needles is also a major pathway, accounting for approximately 25 percent of infections in the United States. Only 10 percent of all infections are attributable to heterosexual contact, although this proportion has been slowly but steadily increasing. Mother to child transmission is also an important pathway, with pregnant infected women having a 25 to 50 percent chance of passing the infection to the child (either during pregnancy, during childbirth, or through breastfeeding), although numerous options exist to control infection from mother to the child, including **antiretroviral drugs.** While MSM still accounts for the majority of HIV cases reported in North America, infection through injection drug use is rising. In Canada, injected drug use accounts for nearly 50 percent of all new infections. Elsewhere, the proportion of infections from injected drug use accounts for 70 percent or more of new infections in China, the Russian Federation, Ukraine, and Vietnam. HIV has also "leaked out" of these high-risk groups into the heterosexual community, aided by contact through prostitution or homosexual contact. The movement of the HIV epidemic into the heterosexual population poses far greater challenges to its control.

In North America and Europe, the openness with which the disease is discussed has helped slow its spread, reflected in the low adult **prevalence** rates[5] of 0.6 percent in North America and less than 0.3 percent in Western Europe (table 3.1).[6] Public education campaigns that have promoted the dangers of risky behavioral choices have been largely successful. Elsewhere, the disease is much more prevalent and threatening. In sub-Saharan Africa, a continent where the epidemic has hit particularly hard, the adult prevalence rate is near 9 percent, with one-quarter to one-third of adults infected in some countries. Here, transmission of the virus is predominately through heterosexual contact, placing a much larger proportion of the population at risk and creating a greater potential for the disease to spread rapidly in

Table 3.1 Regional HIV/AIDS Statistics and Features, 2000

Region	Epidemic Started	Adults and Children Living with HIV/AIDS	Adults and Children Newly Infected with HIV	Adult Prevalence Rate[a] (%)	Percent of HIV-Positive Adults Who Are Women	Main Mode(s) of Transmission[b]
Sub-Saharan Africa	Late '70s Early '80s	25.3 million	3.8 million	8.8	55	Hetero
North Africa and Middle East	Late '80s	400,000	80,000	0.2	40	Hetero IDU
South and Southeast Asia	Late '80s	5.8 million	780,000	0.56	35	Hetero IDU
East Asia and Pacific	Late '80s	640,000	130,000	0.07	13	IDU Hetero MSM
Latin America	Late '70s Early '80s	1.4 million	150,000	0.5	25	MSM IDU Hetero
Caribbean	Late '70s Early '80s	390,000	60,000	2.3	35	Hetero MSM
Eastern Europe and Central Asia	Early '90s	700,000	250,000	0.35	35	IDU
Western Europe	Late '70s Early '80s	540,000	30,000	0.24	25	MSM IDU
North America	Late '70s Early '80s	920,000	45,000	0.6	20	MSM IDU Hetero
Australia and New Zealand	Late '70s Early '80s	15,000	500	0.13	10	MSM
Total		36.1 million	5.3 million	1.1	47	

Source: Reproduced by kind permission of the Joint United Nations Programme on HIV/AIDS (UNAIDS).

[a]The proportion of adults (15–49 years of age) living with HIV/AIDS in 2000 population numbers.

[b]Hetero (heterosexual transmission), IDU (transmission through injecting drug use), MSM (sexual transmission among men who have sex with men).

comparison to when it is contained within a given population. The differences between Africa and elsewhere in the primary transmission route of HIV/AIDS are highlighted in the far higher prevalence rates among women. In sub-Saharan Africa, women make up 55 percent of the infected population, and rates of infection among women equal or surpass male infection rates. Outside of Africa, females typically have lower infection rates. In North America, women represent only 20 percent of the HIV-infected population and 25 percent in Western Europe.

The increased prevalence among men is linked to notions of masculinity and risk-taking, making them candidates for infection.[7] However, their behavior also directly contributes to HIV prevalence among women, who often have less power within sexual relationships, are less able to engage in safe sex, or are unable to decide with whom intercourse occurs. Notions of masculinity and sexual power are not the only factors that facilitate the spread of HIV. Instead, a number of nonexclusive social, behavioral, and biological factors are thought to assist the establishment of the HIV epidemic or drive it to higher levels within the general population, although it is not known exactly how each of these factors contributes to the spread of HIV.[8]

Social and behavior factors include:

- *Condom use.* Condoms effectively protect against the transmission of sexually transmitted diseases **(STDs),** including HIV. Although their availability and use has increased, it is still insufficient to slow the spread of the epidemics. Oftentimes their use may be discouraged by political, cultural, or religious beliefs, and the use of condoms may be stigmatized because of associations with commercial prostitutes. In other cases, condom use could jeopardize relationships, implying potential contact with HIV or engagement in risky behavior. Moreover, condoms do not help in a stable relationship where pregnancy is desired.
- *Multiple sex partners.* The high incidence of multiple sex partners, including pre- and extramarital intercourse, increases the likelihood of infection, particularly when partners are concurrent (i.e., many within a short period of time) rather than serial, relationships that typically occur within monogamous relationships.
- *"Age mixing."* Sexual intercourse between older men and younger women or girls has typically occurred as older and richer men seek out supposedly uninfected populations, coercing or enticing young girls into sexual relationships. Unfortunately, many of the men are already infected and thus introduce HIV to a new generation. Magnifying the problem, girls are less likely to be informed about HIV and how to prevent transmission, even if engaging in consensual sex.
- *Use of prostitutes.* The frequent use of prostitutes, with most clients engaging in unprotected sex, promotes the spread of HIV into the heterosexual population. Prostitution has thrived because of tourism, urbanization, and poverty. In por-

tions of Africa, prostitutes are associated with long-haul trucking, facilitating its spread over long distances and into the family upon returning home.

- *Rapid rates of urbanization.* As males have migrated to urban areas in search of employment, they frequently leave behind wives and families but become involved in new sexual relationships in the city. STD rates are also higher in cities because of the larger population size and the breakdown of traditional social norms that limit sexual contacts. The presence of STDs increases the likelihood of infection, with the individual ultimately returning home to rural areas or smaller villages and exposing the family to HIV.
- *Status of women.* In many developing societies, women are frequently economically or politically disadvantaged. Their lack of power and economic dependence forces reliance upon marriage or prostitution, removing control over the circumstances within which sex occurs or use of safe sex practices. Women may search for alternative ways, including prostitution, to support their children and augment their income.

Biological factors include:

- *High rates of STDs.* STDs, particularly those that cause skin lesions, facilitate the transmission of HIV during unprotected intercourse.
- *High viral load.* HIV levels are typically highest when a person is first infected and again in the late stages of the disease, with higher viral loads increasing the likelihood of transmission.
- *Rates of male circumcision.* Although the epidemiological effect is still debated, countries with high levels of circumcision before puberty have limited epidemics. In some countries with higher prevalence rates, circumcised men have lower rates of infection than uncircumcised ones, even after controlling for other covariates including education, income, and age effects.[9]

Given variations in the prevalence of HIV/AIDS this chapter follows two avenues of discussion. First, it focuses upon the African crisis, illustrating the potential demographic and related social and economic effects, including decreased economic productivity, lowered incomes, and the social costs of a growing population of AIDS orphans. Second, the chapter references the debate over the provision of anti-AIDS drugs in the developing world, a discussion that was heard before the courts in Pretoria, South Africa, in the spring of 2001. Until recently, and in the absence of a cure, the outlook has been bleak for most Africans infected with HIV. New drug therapies, while not providing a cure, have promised to improve health within the developed world. These same drugs remained beyond the reach of most patients within Africa, with drug companies clinging to their need to charge high prices owing to the high cost of drug development and research. Ultimately, the drug companies backed down, agreeing to sell the drugs at significantly reduced rates, an outcome that promises to reshape the epidemic. The final section discusses emerging trends and issues within the HIV/AIDS dialogue, including the ongoing need for public education, the continued threat of HIV/AIDS in the developed world, and the emergent crises within parts of Asia or the Caribbean.

THE AFRICAN CRISIS

The challenges posed by HIV/AIDS vary from place to place, but are perhaps felt most acutely within sub-Saharan Africa, where AIDS has become the leading cause of death. The first case of AIDS was reported in the Congo in the early 1980s, beginning among individuals engaged in high-risk sexual behavior including prostitutes and their clients. The virus quickly spread into the general population where it is much more difficult to control, infecting more women than men and spreading outward from the major centers of population through hierarchical and contagious diffusion and eventually spreading through rural populations.[10] With a current (2000) adult (aged fifteen to forty-nine) infection rate of 8.57 percent, the total number of people with HIV/AIDS in sub-Saharan Africa was 25.3 million. Africa represents 70 percent of the world's cases, and 80 percent of the children living with HIV are found in the African continent.[11]

Although infection rates are high in the region, the prevalence of HIV/AIDS is unequal. While initially centered in the countries of central and eastern Africa, the epidemic has exploded in Africa's southern countries, while prevalence rates remain less than 2 percent in many West African states (figure 3.1). The epidemic peaks in South Africa, where 35.8 percent of all adults (aged fifteen to forty-nine) in Botswana are infected. Growing from just 1 percent in the early 1990s, the prevalence rate in South Africa is now 19.94 percent among adults, giving South Africa the dubious distinction of having more people infected with HIV than any other country. Swaziland, Zambia, Zimbabwe, and Namibia all have adult infection rates greater than 19 percent (25.25, 19.95, 25.06, and 19.5 percent, respectively). In other words, between one in four and one in five adults in South Africa carry the virus. Albeit somewhat lower, prevalence rates among the young tend to track adult infection rates in these countries, ominously pointing to a continuation of the disease in younger generations. In Botswana, it is estimated that 32.55 to 36.07 percent of females aged fifteen to twenty-four years are infected, with infection rates being lower among males (13.68 to 18.00 percent).

Spatial variations in HIV/AIDS prevalence are likely rooted in a complex web of behavioral, social, and biological factors that interact with the continent's varied economic, social, and political systems.[12] The exact reasons for the spatial variation remain unclear, however, and a number of theories have been advanced.[13] One possibility lies in the patterns of sexual activity or networking within sub-Saharan Africa that promotes heterosexual infection. Pre- and extramarital intercourse, age at first intercourse, number of partners, polygamy, the low status of women, wife inheri-

Figure 3.1. HIV Prevalence Rates in Africa, 1999.

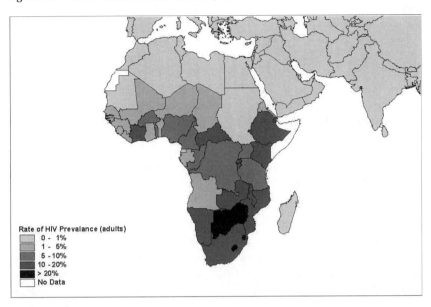

Source: United Nations, 2000.

tance, and use/frequency of contact with prostitutes have been implicated as practices that increase the risk of infection. While there are elements of truth to the networking theory, it is important to place it within the proper social, cultural, and political context of sub-Saharan Africa, rather than creating an ethnocentric version that portrays African societies as sexually promiscuous.[14] A second theory relates to the increased prevalence of other sexually transmitted diseases in sub-Saharan Africa, with sexually transmitted diseases resulting in lesions to the skin, allowing easier infection. A third suggests that the presence of other infections such as malaria or tuberculosis can increase the amount of HIV in the blood, thereby increasing the ability to infect a partner.

While there are now successful models for controlling HIV/AIDS within the continent, many sub-Saharan countries were slow to adopt HIV/AIDS awareness programs or to simply recognize the existence of the virus. The discussion of sex or sexuality was taboo in many societies, and HIV/AIDS carried a stigma that governments and individuals alike tried to avoid, denying it as a problem and failing to invest in public education. Countries lost time in introducing measures to contain HIV because the disease and its significance was not fully understood or governments denied that it was occurring. The Kenyan government denied that AIDS existed in the early and mid-1980s, and along with other governments in the region, rejected condom use. As recently as 1999, the South African president Thabo Mbeki questioned whether HIV causes AIDS.[15] Since then, he has recanted his argument, and the country has moved to the forefront of AIDS awareness and the provision of low-cost AIDS drugs to its population. Economic disparities and poor health systems further hamper HIV/AIDS control. In many countries, access to condoms, anti-AIDS drugs, and health care facilities were limited for economic, political, or cultural reasons, and countries lacked sufficient screening facilities. Many unknowingly carry the virus and infect others, with one estimate suggesting that upward of 90 percent of the infected population are unknowing carriers.[16]

Demographic, Economic, and Social Implications of the AIDS Crisis in Africa

Sub-Saharan Africa is a region coping with the cumulative impact of HIV/AIDS, where the disease has probably lasted longer than elsewhere in the developing world since it is thought to originate there. Here, HIV threatens to destroy decades of progress measured by health and economic indicators, as well as generating personal suffering and hardship. In 2000, it was estimated that 3.8 million sub-Saharans were newly infected with HIV.[17] Although this represents a modest drop from 4.0 million new infections in 1999, approximately a half million of these new infections were in South Africa alone. At a single clinic in Johannesburg, approximately 70 new HIV patients are seen each week.[18]

The most obvious effect of the HIV/AIDS epidemic is the increase in mortality rates.[19] Already high relative to the developed world, mortality rates are expected to be higher in countries that are affected by AIDS than they would be without AIDS within the next decade. Even now, AIDS causes approximately 1 in 5 deaths in sub-Saharan Africa, and mortality rates are expected to climb from fifteen per one thousand to twenty-five per one thousand within the next twenty-five years (figure 3.2). The increase in death rates is even greater in Botswana, a country with an adult prevalence rate of 35.8 percent, and where mortality rates are projected to grow from a current twenty-two per one thousand to thirty-three per one thousand by 2025.[20] Despite higher mortality rates, AIDS was not expected to alter population growth rates, with the expectation that population growth rates would remain positive given high levels of fertility and the effect of population momentum. As recently as 1996, for example, the U.S. Census Bureau projected that AIDS deaths would not slow the overall rate of population growth. Globally, this is still true, but it is not for individual countries. Recent (2000) projections by the U.S. Census Bureau have altered this view, with estimates that Botswana, South Africa, and Zimbabwe will experience negative population growth by 2025. Several other sub-Saharan countries will see their growth rates approach zero within the next twenty-five years, declines that are far faster than would be expected without AIDS.

AIDS deaths are premature deaths, and consequently alter the age structure of the

Figure 3.2.   Estimated Population Growth Rates in Selected African Countries, 2000 and 2025.

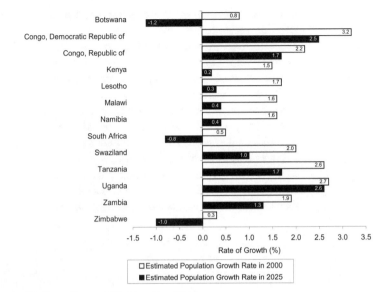

Source: U.S. Census Bureau, 2001, International Database.

population as well as infant mortality and life expectancy, the two traditional markers of development discussed in the previous chapter. AIDS mortality is increasing child mortality in sub-Saharan Africa, reversing improvements in health indicators that had been occurring since the 1970s and 1980s. In Zimbabwe, there has been little decline in child mortality when declines should be expected, and it is projected that the infant mortality rate will be more than twice as high as it would have been without the prevalence of AIDS by 2010. In the same country, 70 percent of deaths before age five are due to AIDS.

AIDS is also associated with declines in life expectancy (figure 3.3) and an increase in death rates (figure 3.4). In Zimbabwe, AIDS is expected to reduce life expectancy (from birth) from its 1997 level of fifty-one years to thirty-nine years in 2010, with further reductions expected by 2025. As of 2001, life expectancy at birth had already fallen to forty years.[21] Without HIV/AIDS, it is estimated that life expectancy would increase to 69.5 years within the next ten years. For children born in Botswana, Malawi, and Rwanda, life expectancies are expected to drop below forty years within the decade and are projected to drop by more than thirty years in Botswana by 2025. This stunning reversal means that the average life expectancy at birth will be just thirty-three years. While declines in life expectancies are not as great in other countries, declines are projected to be greater than twenty years in Zimbabwe (25.5 years), Namibia (20.2 years), and Lesotho (23.5 years). In South

Figure 3.3.   Estimated Life Expectancy at Birth with and without AIDS in Selected African Countries, 2000–2005.

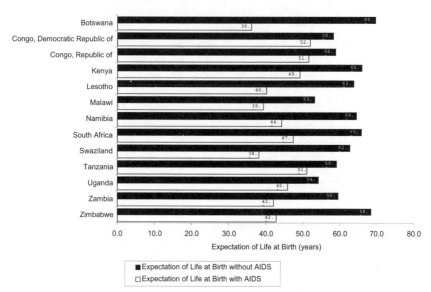

Source: United Nations, 2000.

Africa, fifteen-year-olds have a greater than 50 percent chance of dying from HIV-related causes.[22] Consequently, the traditional population **pyramid,** with a wide base among the young and tapering with increasing age, is being restructured and characterized as a population "chimney" in countries that have high HIV prevalence rates (figure 3.5). Instead, AIDS is "hollowing out" the young adult population, generating a base that is less broad with fewer young children. With fewer women reaching and surpassing their childbearing years and having fewer children, the most dramatic changes occur when young adults who were infected in their adolescence die, substantially shrinking the adult population, particularly those in their twenties and thirties.

But the effect of HIV/AIDS is far more insidious, reaching into almost every corner of daily life and affecting both individuals and societies. In the countries worst affected by the epidemic, HIV occurs against a backdrop of deteriorating public services, poor employment, and poverty, all of which work concurrently to reduce the ability of communities and individuals to cope. Existing evidence suggests that households bear a large part of the burden, with differences in the ability to cope based upon wealth and income.[23] In poor households, the death of an adult member reduces money for food, with poor households receiving little financial help from family and friends. Many other households are unable to cope with the death of a family member, or the burden of care that is associated with either sickness or death.

Figure 3.4. Estimated Death Rates in Selected African Countries, 2000 and 2025.

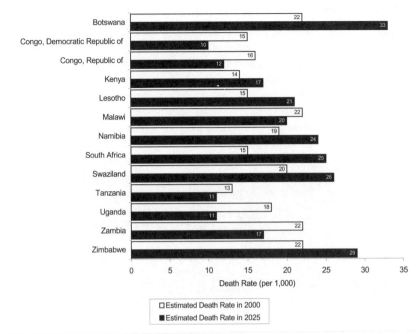

Source: U.S. Census Bureau, 2001, International Database.

Socially, fear and shame are still associated with the disease, hindering prevention and care while potentially exposing others to the virus. Death of just one parent also disrupts life and economic abilities. Even if they are not infected, the responsibility for care of children lies with women. Lacking property and inheritance rights in many African countries, the epidemic compounds the burden placed upon AIDS widows who are faced with the loss of their economic livelihood. Often times, children are left with a future that only reflects what the streets can offer.

Although AIDS tends to kill proportionately more young or middle-aged persons who were infected in adolescence, its effect on the very young is startling and has created a **cohort** of AIDS orphans. Worldwide, it is estimated that 13.2 million children are AIDS orphans, of which 12.1 million are found in sub-Saharan Africa.[24] The number of orphans is expected to balloon to forty million within ten years,[25] with orphaned children facing a variety of social and economic challenges. Economically, the large number of orphans increases the burden of communities and governments to provide food, shelter, health care, or schooling. Young orphans are rarely able to cope with agricultural tasks, leading to crop failure and the death of livestock. Socially, AIDS orphans may be burdened by the psychological damage of seeing a parent die. Immediately relevant is the question of who raises the orphaned child. Grandparents or extended family members are frequently called upon to raise them,

Figure 3.5.   Projected Population Structure with AIDS, Botswana 2025: The AIDS "Chimney."

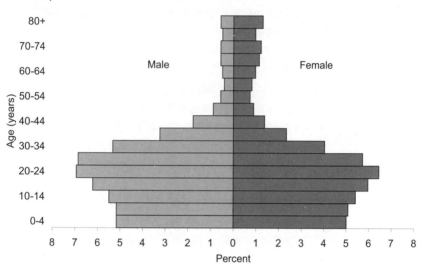

Source: U.S. Census Bureau, 2001, International Database.

but this occurs at the same time as they had expected to have a reduced role in the family. Instead, they are forced into the parenting role once again, including the need to provide economic security. However, the increased number of orphans has altered the ability and willingness of families and communities to help, and the task threatens to outstrip the capacity of the extended family system. For those lacking an extended family, street gangs provide an alternate "family," but one that exposes them to violence, antisocial behavior, as well as STDs or HIV as they exchange sex for food and money. Although the number of orphans is large, this represents only a portion of the children who are affected by HIV. Millions more are living with parents who are ill, becoming primary caregivers for their parents or siblings.[26] Like orphans, they are more likely to drop out of school, more likely to suffer from malnutrition, and may be compelled to work.

HIV/AIDS also threatens the economic stability of countries through a variety of routes by straining already fragile health care systems, decreasing the quality and quantity of labor, reducing economic output, and decreasing the amount of disposable income. The epidemic has increased the demand for health care, along with the costs of providing drugs and maintaining and improving its infrastructure. In 1997, it was estimated that public health spending on HIV/AIDS exceeded 2 percent of GDP in several African nations, which is huge when we realize that total health expenditure accounts for just 3 to 5 percent of GDP in many cases. In other words, greater than 50 percent of health care expenditure goes to HIV/AIDS. Training and the staffing of health centers pose additional hardships, particularly due to AIDS-related illnesses or the death of health care workers from AIDS. Concurrently, non-AIDS patients are frequently crowded out of health care facilities, and tuberculosis is emerging as the leading cause of death among those infected with HIV.

The disease knows no boundaries and spares no occupational or social group. From an educational standpoint, the epidemic threatens the coverage and quality of education. As teachers die from AIDS, African countries will be faced with a teacher shortage and class sizes are likely to increase, while governments are faced with the costs of training replacement teachers over the longer term. Failure to do so or to meet the demand for teachers will result in a population that lacks the skills needed to fully participate within the economy. Moreover, education may not be reaching those who need it the most. This includes orphaned children who may be forced to drop out of school to earn a wage or work on the family farm, or because they can no longer afford school fees. In turn, there is an increased likelihood of infection, with **UNAIDS** studies demonstrating that those with lower levels of education were more likely to engage in casual, unprotected sex.[27] On a larger scale, HIV/AIDS is stripping the ability of sub-Saharan countries to build for the future, robbing them of the ability to generate and supply what Homer-Dixon calls "ingenuity," threatening their very survival.[28]

The impact of AIDS is also felt within the labor force, where it reduces the number of workers and degrades the quality or productivity of work at the same time as it undermines education and the ability of the system to provide the needed skills. Responsible for a large burden of sickness, HIV/AIDS leads to increased absenteeism from work, medical costs, and higher costs for training of new workers. Faced with high prevalence rates and lower productivity, companies may outsource their labor requirements. Alternatively, companies may reduce their investment in areas with high HIV prevalence. Either way, the cost of caring for sick workers is shifted from the company to households or governments and undermines the economic security of workers.

While it is difficult to measure the economic impact of HIV/AIDS, there is growing evidence that as HIV prevalence increases, the growth of national income, measured by GDP, falls.[29] Among countries with prevalence rates greater than 20 percent, GDP growth may be reduced by as much as 2 percent per year. In South Africa, UNAIDS estimates that the overall economic growth in the coming decade may be 0.3 to 0.4 percent per year lower than it would be without AIDS. This translates into a 17 percent reduction in GDP (relative to the estimated GDP without AIDS) by 2010. What this means is that household income will be reduced at the same time as countries spend more on the care of AIDS patients or orphans. AIDS will alter the distribution of income, with the number of households in poverty expected to increase, while poor households will see a drop in income. While the large pool of unemployed may replace unskilled workers, the impact of HIV/AIDS upon the education of future workers will likely cause a shortage of skilled workers. Investment, which promotes long-term economic growth, will suffer as money is diverted into health care expenditures.

ANTI-AIDS DRUGS:
THE PROMISE AND BATTLE

For the first decade of the epidemic, medicine was able to offer relatively little hope for those diagnosed with HIV/AIDS, making it a terminal disease. Scientists searched frantically for a vaccine, but the virus's ability to mutate and the number of strains of HIV have made vaccine development exceedingly difficult.[30] To date, the greatest advances have been associated with protease inhibitors, a class of drugs that were introduced in 1995–96. While not a cure, the drugs reduce the viral load within an infected person, inhibiting the progression of HIV into AIDS. Those with the ability to pay (mainly in the developed world) for these medicines are able to prolong their lives and maintain a relatively good state of health.

At the same time, the developing world has been largely overlooked or bypassed in the rush to find a cure or treatment, even though it endures a disproportionate share of the disease. Any involvement by the drug companies in the developing world has tended to be short term, with allegations that they tested new drugs and therapies on unsuspecting populations. Withdrawing once the trials were completed, the infected populations were left with no drugs and little long-term hope. Arguing the need to cover their high cost of research and development and hiding behind patent laws, drug manufacturers such as Merck, Squibb, and Bristol-Myers insisted on charging developed world prices in the developing world. But the estimated $10,000 to $15,000(U.S.) per year for drugs has placed their availability beyond the reach of most of the HIV-infected population. In countries where per capita health care expenditure could be measured in the tens of dollars and household income is less than $1,000 per year, individuals and governments had little hope of extending drug coverage without dramatically increasing their health budgets. If they did, it was typically at the expense of some other needed program, meaning that the majority of sub-Saharans had little hope of securing treatment. The most that poorer countries could do was prevent new infection through public education programs and perhaps treat a limited number of patients.

Moving to stem rising international criticism of their established pricing policies while protecting their intellectual property rights, drug companies encouraged private deals with individual countries. Under these deals, drug costs would be substantially reduced (up to 90 percent), but the deals would restrict the number of people able to receive the drugs, giving the programs limited reach.[31] More problematic, such stopgap solutions raised a host of ethical issues and slowed the development of longer-term programs. For instance, it is clear that such programs would not be equitable. In other words, who would receive the medicines (children versus adults, wealthy versus poor, newly infected versus long term) and who would make the decisions? Similarly, is it appropriate to limit the supply of needed drugs when 20 percent or more of a country's population is infected? Finally, what is the potential for blackmail and extortion in the distribution of drugs, particularly in countries where corruption is commonplace? Would those that had the greatest need (i.e., the poor) be bypassed as those with more resources or political connections receive the drugs?

In the face of the growing crisis, governments and NGOs (nongovernmental organizations) struggled to enact a coherent AIDS drug plan that would provide drugs to those who needed them. They were faced with a difficult, if not impossible, task. Recognizing their inability to secure drugs through normal market mechanisms, and led by countries such as Brazil and India, governments sought ways to skirt patent laws and provide their population with low-cost drugs.[32] While member countries of the World Trade Organization (WTO) must grant twenty-year patent protection to drugs, they can circumvent the rules. One option is "parallel importing," which allows the importation of a patented drug without the owner's consent. In addition, "compulsory licensing" allows a country to use a patent without consent if the owner does not provide the product at a reasonable market price. By declaring a national emergency, countries can invoke these safeguards, but the process is slow and can take years as it winds its way through hearings and the WTO.[33]

In 1997 Brazil began the production of the generic version of several antiretroviral drugs.[34] While costing the government approximately $3,000 per year per victim, they were offered free to those infected with HIV. To date, the results have been impressive, muting fears that such programs would fail because of an inadequate health care infrastructure that would limit the ability of programs to reach patients and was ill prepared to distribute drugs and monitor compliance in what is a strict drug regimen.[35] Critics noted that even simple, short-term drug programs such as tuberculosis treatment regimens had limited and sporadic compliance in many cases, the result of overburdened and underfunded health care systems. Instead, Brazil successfully built AIDS clinics, despite the relatively poor existing health system, and demonstrated that the poor could take their medication on time, with compliance rates equal to those found in North America. Critics also assailed the program because of its expense. While the program is expensive, it has stabilized the epidemic, paying for itself in reduced death rates from AIDS, reduced hospital stays and charges, reduced sick days, and increased productivity among the infected.

In the face of the mounting AIDS crisis and increasing criticism that its policies were preventing millions from receiving needed care, drug companies were forced to reduce the cost of their anti-AIDS medicines. The United States and other developed countries also placed pressure on the drug companies to alter their policies. A decision by the Clinton administration, for example, stated that the U.S. government would not discourage other countries from producing or acquiring generic drugs, siding against the U.S. drug companies. But even with announced price reductions by the major drug manufacturers for patients in the developing world beginning in 2001, the cost remained at approximately $600 per year per victim.[36] In addition, countries such as Brazil, India, and South Africa were determined to resist drug company pressures and patent laws that were viewed as only benefiting the drug companies. These countries asserted their right to import or produce generic drugs that still promised to be cheaper than the prices offered by the drug companies. Not surprisingly, the major drug companies opposed initiatives within the developing world since they violated patent laws and intellectual property rights, with the companies arguing that Brazil and other generic drug producers essentially stole their intellectual property. The debate over drug pricing appeared elsewhere as well. In South Africa, the government moved in 1997 to allow the importation of generic drugs through parallel importation, a move that was challenged in the courts by the major drug manufacturers who cited the need to protect intellectual property rights, trade, and patent laws (figure 3.6). The legal challenge was heard before a South African court in the spring of 2001 and was seen as a test of the ability of drug companies to protect their patents against governments who were looking for a way to fight the AIDS epidemic. Finally, and setting a precedent, the drug companies backed down, allowing the South African government to import and produce cheap anti-AIDS drugs, potentially rewriting the face of the epidemic in South Africa and elsewhere.[37]

Figure 3.6.   The Drug Companies' Response to AIDS in Africa.

In 2001, the major drug companies took the government of South Africa to court over that country's importation or production of generic anti-AIDS drugs, a violation of existing patent laws. The drug companies ultimately backed down in the face of national and international pressure.

Source: Kirk Anderson, reproduced with permission.

EMERGENT THEMES AND ISSUES

In North America and Europe, HIV/AIDS has seemingly been controlled, attributable to education and prevention, leaving the epidemic largely confined to specific (and typically high-risk) populations. By 1999, HIV infection was no longer among the fifteen leading causes of death in the United States for the first time since 1987 when it was first ranked. Infection rates, and ultimately death rates, dropped as educational programs meant to modify behavior were implemented over the 1980s and 1990s. Antiretroviral drugs have increased survival rates and reduced the number of deaths from AIDS. Mother-to-child transmission of HIV has also been reduced following the introduction of drugs to prevent perinatal transmission.

Not all the news emerging from the developed world is good. Despite the gains made over the past two decades in educating the public and reducing the number of new infections, complacency is not an option. Prevention methods may be stalled, with no further reductions in the number of AIDS cases and deaths in many countries. In some cases, the number of new infections has risen slightly. An increasing proportion of infections through heterosexual contact is especially troubling, indicating that it is spreading into the larger population. There is, therefore, a potential for the prevalence of HIV/AIDS to increase in developed countries, attributable to three effects. First, individuals may be more likely to engage in risky behavior than they were just ten years ago, reversing a trend that had been observed since the emergence of the epidemic. Unlike the 1980s and early 1990s when HIV/AIDS was largely being felt within the gay community, few young homosexual men have seen their friends die from AIDS or other opportunistic infections and are increasingly engaged in high-risk sexual behavior such as unprotected sex. Reports from Toronto, for instance, suggest that HIV infection rates are rising among gay men due to a relapse in unprotected sex behavior.[38] The U.S. Centers for Disease Control and Prevention have similarly noted declines in safe sex and resurgence in HIV among gay men.[39] Similarly, the proportion of injecting drug users who report sharing a needle has increased. Although there is no evidence to indicate that infection rates are currently increasing within this population, the potential exists.

Second, the emergence of antiretroviral drugs, while providing hope and extending life for those with HIV, has led to the mistaken assumption among some that these new drugs *cure* AIDS. At a minimum, AIDS is now seen as a survivable but "chronic" condition, similar to other common afflictions, again reducing the apparent threat of the disease, although there is emerging evidence that the virus is increasingly drug resistant. The hope of longer-term discoveries, such as a cure or vaccine that would eliminate or reduce the threat of HIV/AIDS, has remained but is unlikely in the near future. Furthermore, given the complications posed by the range of virus subtypes and the ability of the virus to mutate, they may never be available. In the absence of a suitable vaccine, prevention is the key.

Third, HIV/AIDS disproportionately impacts racial and ethnic minority groups, and not all groups have benefited equally from the new treatments. No longer confined to homosexuals and injecting drug users, HIV/AIDS is increasingly defined as an epidemic of the poor and minorities. In the United States, for example, HIV/AIDS is found disproportionately among the young who are more likely to be promiscuous or injected-drug users, making HIV the fifth leading cause of death among the young aged twenty-five to forty-four (all races, both sexes).[40] With 45 percent of reported cases in the United States, HIV/AIDS disproportionately affects African Americans: the prevalence rate was almost nine times that of whites in 1998 (84.7 per 100,000 compared to 9.9),[41] and it is the second leading cause of death among black males aged twenty-five to forty-four. The disproportionate impact on racial and ethnic minorities has been increasing, and disparities likely reflect the insurance and medical systems in the United States.[42] Infections are also rising among heterosexual women, particularly in the rural South, where joblessness, substance abuse, poor health care, poverty, low levels of education, and high rates of sexually transmitted diseases increase the risk of infection.[43] Black women, who make up 7 percent of the nation's population, account for a growing percentage of new infections, a rate that reached 16 percent in 1999. Consequently, while the developed world tends to think about HIV prevalence rates as being much lower than those found in other countries, there are populations that have a tremendous potential for explosion similar to what is observed in other parts of the world.

Controlling or stopping the spread of HIV within the developed world therefore continues to require both immediate action and long-term reforms that target cultural factors that promote its transmission. While recognizing the importance of prevention and educational campaigns in slowing the spread of HIV/AIDS is hardly new, it is sometimes forgotten that such campaigns have been the cornerstone of HIV prevention policies over the past two decades. Over the longer term, there is a need for reforms to improve public health care. Over the short term, there is an ongoing need to convince people to change their sexual behavior by reducing the number of partners, promoting condom use, delaying sexual activity, and seeking treatment for STDs. But, standard prevention messages will not be effective for everyone. For example, how the young perceive risk and how their attitudes can be changed will differ from their older counterparts, creating a need for research that clearly identifies the role of behavior and how it can be modified. In a similar way, it is easy to promote condom use and/or the use of clean needles within the injected-drug-user populations. In fact, efforts to contain the spread of HIV/AIDS while restricted in these populations would be successful simply because of the fact that they are identifiable and contained. Once HIV is established within the heterosexual population, prevention campaigns and care of those infected with HIV become more expensive. Yet, drug users and commercial sex workers frequently face criminal charges, making it difficult to work with these populations and preventing them from seeking assistance for fear of identification or arrest.[44] Moreover, these education and intervention programs must be packaged in a culturally appropriate manner so that a number of alternatives are offered, rather than the promotion of just one or two components.

While the outlook might be guardedly positive within the developed world, it is much less so within the developing world where unprotected sex and injecting drug use continue to fuel a heterosexual epidemic even in the face of prevention campaigns. While Africa is feeling the brunt of the epidemic, no country or region is immune from its effects. In fact, the world may have only seen the beginning of the epidemic. By 2000, the Caribbean had the second highest prevalence rate (2.3 percent) outside of sub-Saharan Africa. Approximately 64 percent of the cases occurred in the heterosexual population, reflecting the main mode of transmission through multiple sex partners and unprotected sex.[45] Current rates in Haiti, which has a similar sexual networking pattern as observed in sub-Saharan Africa, exceed 5 percent (and perhaps run as high as 12 percent), making it the only country outside of Africa to have such high rates, and its life expectancy has dropped from fifty-seven to forty-nine years. In the Bahamas, 60 percent of all deaths before age five are due to AIDS. In Eastern Europe, prevalence rates remain low, but an increasing number of infections is worrisome. In the Russian Federation, more new infections were registered in 2000 than in all previous years combined. Most of these infections (greater than 70 percent) could be attributed to injected-drug users, with prevalence rates remaining low among other populations, including homosexuals and pregnant women. But, the estimated number of infections most likely underestimates the true number since the national registration system captures only a portion of all infections.[46] At the same time, increasing numbers of STDs are being reported, which may facilitate the transmission of HIV into the heterosexual population in the near future, with signs already emerging that infection is increasing in the general population. Elsewhere in Eastern Europe, the numbers are increasing as well, with most new cases attributed to injected-drug use, a problem facilitated by the fall of communism, opened borders, economic troubles and unemployment, and decreased police controls that traditionally curbed drug use and prostitution.[47]

The situation is similar in Southeast Asia and the Pacific, where there is a large potential for growth in the number of infections aided by an active sex trade, use of injected drugs, and human migration. In Thailand, where the adult prevalence rate is already 2.15 percent, the potential for growth within the heterosexual population is large. Home to a burgeoning sex trade that reaches throughout Asia and into Europe, use of condoms among commercial sex workers has been historically low, with workers lacking the power to insist that their clients use protection. Use rates have improved with awareness campaigns that have targeted clients. Injected-drug use has furthered the spread of HIV. Cambodia has the highest prevalence rates in the region (4.04 percent), and evidence from Vietnam suggests the virus is rapidly expanding through sexual transmission and injected-drug use. Like the situation in sub-Saharan Africa, measures of life expectancy and infant mortality have been rolled back, reflecting the impact of HIV/AIDS.[48] Life expectancy in Thailand and Cambodia has been reduced by approximately three years. Although longer-term projections made by the U.S. Census Bureau show an increase in life expectancy within these countries, they assume that the virus does not make further inroads into the population. Infant and child mortality has been affected the most in countries that had already reduced mortality due to other causes. Finally, China has only recently acknowledged HIV/AIDS as a problem, despite evidence of a 30 percent growth rate in infections.[49]

There is, fortunately, some room for optimism in the fight against HIV/AIDS, although any report of success is subject to important caveats and exceptions. First, the move by drug companies in 2001 to reduce the price of anti-AIDS drugs and to allow countries to import or produce generic versions of the drugs is significant. Ultimately, this may ensure that the drugs are available for all that need them. It is important to recognize, however, that programs to provide anti-AIDS drugs have yet to be implemented and their success can only be measured in the coming decades. This assumes, of course, that governments and other groups can overcome problems associated with the distribution, financing,[50] and compliance associated with these new programs, and that the emergence of drug-resistant strains does not thwart attempts to control it. While Brazil has shown that programs providing free or low-cost AIDS drugs can work, replicating its success will be difficult in places with lower incomes, poorer health care systems, or greater numbers of infected people. Even in South Africa, where average incomes are higher than most other African nations, the prospect of establishing and maintaining a long-term drug program is nothing short of daunting. Moreover, there is concern whether generic drug makers, particularly small or unknown companies that might spring up to fill the need for drugs, can provide reliable versions of the antiretroviral drugs. Products that are not full strength or differ in the way the body absorbs the medicine could promote the growth of drug-resistant viruses or fail the patient, and contaminated or substandard drugs could kill.

Similar difficulties arise in the prevention of mother to child transmission. Although the risk of infection can be reduced dramatically through drug intervention, including AZT and other antiretrovirals that have proven effective, they require strict compliance and are expensive, relegating their use to a small number.[51] Recent research has shown that the antiretroviral drug nevirapine can be administered to the mother during labor and to the infant after birth at one-tenth the cost of AZT (about $4[U.S.]) with the same effectiveness as AZT. Geography, however, means that distribution and awareness of the drug remain problems. Other interventions, including the use of infant formula rather than breast milk (which can pass HIV) or caesarian delivery of children, have proven effective in reducing HIV transmission in developed countries but are not always available or are costly in the developing world. Moreover, breastfeeding is near universal in Africa. Short of these interventions, improved antenatal care, confidential counseling and testing of women (many women are reluctant to be tested for HIV), short-course drug therapy, and strengthened family planning programs would be beneficial in slowing the spread of the disease.

Also, there are some indications that the rate of new infections may be leveling off in sub-Saharan Africa, with Uganda frequently offered as the poster child.[52] Since 1992, HIV infection levels have steadily declined, especially among young women aged fifteen to nineteen years. In 1992, HIV prevalence among pregnant women was approximately 30 percent only ten years after the virus had appeared. By 1996, the rate had dropped by 50 percent and had dropped by up to 70 percent among young women (from 28 percent in 1992 to 8 percent in 1997). Similarly, infection rates have been observed to decline in Zambia, where the percentage of pregnant girls aged fifteen to nineteen infected with HIV in the capital, Lusaka, has dropped by almost half in the past six years. Likewise, the percentage of unmarried women who were sexually active fell from 52 to 35 percent between 1990 and 1996, reducing the risk of infection.[53] A number of reasons account for this change, including education that has promoted delayed sexual activity, use of condoms, and limiting the number of sexual partners. In addition, the slight leveling off in the number of new infections may reflect the duration of the disease, leaving behind a relatively small pool of uninfected people. Unfortunately, Uganda's experience is not the rule. With only a few areas showing stabilization in the prevalence of HIV/AIDS, the epidemic has not yet peaked in Africa and may quickly expand if countries in western Africa, including Nigeria, which currently has a relatively low prevalence rate (5.06 percent), begin a rapid increase in the number of HIV/AIDS cases.

Clearly, the fight against HIV/AIDS in the developing world cannot be relaxed. Instead, governments and NGOs are still faced with the crises of providing health care to a growing population, reducing the number of new infections, and coping with the cumulative impact of HIV/AIDS. Many countries have intervention programs that includes a comprehensive AIDS program promoting condom use, sexual abstinence, delayed intercourse, social openness and ability to discuss HIV/AIDS, and mutual fidelity between partners, but they vary in their effectiveness and in the populations they reach. Promoting the status and equality of women through improved education, employment, income, and political opportunities is crucial.[54] In addition to linkages to fertility control, status and equity have a direct bearing upon whether they protect themselves from HIV infection and the resources available to them. While chapter 1 referenced the linkage between fertility, health, and the provision of basic health care services, a similar linkage could and should be made with HIV and STDs, with clinics offering education and screening services. Improved primary or basic health care is also essential. If a primary health care system is to be promoted, access to HIV/AIDS education and drugs can easily be made available to a much wider public. Unfortunately, access to AIDS drugs may yet reflect a landscape of geography and class, with people near hospitals and with jobs that provide drug coverage having the best chance; while the poor and those in rural areas will have far fewer opportunities. Most likely, the success of education and drug programs will require the assistance of the developed world to cover cost shortfalls and help establish the health care network.

Finally, the battle against the epidemic must also be contextualized by socioeconomic and political instability. While allowing the epidemic to grow, the epidemic may also encourage economic and political instability, creating a self-reinforcing loop. Such instability may increasingly characterize countries that have been hard hit by HIV/AIDS, devastating their economies. Not only does AIDS impact the age structure of the population, but it also jeopardizes future economic growth by removing economically active adults from the workforce and reducing economic output. Just as it removes the young and educated from the labor force, HIV/AIDS threatens the leadership structure of countries. Declining incomes and decreased economic opportunities have the potential to create an environment that fosters political instability as populations search for answers, assistance, and guidance.

NOTES

1. Peter Gould, *The Slow Plague: A Geography of the AIDS Pandemic* (Oxford: Blackwell, 1993).

2. Gina Kolata, "The Genesis of an Epidemic: Humans, Chimps, and a Virus," *New York Times*, 4 September 2001, 3(C).

3. John R. Weeks, *Population: An Introduction to Concepts and Issues,* 7th edition (Belmont, Calif.: Wadsworth, 1999).

4. Statistics are for all years (1985–99), all races, both sexes. National Center for Health Statistics. <http://www.cdc.gov/nchs/> (20 April 2001). The specific statistics can be found at <http://www.cdc.gov/nchs/fastats/aids-hiv.htm> (20 April 2001).

5. UNAIDS defines the adult population as those aged fifteen to forty-nine, since this is the most sexually active age group and therefore subject to the greatest risk of infection. Although the risk of infection continues beyond age fifty, it is thought that most of this group who engage in high-risk behavior are already infected.

6. All HIV prevalence rates within this chapter are drawn from UNAIDS <http://www.unaids.org> (June 2001).

7. Gould, *The Slow Plague.*

8. Thomas J. Goliber, "Population and Reproductive Health in Sub-Saharan Africa," *Population Bulletin* 52, no. 4 (December 1997).

9. <http://www.unaids.org/epidemic_update/report_dec00/index_dec.html #full> (16 April 2001).

10. Gould, *The Slow Plague.*

11. <http://www.unaids.org/epidemic_update/report_dec00/index_dec.html #full> (16 April 2001).

12. See the edited volume of *African Rural and Urban Studies* 3, no. 2 (1996) for a discussion of AIDS in sub-Saharan Africa. See also <http://www.unaids.org/epidemic_update/ report_dec00/index_dec.html#full> (16 April 2001).

13. Lawrence K. Altman, "The AIDS Questions That Linger," *New York Times*, 30 January 2001, 1(D). For an academic analysis of the spread of HIV/AIDS in Africa, see Bakama B. BakamaNume, "The Spatial Patterns of HIV/AIDS Infection in Uganda: 1987–1994," *African Rural and Urban Studies* 3, no. 2 (1996): 141–162; Peter Gould, *The Slow Plague: A Geography of the AIDS Pandemic* (Oxford: Blackwell, 1993); Veronica Ouma, "A Spatial-

Temporal Analysis of HIV/AIDS Diffusion in Kenya: 1986–1993," *African Rural and Urban Studies* 3, no. 2 (1996): 113–140.

14. Ezekiel Kalipeni and Joseph Oppong, "Rethinking and Reappraising AIDS, Health Care Systems, and Culture in Sub-Saharan Africa—Introduction," *African Rural and Urban Studies* 3, no. 2 (1996): 7–11.

15. See, for example, Helen Schneider and Joanne Stein, "Implementing AIDS Policy in Post-Apartheid South Africa," *Social Science and Medicine* 52 (2001): 723–731.

16. Gould, *The Slow Plague.*

17. In 2000 alone, it is estimated that 5.3 million people worldwide were infected with HIV.

18. Rachel L. Swarns, "Drug Companies Begin Talks with South Africa," *New York Times*, 18 April 2001, 2(C).

19. Goliber, "Population."

20. Projected life expectancies, mortality rates, and infant mortality rates included within this chapter are drawn from the U.S. Census Bureau's International Data Base (IDB). <http://www.census.gov/ipc/www/idbsum.html> (19 April 2001).

21. *World Population Data Sheet* (Washington, D.C.: Population Reference Bureau, 2001).

22. <http://www.unaids.org/epidemic_update/report/index.html#table> (16 April 2001).

23. UNAIDS, *AIDS Epidemic Update: December 2000* (Geneva: UNAIDS). This report is available at <http://www.unaids.org/epidemic_update/report_dec00/index_dec.html#full> (18 April 2001).

24. <http://www.unaids.org/epidemic_update/report/index.html#table> (16 April 2001).

25. <http://www.unaids.org/epidemic_update/report_dec00/index_dec.html#full> (18 April 2001).

26. See *USAID Efforts to Address the Needs of Children Affected with HIV/AIDS* (Washington, D.C.: USAID, 2000). It can be found at: <http://www.usaid.gov/pubs/hiv_aids/> (20 April 2001).

27. <http://www.unaids.org/epidemic_update/report_dec00/index_dec.html#full> (16 April 2001).

28. Thomas Homer-Dixon, *Environment, Scarcity, and Violence* (Princeton, N.J.: Princeton University Press, 1999).

29. <http://www.unaids.org/epidemic_update/report_dec00/index_dec.html#full> (16 April 2001).

30. Two types of HIV are currently recognized: HIV-1 and HIV-2. Both are transmitted in identical ways and cause clinical AIDS. HIV-2 is less easily transmitted and has a longer incubation period. HIV-1 is the predominant virus worldwide, having several subtypes (A-J, O, and N) that vary by geographic area. Subtypes A and D, for example, are found in sub-Saharan Africa, and B in North America, Japan, Australia, and Europe. They differ primarily by their genetic makeup and may vary in their transmission routes. Subtype B is most prevalent among homosexuals and injected-drug users, and subtypes E and C are associated with heterosexual transmission. See <http://www.unaids.org/hivaidsinfo/faq/variability.html> (22 April 2001).

31. Although most deals were not made public, it was reported that the Ugandan government negotiated a cost of approximately $500 a month per patient. In Senegal, the price was

reduced to a yearly cost of approximately $1,000, but the program was apparently limited to a few hundred individuals. See Tina Rosenberg, "Look at Brazil," *New York Times Magazine*, 28 January 2001, 3–7.

32. Gumisai Mutume, "Pressure Mounts for Cheaper Anti-AIDS Treatment," <http://www.prb.org/regions/africa/pressure.html> (27 February 2001).

33. Drug companies have argued that if countries turn to compulsorily licensing, the development of new AIDS drugs would be reduced. Drug companies have also wanted to prevent this to protect their profits and intellectual property rights in the developed world, fearing the illegal importation of cheaper drugs.

34. Rosenberg, "Look at Brazil."

35. To be successful, the drug cocktail, including AZT, ddI, and protease inhibitors, must be taken following a strict regimen and must be taken for the remainder of the victim's life, given current scientific thinking. Current drugs do not remove the virus from the body, but simply reduce it to low numbers and slow its ability to reproduce. Patients may stop taking the drugs, given adverse side effects associated with many, when their health is improved. Failure to comply will result in the virus returning at full strength and decreased effectiveness.

36. Price reductions were offered in response to the cost of generic drugs entering the market. Rachel L. Swarns, "AIDS Drug Battle Deepens in Africa," *New York Times*, 8 March 2001, 1(C); Rachel L. Swarns, "AIDS Obstacles Overwhelm a Small South African Town," *New York Times*, 29 March 2001, 3(C).

37. Andrew Pollack, "News Analysis: Defensive Drug Industry Fuels Fight Over Patents," *New York Times*, 19 April 2001, 1(A).

38. <http://cbc.ca/news/indepth/aids/next.html> (4 February 2001).

39. Lawrence K. Altman, "Swift Rise Seen in HIV Cases for Gay Blacks," *New York Times*, 1 June 2001, 1(A); Sheryl Gay Stolberg, "In AIDS War, New Weapons and New Victims," *New York Times*, 3 June 2001, 1(A).

40. The U.S. National Center for Health Statistics publishes yearly statistics on cause of death, with the most recent year being 1998. See <http://www.cdc.gov/nchs/>.

41. The Kaiser Family Foundation, "The State of the HIV/AIDS Epidemic in America," April 2000.

42. *MAP: The Status and Trends of the HIV/AIDS Epidemics in the World.* <http://www.unaids.org/hivaidsinfo/statistics/june00/map/map_stats_2000.doc> (18 April 2001).

43. Kevin Sack, "AIDS Epidemic Takes Toll on Black Women," *New York Times*, 3 July 2001, 1(A).

44. *MAP: The Status and Trends of the HIV/AIDS Epidemics in the World.*

45. Tony Fraser, "Caribbean Faces AIDS Epidemic, *Population Today* 28, no. 7: 10.

46. <http://www.unaids.org/epidemic_update/report_dec00/index_dec.html #full> (16 April 2001).

47. <http://www.unaids.org/epidemic_update/report_dec00/index_dec.html #full> (16 April 2001).

48. *MAP: The Status and Trends of the HIV/AIDS Epidemics in the World.*

49. Bates Gill and Sarah Palmer, "The Coming AIDS Crisis in China," *New York Times*, 16 July 2001, 19(A).

50. Even at sharply reduced prices, AIDS drugs remain out of reach of much of the population. Governments or other groups will likely be required to bridge the gap.

51. See *USAID Efforts to Prevent Mother to Child Transmission of HIV/AIDS*, (Washington, D.C.: USAID, 2000). It can be found at <http://www.usaid.gov/pubs/hiv_aids/> (20 April 2001).

52. Yvette Collymore, "Uganda Beats Back HIV/AIDS," *Population Today* 27, no. 11 (November 1999): 5.

53. <http://www.unaids.org/epidemic_update/report_dec00/index_dec.html #full> (16 April 2001).

54. See Lori S. Ashford, "New Population Policies: Advancing Women's Health and Rights," *Population Bulletin* 56, no. 1 (March 2001).

4

❧

Immigration: Closing or Opening the Door?

S andwiched between life and death, the human population is relatively free to move. As a measurable concept, population movement is harder to define than birth or death events, dependent upon time and space constraints, yet it has a large potential for altering the distribution of the population.[1] Migration has become increasingly important as a vehicle for population change, with three dominant themes, namely, rural to urban migration, international labor migration (legal and illegal), and refugee flows. Out of all population movements, international migration perhaps generates the greatest political, economic, and demographic interest, owing to the large numbers of individuals who cross international borders. Fundamentally an economic process, international migration is motivated by a combination of "push" factors in the origin, including poor employment prospects, large populations, and low wages, with the major sending regions defined by Asia, North Africa, and Latin America. Principal receiving countries include the United States, Canada, Australia, Western Europe, Scandinavia, and Russia,[2] where higher wages and increased opportunities serve as immigrant "pulls."

Articulated by Douglas Massey and colleagues, immigration is a complex demographic process.[3] Diverse theories to explain immigration include neo-classical theory (supply/demand of labor), dual labor markets within developed countries where immigrants fill undesirable and low-paid positions, networks or "chain immigration" that reflect the persistence of immigrant flows, institutional theories that postulate institutions that promote or organize flows, and cumulative causation theories. Notwithstanding the diversity of these theories, no single theoretical viewpoint captures all the nuances of immigration. In part, this is because national policies have also created and influenced immigration flows, either intentionally or unintentionally. In the past, immigration was an important component of nation building in Canada, the United States, Australia, and New Zealand, and indeed

89

remains a "myth" within many of these countries. The enduring and near mythical status attained by places like Ellis Island in New York, Canada's Pier 21 in Halifax, or Australia's settlement by ex-convicts are important components of each nation's development and psyche. Countries have also encouraged labor recruitment through programs such as the **Bracero** program, which recruited Mexican laborers for work in the United States, or Germany's "guest-worker" program. Consequently, immigrant decisions must be set within the broader context of national policies that promote or impede immigration.

Notwithstanding the historical significance of immigration flows, the developed world debated the costs and benefits of immigration throughout much of the twentieth century, and governments have moved to limit the number of allowed entrants. Despite the increased emphasis placed on immigration control, there is growing concern that receiving states have effectively lost control over their borders. This **"immigration gap"**—the difference between immigration policy and outcome, articulated by Cornelius, Martin, and Hollifield[4]—is due to a variety of national and international factors. Globalization, economic restructuring, liberal politics, and state policies that have encouraged immigration have worked to undermine state attempts to control it, provoking public opposition and calls for even tighter immigration policies.

In Europe, national identity and concerns with cultural and linguistic protection and differences between foreigners and the native-born have driven a backlash against immigrants. In Germany, anti-immigrant sentiment is driven by cultural and religious differences along with economic concerns. This backlash has increasingly driven European politics through forums such as Germany's "skin heads," France's Front National, and Austria's Freedom Party, all of which espouse anti-foreigner sentiments.[5] Anti-immigrant groups are finding increasing political strength elsewhere in Europe, including Spain and Italy where anti-immigrant violence has erupted, even though they, like other European countries, need foreign workers owing to declining birthrates and an increasing elderly population. Like other European countries, Spain and Italy have never defined themselves as immigrant importers and have only imported labor recently. Rather, they have historically been exporters of labor, and the shift from exporter to importer is difficult for the average person to accept, made even more difficult by large numbers of illegal immigrants.

The fact that Canada, the United States, and Australia define themselves as "nations of immigrants" may only serve to delay large-scale anti-immigrant backlashes. In North America, concerns center on the economic and fiscal effects of immigration, including whether immigrants negatively influence wages and employment among the native-born. The ability of immigrants to adjust to North American society, including questions of adjustment or assimilation, has also dominated policy and lay discussions. In the United States, these concerns have intensified owing to illegal immigration. In fact, anti-immigrant sentiments are already present within the United States in response to the perceived negative consequences associated with immigration, including changes to the larger society, its institutions, and economic effects. Academically, many of these concerns are captured in the "Balkanization" debate, a literature that suggests significant and negative spatial segmentation by race and ethnicity associated with labor-force competition between the native- and foreign-born populations.[6] Invoking Ellis and Wright's arguments, the use of Balkanization evokes a negative interpretation of immigration, ethnic antagonism, spatial disintegration, and a pessimistic view of the ability for groups to exist peacefully. From a legislative perspective, California's **Proposition 187,** welfare reform, and a refocusing of resources on the U.S.–Mexican border to staunch illegal immigration provide sufficient evidence of mounting American concern with immigration. Canada, on the other hand, has largely avoided protracted immigration debates. Immigration there is viewed as an asset, its immigration policy is clear and has largely succeeded, although illegal immigration and refugee flows represent areas of increasing concern.

Spotlighting the policy and political implications associated with immigration, the current chapter considers legal and illegal immigration from the European and North American viewpoint. Most developed countries have instituted restrictions and barriers to immigration and recast immigration as a national security issue. But, if a country tries to close the door to immigration, will it succeed? Experiences from Europe and the United States, including the 1986 Immigration Reform and Control Act **(IRCA)** and recent clampdowns on illegal border crossings, suggest not. In fact, restricting legal immigration may only serve to increase illegal immigration or other "backdoor" immigration through family reunification programs or seasonal worker admission. Both Europe and the United States are now faced with a large gap between the realities of controlling immigration and politics, caught between the desire by employers for cheap labor and U.S.-born workers whose power and livelihood are threatened.[7] In Europe, anti-immigrant sentiment is more pronounced. While immigration is often portrayed as an economic issue within the receiving country, it also engages a rather thorny question of who (or what) constitutes a "nation." Such issues lie at the root of anti-immigrant violence in Europe and right-wing political parties that have risen in response to perceived threats to national identity.

POLICY AND REALITY: THE "IMMIGRATION GAP"

Over the past hundred years, most governments have attempted to control the movement of populations into and out of their countries, and state governments wrote and rewrote immigration law throughout the later half of the 1900s to reflect emerging economic and demographic needs as well as the reality of the civil rights movement. While many policies appeared to succeed at first, states have found it increasingly difficult to control immigration since the 1980s. Despite their best attempts to impose tighter entry restrictions and other controls,[8] labor-importing states are faced with an immigration control crisis, defined by Wayne Cornelius and his colleagues as the "gap" between immigration control policies and their outcomes. While desiring to control immigration, the reality is that governments have less confidence in their ability to control immigration now than fifteen to twenty years ago. The gap between immigration policy and reality is aided and abetted by three concurrent factors.[9]

First, various domestic factors have limited the state's ability to control its borders. For example, programs such as Germany's guest-worker program or the Bracero program in the United States were meant to be short term, with workers cycling in and out of the country as needed. The very existence of such programs, however, legitimized and concretized the movement of workers across international borders, connected regions, and created pathways for future immigrants, spreading information about jobs and receiving areas. Existing immigrant communities within the receiving regions have served as anchors for new arrivals, cushioning the stress of relocation. When states have attempted to restrict immigration, these networks maintain flows through illegal immigration and family reunification. Likewise, policies meant to close the border have created permanent residents from temporary workers. Concerned with labor shortages, employers maintained their existing pool of immigrant workers. Workers, on the other hand, feared that they would not be able to return should they leave their host countries. Instead, they remained. Both France and Germany have, at different points in time, declared their borders closed to further immigration, only to see the numbers of foreign born increase through family reunification clauses or other "backdoor" immigration routes, including illegal immigration. Similarly, U.S. domestic policies have failed to deter illegal immigration. Nowhere is this better illustrated than through IRCA, which sought exemptions for California's agricultural growers to continue to use undocumented workers at the same time as other employers were required to verify the employment eligibility of workers.

Second, a number of factors from outside the state have contributed to the gap between policy and reality, including globalization and economic restructuring. Globalization opens economies to greater trade and capital flows and increases demands for cheap labor within industrialized countries. Stopping or controlling immigration becomes increasingly hard because of the underlying demand for inexpensive labor. With globalization, employers have shown an increasing insensitivity toward economic fluctuations. That is, employer demand for cheap labor remains strong even in conditions of relatively high unemployment, and employers have been successful in recruiting workers and coopting state policies for their benefit. Concurrently, population growth and economic restructuring within the labor exporting countries promote economic and social disparities and create a ready pool of labor that encourages emigration. A second exogenous factor is that advances in communications and transportation technology are increasingly accessible to immigrants, aiding the expansion of international migration networks and sustained immigration flows.

Third, the rise of liberalism and the extension of human rights to foreigners within developed countries have further legitimized their position within host countries, hampering state efforts to control immigration. Policies aimed at protecting rights have helped immigrants get into countries (e.g., **asylum**) as well as to remain within the host country. Canada, for instance, has had problems in the administration of its refugee policy,[10] and Germany's generous asylum policies were seen as a quick and easy way to gain entry. Although some of the rights acquired by the foreign-born in the 1960s and 1970s have been lost through new legislation, they remain a barrier to immigration control.

THE NORTH AMERICAN EXPERIENCE: THE DOORS REMAIN OPEN

Both the United States and Canada have long prided themselves on being nations of immigrants, with immigrants arriving in search of economic opportunity, political or religious freedom, or to reunite with their families. Despite the long history of immigration to both countries, public attention has increasingly focused on the size, origins, and implications of large-scale immigration.[11] Over the past fifty years, polling has charted increasing opposition to immigrants within the United States. Ongoing and emerging debates reflect associated concerns: How will immigrants assimilate or incorporate themselves within the host society? How will the larger society be changed? Will society become "Balkanized" along ethnic or racial lines?

Discussions of the costs and benefits of immigration reflect a long-running debate found within most countries that receive a large number of immigrants. Answering this question cuts across economic, social, fiscal, and demographic perspectives.[12] Undoubtedly, public awareness is higher in primary magnets for immigrants, including California, New York, Illinois, Florida, and New Jersey in the United States, and Ontario, Quebec, and British Columbia in Canada. But concerns with the impact and number of immigrants are not limited to these areas. Recent reports, including the U.S. Census 2000 data, indicate that the foreign-born are increasingly found in areas that have not been traditional destinations for immigrants.[13] States such as Iowa, which could hardly be described as immigrant "magnets," are now counting larger foreign-born populations, where the new arrivals frequently fill low-paying or unskilled positions, and their presence forces communities to deal with issues of immigration and assimilation that had previously been unheard of in small-town America.

Economically, the bulk of evidence from Canada, the United States, and elsewhere indicates that immigration has a rather minimal but positive impact on economic well-being.[14] Immigration most directly benefits the immigrants themselves, making them financially better off in their host country relative to their origin, even though they tend to earn less on average than the native-born and are predominately found in low-paying, low-skilled positions within the workforce. Domestically, immigrants increase the supply of labor, boost production and demand for goods, and have commonly been regarded as a potent short-term policy tool allowing skill shortages to be alleviated quickly. Although the economy as a whole may gain, immigration will also create losers, including the less-skilled native-born who compete directly with immigrants in the job market and who may see wages fall. Again, however, the available evidence suggests that immigration has only a small negative impact upon the wage and labor opportunities of the native-born. In the formal sector, minimum wage laws, unions, and low unemployment rates have ensured "wage stickiness," although workers in the informal economy or regions that receive large numbers of immigrants may be somewhat more disadvantaged.

Fiscally, the debate whether immigrants pay more in taxes than they receive in benefits is contentious. In an analysis of the impacts of immigration on U.S. society, the National Research Council (NRC)[15] found that immigrant-headed households make small positive contributions to federal tax revenues.[16] At the state and local levels, the picture is less clear, with net fiscal burdens reported in immigrant receiving states such as New Jersey and California. In other words, the NRC calculated that immigrants receive more in services than they pay in taxes in these two states. However, the increased burden is explained by the fact that both states are important immigrant destinations with large numbers of immigrants. In turn, immigrant households tend to have a greater number of school-age children and therefore receive more transfers. Likewise, immigrant households tend to have lower incomes and less property, so they consequently pay lower taxes. Fiscal burdens may be particularly acute at the local scale. In Phoenix, Arizona, the burgeoning Hispanic population, many of whom are believed to be illegal, has exerted pressures on institutions such as local school boards, hospitals, and libraries, even as their presence has been acknowledged to sustain the state economy.[17] If the state or federal government does not reimburse local costs, the burden would fall to local taxpayers, a situation in which it is easy to imagine increased calls for immigration control.

Long-term projections of the fiscal costs and benefits of immigration reveal that they balance over the lifetime of immigrant residency. Immigrants, like the native-born, pose greater burdens during childhood and old age, owing to the costs of education and health care. During their labor force years, they tend to make a net fiscal contribution. Fiscal burden also varies by origin and education, with European and North American immigrants making a net fiscal contribution. On the other hand, immigrants from Central and South America create a fiscal burden owing to lower incomes, lower levels of education, and more school-age children than other households. Importantly, it must be realized that education and service provision to the poorly educated or low-income native-born pose similar fiscal burdens. In other words, the question of fiscal burden is not just an "immigrant" issue.

Demographically, immigration has frequently been touted as a cure to an aging population. As noted in chapter 1, most developed countries have entered a period of below-replacement fertility. Economic development, associated with urbanization, industrialization, economic uncertainty, and the welfare state, has translated into a reduced need or desire for children. The result is an increasing proportion of elderly and a decreasing share of the population aged fifteen years and younger. In effect, we are seeing a fundamental change in the age distribution of the population away from the traditional "pyramidal" structure with a large share of the population concentrated in the younger age groups, toward a "rectangular" age structure with a more even distribution of the population across ages. In response, immigration could be used to offset the demographic implications of an aging population if young immigrants were targeted as the most desirable entrants. Most studies, including those of the NRC, have found that immigration merely postpones or alleviates the onset of an aging population. In part, family reunification offsets the desired demographic effects as young adults sponsor their parents. Moreover, the dynamics of demographic change now under way within the developed world imply that the population will continue to statistically age in the coming decades.

Instead, the most visible impact of immigration will be changes to the cultural, racial, or ethnic composition of receiving countries as immigrants account for an increasing share of population, issues that most developed countries are already grappling with. Socially, opposition to immigration has frequently focused on the perceived cultural and racial differences between immigrants and the native-born. But this raises debates associated with whether the receiving country has one culture or many. In Europe or Canada, the answer to this question is simple but reflects near polar ends of the spectrum. Most European states see their borders encompassing a single nationality, hence the concern with increasing numbers of foreigners and their "dilution" of national identity. Canada, on the other hand, is a multicultural society, an agenda that has been fostered and actively promoted by the federal government for the past thirty years. In the United States, the answer is less clear but no less important. The unified vision of the "melting pot" contrasts with the reality of immigration. Immigration to the United States may have altered impressions of culture, but it does not necessarily suppress the cultural identity of immigrants, making the United States a de facto multicultural society as well (figure 4.1). Even among groups that have been long-term residents of the United States, such as Germans or Scandinavians, their cultural heritage is embraced and the identity of these groups has left lingering impressions upon the cultural and economic landscape.[18]

The United States

For much of the first century of its existence, U.S. immigration was largely unrestricted, and it wasn't until 1875 that the Supreme Court ruled that the federal government had authority over immigration.[19] The years between 1875 and 1920 witnessed the increasing regulation of entry into the United States, aimed at excluding those with criminal records, diseases, unacceptable moral standards, anarchists, and particular groups. The 1882 Chinese Exclusion Act represented the first of several acts that restricted Asian immigration, with the Japanese excluded in 1907, and all Asians excluded in 1917. During the 1920s, national quotas were established that

Figure 4.1.   The United Immigrants of America.

THE UNITED IMMIGRANTS OF AMERICA

With an increasingly diverse immigrant population, the United States must acknowledge that it is truly a nation of immigrants, with a multicultural, not melting pot, society.

Source: Kirk Anderson, reproduced with permission.

favored northern and Western Europeans in an effort to maintain the racial and ethnic mixture in the United States. The 1921 act was the first to place quantitative restrictions on immigration, with annual immigration from a country limited to 3 percent of the number of foreign-born from that country that resided in the United States in 1910 when northern and Western Europeans dominated the country. In effect, the law shifted immigrant origins away from regions that were not favored, including southern and eastern Europe, emphasizing instead an Anglo-Saxon immigration agenda. Interestingly, the quotas did not place restrictions on immigrants from the Western Hemisphere. Canadians were seen as no different from the existing American population stock, and immigration from Central and South America was not deemed a problem. In subsequent years, quotas were made increasingly tight, altering either the percentage or pushing back the base year, further reducing the number of immigrants allowed entry. But by imposing restrictions on immigration, a new category of illegal immigrants was created. In response, Congress established the U.S. Border Patrol in 1924, charged initially with apprehending illegal entrants.

The blatantly racist restrictions within American immigration policy were not removed until 1952 with the passage of the Immigration and Nationality Act. The act introduced a preference system for those with needed skills. For the first time, limits were placed on the Western Hemisphere and a preference system was set in place, with priority given to family members of American citizens and permanent residents, as well as those with needed job skills. The **quota system** was finally lifted in the 1965 revisions to the Immigration and Nationality Act, replacing it with hemispheric limits and having a significant impact upon the nature of American society. Although it was unintended, the family preference category dramatically shifted immigration away from traditional origins such as Europe and toward new origins in Central and South America and Asia. Prior to 1965, Europeans represented the majority of immigrants arriving in the United States, but represented less than 14 percent in 1998. Instead, approximately 38 percent of all immigrants were from the Americas by 1998, with Mexico representing the single largest origin (20 percent).[20] With 33 percent of immigrants, Asians were the second-largest group. Minor adjustments were made to the Immigration Act through the 1970s and 1980s, a period marked by an increasing awareness of the scope of illegal immigration, with the Immigration Act of 1990 being the last major revision. Although family reunification remained a significant component, the act increased the number of immigrants admitted on a yearly basis and expanded the number of visas given on economic grounds to 140,000 per fiscal year (tables 4.1, 4.2).[21]

In framing its immigration policy, U.S. legislators have attempted to balance competing economic, social, and humanitarian goals. But these competing interests have lead to policy gridlock, a fragmented policy agenda, and unanticipated consequences, resulting in an emerging gap between the *goals* of national immigration policy and the *results* of those policies.[22] In her analysis of U.S. immigration, Kitty Calavita argues that historical and current policies are best summarized as a triad of opposites between employers and workers, between an economy that needs unskilled workers and the political class that is unwilling to confront the conflicts this creates, and between human rights and border control.[23]

The contradictions inherent in U.S. policy can be observed in the Bracero program (1942–64) of contract labor importation, which legitimized migrations between Mexico and the United States. In legitimizing immigration, it created long-term connections between the two countries and essentially condoned illegal immigration. IRCA of 1986 further exemplified these contradictions. Meant to solve the problem of illegal immigration, employer sanctions were put in place for those who hired undocumented workers. At the same time, IRCA immediately provided exemptions for California's agricultural growers to continue to use undocumented workers under the Special Agricultural Workers (SAW) program. Immigration control was further undermined when IRCA failed to require employers to check the veracity of legal documents. IRCA also provided amnesty for illegal **aliens,** allowing them to apply for legal status if they had been resident in the United States prior to January 1, 1982. While nearly three million immigrants were legalized, the amnesty

Table 4.1 Class of Admission of Legal Immigrants to the United States, Fiscal Years 1996–1998

	1996		1997		1998	
	Number	Percent	Number	Percent	Number	Percent
Total, all immigrants	**915,900**	**100.0**	**798,378**	**100.0**	**660,477**	**100.0**
New arrivals	421,405	46.0	380,719	47.7	357,037	54.1
Adjustments	494,495	54.0	417,659	52.3	303,440	45.9
Preference immigrants	**411,673**	**45.0**	**303,938**	**38.1**	**268,997**	**40.7**
Family-sponsored immigrants	**294,174**	**71.5**	**213,331**	**70.2**	**191,480**	**71.2**
Unmarried sons/daughters of U.S. citizens	20,909	7.1	22,536	10.6	17,717	9.3
Spouses of alien residents	182,834	62.2	113,681	53.3	88,488	46.2
Married sons/daughters of U.S. citizens	25,452	8.7	21,943	10.3	22,257	11.6
Siblings of U.S. citizens	64,979	22.1	55,171	25.9	63,018	32.9
Employment-based immigrants	**117,499**	**28.5**	**90,607**	**29.8**	**77,517**	**28.8**
Priority workers	27,501	23.4	21,810	24.1	21,408	27.6
Professionals with advanced degrees	18,462	15.7	17,059	18.8	14,384	18.6
Skilled workers, professionals, other workers	62,756	53.4	42,596	47.0	34,317	44.3
Special immigrants	7,844	6.7	7,781	8.6	6,584	8.5
Employment creation	936	0.8	1,361	1.5	824	1.1
Immediate relatives of U.S. citizens	**300,430**	**32.8**	**321,008**	**40.2**	**283,368**	**42.9**
Spouses	169,760	56.5	170,263	53.0	151,172	53.4
Children	63,971	21.3	76,631	23.9	70,472	24.9
Orphans	11,316	3.8	12,596	3.9	14,867	5.3
Parents	66,699	22.2	74,114	23.1	61,724	21.8
Refugees and asylees	**128,565**	**14.0**	**112,158**	**14.1**	**54,645**	**8.3**
Refugee adjustments	118,528	92.2	102,052	91.0	44,645	81.7
Asylee adjustments	10,037	7.8	10,106	9.0	10,000	18.3
Other immigrants	**70,597**	**7.7**	**58,726**	**7.4**	**52,512**	**8.0**

Source: U.S. Immigration and Naturalization Service, *Statistical Yearbooks 1996–1998.*

Table 4.2   Immigrants Admitted to the United States by Selected Country of Birth, Top Ten Origins, Fiscal Years 1996–1998

Rank	1996			1997			1998		
	Country	Number	Percent	Country	Number	Percent	Country	Number	Percent
—	All Countries	915,900	100.0	All Countries	798,378	100.0	All Countries	660,477	100.0
1	Mexico	163,572	17.9	Mexico	146,865	18.4	Mexico	131,575	19.9
2	Philippines	55,876	6.1	Philippines	49,117	6.2	China, People's Rep.	36,884	5.6
3	India	44,859	4.9	China, People's Rep.	41,147	5.2	India	36,482	5.5
4	Vietnam	42,037	4.6	Vietnam	38,519	4.8	Philippines	34,466	5.2
5	China, People's Rep.	41,729	4.6	India	38,071	4.8	Dominican Republic	20,387	3.1
6	Dominican Republic	39,604	4.3	Cuba	33,587	4.2	Vietnam	17,649	2.7
7	Cuba	26,466	2.9	Dominican Republic	27,053	3.4	Cuba	17,375	2.6
8	Russia	19,688	2.1	El Salvador	17,969	2.3	Jamaica	15,146	2.3
9	Jamaica	19,089	2.1	Jamaica	17,840	2.2	El Salvador	14,590	2.2
10	Haiti	18,386	2.0	Russia	16,632	2.1	Korea	14,268	2.2

program did not meet its goal of reducing illegal immigration over the long run. Instead, apprehensions of illegals entering the country skyrocketed within three years, and it was clear that others were rushing to fill the need for illegal labor. Subsequent studies demonstrated that the law did not provide a substantial deterrent to illegal immigration.[24] More recently, and given the tight economic conditions and low unemployment rates of the late 1990s, reports suggested that the **INS** (Immigration and Naturalization Service) was no longer pursuing illegal aliens once inside the United States. This quiet agenda catered to employer demands for inexpensive labor and is reminiscent of the Bracero program, where apprehended illegal Mexicans were returned to the Mexican side of the border, only to be immediately issued papers for legal employment in the Bracero program. Such mixed signals further encourage migration from labor exporting countries.

Ultimately, the imbalance between policy goals and realities may engender greater hostility toward immigrants, placing increased pressure on the government to restrict immigration. In 1986, for example, 1,615,854 illegal aliens were apprehended along the U.S.–Mexico border, and aliens were brazenly entering the country by running directly past immigration agents at border crossings. Such images provoked fears that the United States had lost control of its borders, and calls for tighter restrictions intensified. Searching for ways to control immigration and responding to public concerns, legislators moved to restrict immigrant access to welfare and social benefits, seen through California's Proposition 187 and welfare reform in 1996, and to make entry more difficult, exemplified by increased border patrol measures.

California's Proposition 187,[25] which was designed to remove public funding from all illegal immigrants, polarized immigration viewpoints within the state and pushed local immigration concerns into the national and international spotlight.[26] Propelled by the real and perceived costs posed by illegal immigrants, including welfare (ab)use, criminal activities, and employment costs, California lawmakers attempted to curb the tide of illegal immigration into the state and encourage some who were already resident to leave. Proposition 187 was designed to exclude illegal immigrants from schools and colleges, deny nonemergency health care to illegal aliens, require the police to verify the legal immigrant status of all people arrested, and require teachers and health care workers to report illegal aliens to the INS. While its provisions did not affect legal immigrants within the state, it nonetheless created an atmosphere in which all people of color, both legal and illegal, became suspect. Internationally, both Mexico and El Salvador expressed concern with Proposition 187, citing human rights violations. More realistically, both were likely concerned with the potential negative economic effects associated with a large number of returning workers.

Passed by public vote in November 1994 with 59 percent of the vote, the Proposition 187 received broad-based support throughout the state and revealed the depth of frustration among California's voters with illegal immigration. Shortly afterward, a federal court ruled Proposition 187 to be unconstitutional, citing the fact that immigration was a federal, not state, matter, and that federal law requires free public education to all children. The widespread support for Proposition 187 had considerable ethnic and spatial variation in voting behavior, stressing the complexity of the immigration debate and providing insight into public reaction to immigration and anti-immigrant sentiments.[27] Ethnic divisions in voting patterns followed expected divisions, with 63 percent of white non-Hispanics voting in support of the proposition. Greater support was found among middle- or upper-income white and Republican voters, expressing a simple anti-immigrant sentiment. African Americans and Asians were moderately likely to support the measure, voting 56 and 57 percent in favor, respectively, while only 31 percent of Hispanics supported Proposition 187. Analysis of the vote at the local scale shows additional variations, with greater support among Hispanic neighborhoods with higher socioeconomic status, suggesting a desire to control illegal immigration and mirroring white, non-Hispanic sentiments. Even in inner-city Hispanic communities, there was a surprising degree of support for the measure.

William Clark, a professor of geography at the University of California, suggested that voter response to Proposition 187 could not be defined simply as nativist or racist reactions, but instead reflected local responses to immigration. Recalling the findings of the NRC, Californians were forced to deal with the real and perceived consequences of immigration locally, where potentially significant (and costly) fiscal effects were more likely to occur.[28] Thus, Proposition 187 may simply have been a reaction to high immigration levels in the late 1980s, local fiscal implications, and the recession of 1990–91 that seemingly increased the cost of service provision by the state and local governments. Clark also suggested that the voting behavior placed California's concerns at odds with the national role of the United States as a receiver of immigrants, along with business's desire for low-cost labor.[29] A darker implication is raised by George Sanchez, who argued that Proposition 187 presented immigrants as scapegoats for California's economic problems in the early 1990s.[30]

Revisions to welfare in 1996 placed immigration concerns within a national forum. Officially known as the Personal Responsibility and Work Reconciliation Act, the act fundamentally altered welfare provision in the United States by cutting money to welfare programs, giving states greater control over spending, and enacting work and duration restrictions to programs. Although its impact upon the native-born was just as significant, welfare reform directly targeted immigrants and their use of programs. Revisions barred most legal immigrants from receiving Supplemental Security Income (SSI) and food stamps, two programs where immigrants received proportionately more benefits than the native-born.[31] At the time, it was estimated that upward of 500,000 aliens lost their eligibility for SSI. An additional one million were estimated to lose their eligibility to receive food stamps. Aliens legally admitted to the United States after August 22, 1996 (the date revisions took effect), were also barred from federal means-tested programs during their first five years of residency. States were also eligible to bar qualified aliens from receiving Temporary Assistance for Needy Families (TANF),[32] Medicaid, and Title XX social services, which funded, among other programs, childcare and elderly services. Although objecting to provisions restricting eligibility for public benefits, President Clinton signed the bill. In subsequent years, several directives and new bills worked to soften the impact of the restrictions upon immigrants, and many state governments provided additional funding to services.

Ultimately, the "first line of defense" against illegal entry falls to the U.S. Border Patrol, which works within the INS to detect and prevent the smuggling or entry of illegal aliens into the United States. In response to increasing concerns with the numbers of illegal immigrants entering the country, the Border Patrol has increased the scope of its operations since 1994 along the southern border with Mexico, the primary entry point from Central and South America. A series of operations, including Operation Gatekeeper in San Diego, Operation Hold-the-Line in El Paso, and Operation Safeguard in Tucson were meant to control the border in each of these areas by cutting off avenues of illegal entry. Most operations included a variety of interventions such as new fencing and use of new technology including infrared scopes, underground sensors, and computer tracking of illegal entrants to deter illegal entry. By INS measures, these programs have been highly successful, reducing the number of apprehensions from over 450,000 in 1994 to 284,000 apprehensions in 1997 (a seventeen-year low) within the San Diego sector alone.[33] Programs in other sectors have reported similar successes (table 4.3).

The reality is that these programs may be somewhat less effective than advertised. While reducing the number of crossing attempts at key locations such as San Diego or El Paso, the deterrence effect of increased surveillance and capture has diverted the streams of illegal aliens to areas that have not received the same degree of attention from the Border Patrol.[34] Operation Hold-the-Line at El Paso, Texas, for instance, succeeded only in reducing local border crossings (i.e., local domestic workers who traveled short distances), but failed to deter long-distance, illegal labor migration. Instead, crossings were diverted to Arizona, where the number of apprehensions increased, or elsewhere along the border.[35] The problem is also indirectly seen in the **Border Safety Initiative (BSI),** a binational program initiated in 1998 between the United States and Mexico. With increasing risk of apprehension in traditionally high traffic areas, illegal entry has shifted to hazardous areas such as deserts or mountains.[36] Meant to reduce injuries and fatalities along the southwest border, one of the primary aims of the BSI has been public education with respect to the risks associated with illegal crossings, especially as illegals who are little prepared for the hardships of these locations are forced to cross in remote areas.

In placing additional resources along the border and proposing other policies aimed at controlling illegal immigration, the U.S. government was effectively recasting the immigration debate as a national security issue. George Sanchez,[37] for example, argues that such politics represent a resurgence of American nativism. This new nativism reflects rising concerns that nonwhites will soon represent the majority within American society,[38] the perceived drain on public resources by immigrants, an increasing fear of linguistic differences, and fear that whites are increasingly losing

Table 4.3 Yearly Border Patrol Apprehensions, Fiscal Year 1992–1998

Border Patrol Sector	1992	1993	1994	1995	1996	1997	1998
All Southwest	**1,145,574**	**1,212,886**	**979,101**	**1,271,390**	**1,507,020**	**1,368,707**	**1,516,680**
San Diego, CA	565,581	531,689	450,152	524,231	483,815	283,889	248,092
El Centro, CA	29,852	30,058	27,654	37,317	66,873	146,210	226,695
Yuma, CA	24,892	23,548	21,211	20,894	28,310	30,177	76,195
Tucson, AZ	71,036	92,639	139,473	227,529	305,348	272,397	387,406
El Paso, TX	248,642	285,781	79,688	110,971	145,929	124,376	125,035
Marfa, TX	13,819	15,486	13,494	11,552	13,214	12,692	14,509
Del Rio, TX	33,414	42,289	50,036	76,490	121,137	113,280	131,058
Laredo, TX	72,449	82,348	73,142	93,305	131,841	141,893	103,433
McAllen, TX	85,889	109,048	124,251	169,101	210,553	243,793	204,257
All other sectors	**53,986**	**50,604**	**52,567**	**52,812**	**42,856**	**44,246**	**39,096**
Blaine, WA	4,217	4,473	3,999	4,067	2,224	2,684	2,403
Buffalo, NY	1,715	1,483	1,177	1,634	2,090	2,065	1,640
Detroit, MI	1,504	1,291	1,214	1,424	1,304	1,500	1,768
Grand Forks, ND	916	1,162	1,237	1,451	1,334	1,978	905
Havre, MT	1,277	1,237	1,298	1,456	1,483	2,813	1,145
Houlton, ME	919	775	352	293	247	309	307
Livermore, CA	23,184	21,148	23,282	17,956	12,756	10,607	11,633
Miami, FL	6,980	6,212	7,865	11,981	8,258	8,305	6,065
New Orleans, LA	5,031	4,919	4,013	5,389	8,642	9,094	8,008
Ramey, PR	3,551	3,587	4,364	3,218	1,454	896	1,244
Spokane, WA	1,690	1,753	2,061	1,992	1,352	2,331	2,176
Swanton, VT	3,002	2,564	1,705	1,951	1,712	1,664	1,802

Source: U.S. Immigration and Naturalization Service.

political and economic ground to nonwhites with the approval of the government. The immigrant backlash is clearly exclusionary in character. Among the lay public, the rise of nativism is expressed through writings such as Peter Brimelow's 1995 *Alien Nation: Common Sense about America's Immigration Disaster*,[39] in which he argues that immigrants are responsible for increased crime, the crisis in social security and welfare, and lowered education standards, which he believes may ultimately lead to the destruction of America. The academic debate is no less straightforward, with a number of studies identifying immigrants as a drain on taxpayers, despite the bulk of evidence showing the opposite.[40] Even if unjustified, these concerns have become dominant themes within the immigration debate.

Amid the current and ongoing discussions of immigration within both the academic and political arenas, we sometimes lose sight of the fact that "nothing is new." In fact, the debate and controversies associated with immigration are well trod, existing in one form or another since the foundation of the United States, albeit reinvented in light of shifting realities, origins, politics, and economies. At various points, the foreign-born have been blamed for every possible social problem—crime, urban unrest, environmental degradation, and unemployment—largely because they have proven to be an easy and visible target. Past nativism resulted in the quota system and exclusionary immigration policies. At the time of the American Revolution, Benjamin Franklin and Thomas Jefferson openly expressed their doubts whether German Protestants could ever become Americans. The massive influx of immigrants in the mid-nineteenth century opened debates over immigration and called for its control, with Americans objecting to the large numbers of arriving Irish Catholics. Later in the century, the arrival of southern Europeans engendered the same responses. Politically, the "Know-Nothings" asserted that immigration was driving the native-born into poverty, but surprisingly did not call for restrictions on the number of immigrants,[41] something that would not be implemented until the 1920s. Economically, the 1850s witnessed an increase in labor militancy as workers demanded greater protection in the face of changing industrial production and the influx of unskilled workers.

Although there is a familiar ring to it, the nativism that is currently stalking American immigration policy differs from historical interpretations in two important respects. First, as articulated by Sanchez, hostility toward immigrants has taken on a new meaning (and urgency) as immigrants are fitted to established white versus black racial patterns, making racism against Latin Americans or Asians an extension of the dominant white-black racism. Within the Cuban-American community, for example, skin color defines alternate social and economic worlds for "black" and "white" Cubans, with "black" Cubans increasingly coopted into the African American community and alienated by their "white" conationals.[42] The use of black and white lens to view immigrants tends to dull awareness of other racial tensions and identities, and it is made more problematic by its denial of alternate realities. The implication of this renewed nativism is an increasing identification between race and immigration, which could threaten to close the doors to immigration and is likely to be reflected in future policy agendas, particularly if the economy does not perform as well as it did during the 1990s.

Second, the new nativism is rooted in economic restructuring that is transforming America's economic landscape. Unlike the past, when rising unemployment triggered calls to restrict immigration, the new economy has actually increased the demands for immigrants in low-wage, low-skilled, and part-time jobs, engendering anti-immigrant sentiments. Instead, the new economy is characterized by an increased proportion working in the secondary sector[43] and a transformation of traditional, well-paying jobs into part-time positions, reducing wages and eroding economic security. The anxiety associated with economic insecurity and decreasing economic opportunities is directed toward immigrants, even as demand remains strong for immigrants.

Canada

Canadian immigration policy is similar to U.S. policy at first glance, but important differences emerge, including Canada's attempt to forge a clear economic, demographic, and political agenda and the relatively small gap between policy and reality. Historically, immigration was important in the evolution of Canadian society and its economy, helping it move from a resource-based to an industrial economy via the importation of immigrants who settled and farmed the western provinces. As early as 1868, the Canadian government became involved in immigration through its Free Grants and Homestead Act. With the lure of free land, the act encouraged agricultural workers to emigrate to Canada and aid in the settlement of western territories. In the decades after Confederation, immigration served two purposes. First, it allowed the Canadian government control over its western territories and kept them from the orbit of American control. Second, the government of Prime Minister Wilfrid Laurier (1896–1911) viewed immigration as a nation-building tool, laying the infrastructure for Canada's development in the twentieth century, as mining, lumber, and railway interests required laborers. Laurier's government particularly encouraged the immigration of agricultural workers from countries that had not traditionally supplied Canada with immigrants, leading to immigration from Russia, Italy, and Austria-Hungary. The policies were so successful that Canada saw its population grow by 40 percent between 1900 and 1914, with approximately 25 percent of the Canadian population in 1914 being foreign-born.

Not surprisingly, it also lead to concerns over the ability of Canada to assimilate these new arrivals. Drawing heavily on American literature and accepting the preference for northern Europeans, James S. Woodsworth, a Methodist minister and politician, advocated restricting immigration in the early twentieth century and encouraged the rapid assimilation of those already settled.[44] While Canada encouraged European immigration, nonwhite immigration was restricted or severely limited. Deeming the Chinese as unable to assimilate in Canadian society, the government passed the Chinese Immigration Act in 1885, which imposed a "head tax" on Chinese immigrants. Further restrictions in 1907 and 1908 limited immigration from Japan and India as well. Laws enacted in 1906 and 1910 placed diseased persons and those advocating violent political change on the restricted list.

The post–Second World War era saw a continuation of these immigration policies, with the government of Prime Minister William Lyon Mackenzie King charting a careful course between concerns over too many immigrants, stressing the need to integrate returning soldiers, increasing immigration for domestic economic development, and assisting Europeans displaced by the war. King's vision of immigration policy encouraged immigration from traditional sources so as not to alter the character of the population, even as he allowed entry of Ukrainians, Russians, Poles, and Jewish survivors of death camps through the auspices of family reunification, a policy that could hardly be contested. By 1953, however, with concerns over immigration again surfacing, revisions to the Immigration Act allowed the government to prohibit the entry of immigrants based on nationality, national security, and ethnicity. Preference was again given to those of British or French birth, representing Canada's two founding countries, along with those from the United States, with a second preference including Western European countries.

It was not until 1962 that national origin restrictions were finally lifted. Like the United States, this has meant a fundamental shift in the origins of immigrants. Prior to 1962, most immigrants originated in Europe. As of 1998, Asia represents the largest origin region (48 percent), with China contributing 11 percent. Europe was the second largest origin (22 percent), and Africa and the Middle East combined the third-largest origins (18 percent).[45] In 1967, the "points system" was established, a policy that has since become an important tool shaping immigration to Canada in the late twentieth century (table 4.4). Economic immigration was encouraged through the selection of immigrants with preferred education, age, training, skills, and language abilities. Although immigration policy has been revised numerous times since its most dramatic reorientation in 1962, the policies of nondiscrimination, family reunion, humanitarian assistance, and the promotion of its economic and social goals have remained at its core. Amendments to the Immigration Act in 1976 introduced yearly target levels for immigrants, determined after federal consultation with provinces and other organizations concerning demographic and labor needs along with social and cultural considerations.

Since 1967, immigration policy has been designed to promote economic development and demographic stability over fears associated with an aging population and its economic consequences. Out of approximately 200,000 to 225,000 entrants per year, family class entrants represented just 29 percent of all entrants in 1998, down from a high of approximately 45 percent in the 1980s (table 4.5).[46] While family reunification remains an important component of immigration policy, Canada has instead attempted to create a more specific agenda that focuses on economic growth, while U.S. policy has fluctuated between humanitarian, economic, and social agendas. Although politicians and academics alike debate the success, logic, and

Table 4.4   Canada's Immigration Point System, 2001

Factor	Maximum Points	Points Calculation
1. Age	10	Under 17: 0 points 17–20: increasing points 21–44: 10 points 45–48: decreasing points Over 48: 0 points
2. Education	16	Less than high school diploma: 0 points Various types of post-secondary training: 5–15 points Second or third-level university degree: 16 points
3. Occupation	10	No listed occupations for which candidate is qualified: 0 points Intermediate points awarded on basis of qualified positions: 1–9 points Candidate has arranged employment in Canada or has a designated occupation with high specific occupation preparation value: 10 points
4. Education and training	18	If the candidates occupation is listed, then the number of points under the ETF[a] column for that occupation is recorded If the candidates occupation is arranged and validated by a Human Resource Canada Center but is not listed, the ETF points will be shown on the notification of arranged employment
5. Arranged employment	10	Arranged employment: 10 points A member of the clergy and possess a letter from a congregation in Canada offering a permanent salaried position: 10 points A family business job offer from a close family member in Canada, which has been approved by local Canada Immigration Center: 10 points
6. Work experience	8	The points are calculated based on the number of years worked in the intended occupation after completion of formal training, and, the number of points scored on the ETF for the occupation
7. Language ability	15	Speaks English and French with difficulty: 0 points Comprehension of both languages: 1–14 points Fluent in both English and French: 15 points
8. Demographic factor	8	Points are set by the federal government to adjust the volume of annual immigration; 8 points are awarded as of January 2001
9. Relative in Canada	5	Applicant has a brother, sister, mother, father, grandparent, aunt, uncle, niece, or nephew as a permanent resident or Canadian citizen living in Canada
10. Personal suitability	10	These points are awarded based on a personal assessment of a Canadian visa officer; the points are based on adaptability, motivation, initiative, and resourcefulness. The purpose is to predict whether the applicant and family will be able to settle successfully in Canada

Source: Derived from Citizenship and Immigration Canada (CIC) <www.cic.gc.ca/english/immigr/guide-ce.html> (16 May 2001).
[a]ETF = Education/Training Factor.

Table 4.5 Class of Admission of Legal Immigrants to Canada, 1997–1999

	1997 Number	1997 Percent	1998 Number	1998 Percent	1999 Number	1999 Percent
Total, all immigrants	**216,104**	**100.0**	**174,159**	**100.0**	**189,816**	**100.0**
Family-sponsored immigrants	**59,953**	**27.8**	**50,880**	**29.2**	**55,216**	**29.1**
Spouses	30,119	50.2	28,312	55.6	32,798	59.4
Fiancé(e)s	3,079	5.1	1,917	3.8	1,733	3.1
Son or Daughter	4,552	7.6	4,010	7.9	3,983	7.2
Parent or Grandparent	20,213	33.7	14,199	27.9	14,463	26.2
Other[a]	1,990	3.3	2,442	4.8	2,239	4.1
Employment-based immigrants	**125,465**	**58.1**	**94,967**	**54.5**	**105,404**	**55.5**
Skilled workers	105,538	84.1	81,191	85.5	92,394	87.7
Skilled workers—principal applicant	44,898	42.5	35,903	44.2	41,482	44.9
Skilled workers—dependent	60,640	57.5	45,288	55.8	50,912	55.1
Business class	19,927	15.9	13,776	14.5	13,010	12.3
Entrepreneur—principal applicant	2,806	14.1	1,770	12.9	1,667	12.8
Entrepreneur—dependent	7,600	38.1	4,847	35.2	4,485	34.5
Self-employed—principal applicant	1,258	6.3	823	6.0	833	6.4
Self-employed—dependent	2,669	13.4	1,802	13.1	1,761	13.5
Investor—principal applicant	1,520	7.6	1,225	8.9	1,138	8.8
Investor—dependent	4,074	20.4	3,309	24.0	3,126	24.0
Refugees	**24,130**	**11.2**	**22,700**	**13.0**	**24,367**	**12.8**
Government sponsored	7,671	31.8	7,397	32.6	7,442	30.5
Privately sponsored	2,312	10.8	2,169	9.6	2,331	9.6
Landed in Canada	10,626	44.0	10,178	44.9	11,790	48.4
Dependents who live abroad	3,221	13.4	2,956	13.0	2,804	11.5
Other immigrants	**6,174**	**2.9**	**5,415**	**3.1**	**4,767**	**2.5**

Source: Citizenship and Immigration Canada.
[a]Applies to orphans under 18, potential adoptees under 13, and other miscellaneous groups.

coherence of immigration policies, economic immigrants now represent over 50 percent of admittances, and the Canadian government has sharpened economic immigration as a tool to promote the economic development of Canada. Economic immigrants include skilled workers and business immigrants and their families, as well as "investor" and "entrepreneur" immigrants. Federal immigration policy has also shifted, focusing more upon language, education, work experience, and the adaptability of immigrants to a changing labor market.

Like its larger neighbor to its south, Canada has dealt with questions pertaining to the social, economic, and cultural incorporation of new immigrants. Canada's immigration policy has been described as consensual and open, owing in part to the relatively small gap between policy goals and outcomes,[47] and it has enjoyed relatively unique success with respect to immigration. Indeed, immigrants continue to be viewed as an asset and important part of Canada's economic strategy, and it is easy to point out the cultural diversity of metropolitan centers. Culturally and socially, Canada has actively pursued policies aimed at the incorporation of immigrants into society while simultaneously recognizing their diversity. Fundamental to this thinking was the liberalization of immigration policy in 1962, which encouraged immigration from nontraditional source countries, the introduction of the "points" system in 1967, and federal multicultural policies. First enacted in 1971 under Prime Minister Trudeau and enhanced in 1988, multiculturalism reshaped thinking associated with the long-term adjustment of immigrants to Canadian society, allowing the expression and preservation of ethnocultural affiliations.

While multiculturalism has given social and economic confidence and expression to various ethnic groups and episodes of racism or discrimination are relatively infrequent, it has not been without its critics. Multiculturalism has been accused by critics of fostering social isolation by emphasizing the preservation of cultural traditions.[48] Multiculturalism may in fact work to opposite ends, promoting equal participation that necessarily requires societal integration on the one hand, while simultaneously promoting ethnic distinctiveness on the other. Ambivalence toward multiculturalism policies and the desirability of ethnic identity and its retention are also found within the Canadian public. That is, while multiculturalism is officially promoted, Canadians continue to desire and expect movement by immigrants toward some single (typically middle-class) and unifying culture. Immigrants are expected to realize that they are entering a society where the dominant structures are English and French, and that they will need to integrate themselves into these structures in order to participate effectively. Multiculturalism may merely provide the veneer of ethnic and racial self-identity and expression within the immigrant community.

The incorporation of immigrants into the fabric of Canadian society has not been seamless. In 1957, 95 percent of all immigrants were from Europe or the United States, with the single largest group represented by the United Kingdom. By 2000, this group accounted for less than 30 percent of new arrivals, with the leading single origins shifting to Hong Kong, Poland, Lebanon, China, India, Vietnam, and the

Philippines (table 4.6). Groups have experienced different settlement processes and reception. During recessions of the 1970s, 1980s, and early 1990s, their arrival coincided with pressures for jobs and the provision of public services, leading to social problems and raising questions regarding Canada's ability to economically and socially absorb these new immigrants. Fears of increased unemployment, ethnic or racial tensions, and pressures on the welfare system were felt within the political system and expressed by the electorate with calls to curb immigration numbers. Given a lingering recession and high unemployment rates, the right-wing conservative Reform Party, in the 1993 federal election campaign, called for a reduction in the number of immigrants allowed entry each year. Nevertheless, the governing Liberal Party maintained immigration numbers in subsequent years. As recently as the fall 2000 federal election campaign, the Canadian Alliance Party (successor to the Reform), was labeled "anti-immigrant" after a member betrayed her party's immigration position by talking of the "Asian invasion."

Other recent expressions of anti-immigrant sentiments further indicate that anxieties associated with immigration have not disappeared. At best, they may simply have been swept under the carpet by a robust economy in the late 1990s. While the federal government debated immigration policy, Toronto grappled with the economic and social incorporation of Somali and Chinese immigrants, with local politics reflecting negative public opinion from time to time.[49] Likewise, the return of Hong Kong to Chinese control in 1997 saw the arrival of large numbers of Hong Kong Chinese into Vancouver, significantly altering the social, ethnic, and economic facade of the city. While welcomed in some respects, Hong Kong immigrants and investors faced a mixed reception, including open (but modest) hostility due to their impact upon the local housing market via the increase of rents, the construction of "monster homes," and the loss of Anglo-Canadian heritage in older residential neighborhoods. Linguistic and cultural tensions have also arisen, particularly in Quebec, where new arrivals tend to adopt English rather than French. Since the mid-1970s, with the introduction of Bill 101, Chartre de la langue française, which limited the use of the English language within the province, the Parti Quebecois has targeted the foreign-born on numerous occasions. The most recent and perhaps most prominent case was in 1995, when Jacques Parizeau, at that time the leader of the separatist Parti Quebecois, blamed the ethnic vote for the narrow defeat of the sovereignty referendum, alienating Quebec's foreign-born population.

Canadians have also only recently recognized illegal immigration as a problem, yet it is reasonable to assume that Canada must also be a destination. Indeed, upward of 200,000 may be in Canada illegally.[50] Historically, illegal immigration into Canada has been assumed relatively small, with most arriving as visitors and then overstaying once in Canada. This complacency changed in the 1990s, as evidence revealed the presence of illegal immigrants within Canada. One estimate counted as many as fifteen thousand Chinese entering the country illegally over the 1990s. If the alarm bells were not yet ringing, they did in 1999 and 2000, when several boatloads of illegal immigrants from China were intercepted off the coast of

Table 4.6 Immigrants Admitted to Canada by Selected Country of Birth, Top Ten Origins, 1997–1999

	1997			1998			1999		
Rank	Country	Number	Percent	Country	Number	Percent	Country	Number	Percent
—	All Countries	24,130	100.0	All Countries	22,700	100.0	All Countries	24,367	100.0
1	Bosnia-Herzegovina	3,677	15.2	Bosnia-Herzegovina	3,590	15.8	Bosnia-Herzegovina	2,692	11.1
2	Sri Lanka	2,564	10.6	Sri Lanka	2,130	9.4	Sri Lanka	2,606	10.7
3	Afghanistan	1,674	6.9	Iran	1,472	6.5	Afghanistan	1,814	7.4
4	Iran	1,665	6.9	Croatia	1,285	5.7	Iran	1,440	5.9
5	Iraq	1,346	5.6	Afghanistan	1,278	5.6	Somalia	1,376	5.7
6	Croatia	996	4.1	Somalia	1,195	5.3	Croatia	1,187	4.9
7	Bangladesh	795	3.3	Iraq	947	4.2	Pakistan	1,088	4.5
8	India	770	3.2	India	829	3.7	Iraq	915	3.8
9	Pakistan	752	3.1	Pakistan	723	3.2	Algeria	694	2.9
10	Somalia	729	3.0	Sudan	614	2.7	India	694	2.9

Source: Citizenship and Immigration Canada.

British Columbia. Most had paid hefty sums, reportedly up to $100,000 (Canadian), to "snakeheads" who smuggled them into Canada, or ultimately the United States. Burdened with repaying the cost of smuggling, along with an additional 18 percent interest rate, it would take years for illegal immigrants to repay their smugglers. Low wages paid by employers who knowingly take advantage of their illegal status and need for work make them virtual slaves within the underground economies in cities like Toronto, Vancouver, and Montreal.[51]

The issue of illegal immigration into Canada is complicated by the fact that many illegal entrants quickly seek refugee status, a route toward legalization of their status that provides constitutional protections. As such, illegal immigration into Canada is closely associated with refugee issues, a topic discussed in the following chapter. Canadian officials have initiated a clampdown on illegal immigration, but it remains too early to evaluate the success of these policies. Like other developed countries, however, Canada is likely to have a difficult time stemming the flow of illegal immigrants. Instead, economic and social conditions within sending countries, such as China, and the rise of liberal policies that extend rights to these groups explain the difficulty of controlling immigration.

THE EUROPEAN EXPERIENCE: THE RISE OF ANTI-IMMIGRANT SENTIMENTS

In contrast to the North American experience where immigration laid national foundations, most European countries have engaged the immigration debate only recently, becoming, as described by several authors, "reluctant" importers of labor.[52] Rather than immigrant destinations, most Western European countries have been traditional exporters of labor. Germany, for instance, was primarily a source of **emigrants** up to the 1950s, exporting its population to Canada, the United States, or elsewhere, while countries such as Spain have exported their labor to other European destinations. Western European countries became importers of labor in the post–Second World War era, increasingly looking outside their borders for labor, as their domestic labor force declined, and stimulating large-scale immigration from the periphery of Europe.

The shift from labor exporters to labor importers is a significant one. Although the European Union has moved toward an integrated immigration policy in recent years, the immigration debate remains divisive, capturing the attention of governments, policymakers, and citizens. Moreover, early experiences with immigration were diverse and have had long-lasting effects, ultimately leading to growing nationalism and **xenophobia.** The current immigration debate in Europe is driven by four nonexclusive realities, namely, the demographic realities faced by European nations, the sanctioned importation of labor that has served to legitimize ongoing movements, the increasing political liability of immigrant populations within European countries, and fears of uncontrolled immigration from the developing world.

First, without immigration, the population and labor force of most European nations is expected to shrink. Already, with a TFR of 1.3, which is well below the replacement level, and a natural increase of –0.1 percent, Germany's population is declining. More generally, low TFR (1.6 in Western Europe) and a growing elderly population (16 percent of Western Europe's population is aged sixty-five or over) drive the demographic need for sustained immigration in one form or another. With aging populations, many are also faced with a growing shortage of skilled workers entering the labor force, and the economic implications of not importing labor are significant. Most observers believe, for example, that Germany's rise as an industrial power would not have been possible without foreign guest workers. To ease labor shortages, Europe has considered increasing child bonuses and other incentives to encourage fertility, but such programs have had limited success. Alternatively, immigration can bolster population numbers, but using immigration to prevent population decline, to maintain Europe's social welfare programs, to increase fertility rates, or to maintain the ratio of workers to dependents would require a massive increase in immigration numbers. The United Nations Population Division estimates, for example, that immigration into the European Union would need to increase to 1.1 million per year to maintain the labor force. If saving social welfare programs is the goal, immigration numbers would need to increase an incredible thirty-seven times.[53]

Second, like the United States, many European governments have directly sanctioned the movement of workers, creating linkages between sending and receiving areas that remain strong and continue to provide a willing pool of labor. Employers too have promoted the use of low-cost workers in production. In France, its history of liberal immigration and naturalization policies has kept the door open to immigration. The government sanctioned worker recruitment, but it had very little control or authority. France's immigration policy was complicated by the end of its colonial era in the 1950s and 1960s, creating a special class of immigrants from North Africa who were protected by a society that emphasized rights of the individual.[54]

After publicly declaring that it was not a nation of immigrations, Germany too is faced with a gap between immigration policy and the reality that greater than one million newcomers entered the country each year through the 1990s, with most arriving from non–European Union countries.[55] The gap between policy and results has led to widespread dissatisfaction, with 60 percent of Germans wanting immigration reduced or stopped, increasing support for anti-foreigner political parties, and increasing violence against the foreign-born. This divergence can largely be attributed to Germany's guest-worker program. With economic recovery in the post–Second World War era, the need for labor prompted German industry to actively recruit workers from Spain, Italy, Greece, Turkey, and Portugal. The state-sanctioned guest-worker program was based on the assumption that guest workers could be rotated in and out of the country as needed or as economic conditions dictated. Over the long term, the rotation policy did not work: workers needed longer to realize their financial goals, and employers were reluctant to let employees go, given their investment in the workers. In the interim, guest workers sent for their families. While this benefited employers, since wives were also eligible to work, stays were prolonged and the number of nonworking immigrants rose substantially, further legitimizing the presence of foreigners within Germany.

At the peak of the program in 1972, guest workers comprised 12 percent of the German labor force, but problems were emerging as the German public recognized the dilemma of immigrant labor. The assumed temporary nature of guest workers was also acknowledged to have failed, with many of the temporary workers becoming "permanent" residents. Most Germans opposed the reality of a large, settled foreign population, and in the face of mounting concerns, the German government stopped further labor recruitment in 1973. At the same time, Germany improved the status of workers currently resident within the country and encouraged family reunification, meaning that the number of foreigners within the country actually increased as workers brought their families into Germany rather than leaving and risk being denied reentry.

A second element is Germany's generous asylum law that entitled individuals to public assistance, accommodation, and a German work permit, making Germany an increasingly strong magnet during the 1980s. The upsurge in the number of asylum seekers, from approximately 100,000 per year in the mid-1980s to over 430,000 less than ten years later, fueled anti-immigrant tensions as local taxpayers footed the bill. As the number of asylum seekers rose, so did violence and attacks on foreigners. The collapse of the Soviet Union added to Germany's immigration concerns with a flood of returning ethnic Germans and asylum seekers.

Spain's first comprehensive immigration policy was not drafted until 1985 as it prepared to enter the European Union and sought to restrict immigration from non-European countries. With a large number of illegal immigrants relative to its total foreign-born population,[56] Spanish immigration policy has attempted to balance between keeping the doors open to needed legal workers while closing the doors to illegal immigrants, a policy that has met little success. Spain's large underground economy has generated a flow of illegal aliens, a group that is economically important, predominately working in service, construction, or agricultural occupations, which many Spaniards avoid because of low pay or poor working conditions. The Spanish government has also granted amnesty to illegal aliens within the country. As with the case of IRCA in the United States, however, amnesty programs actually generated illegal immigration. Despite indicating that it would not support any further legalization programs (it had three legalization programs between 1985–91), it offered amnesty to illegal immigrants again in 1999.[57]

Third, what was once a sanctioned movement of labor has since become a political liability. Throughout Western Europe, the arrival of workers, particularly non–European Union immigrants and their families, has created deep ethnic and racial divisions within the respective societies. Most European countries view immigration as socially disruptive, yet the European Union receives several hundred thousand immigrants a year, with immigrants primarily entering France, Germany, Italy, and the United Kingdom.[58] Even if foreign workers and their families are in a country as legal guest workers, they are still unwanted as permanent additions to the population. More so than in North America, Europe is concerned with the maintenance of national culture, language, and identity in the face of immigration, with the threat to national culture frequently used to justify restricting immigration. Immigrants are associated with increased crime and face discrimination in housing or labor markets and are seen as "idle" or "lazy," relying upon the state for support (figure 4.2). Nativism, xenophobia, and violence have become common in many countries, fed by fears of the dilution of national identity or the collapse of overburdened social welfare institutions. In response, right-wing parties such as the French Front National or Austria's Freedom Party, which speaks of "overforeignerization," have found ample political support expressed in such events as the violent riots that rocked Britain's northern cities in the summer of 2001.

Increases in the expression of nativism and racism reflect Europe's deep-rooted concerns regarding the ability to integrate immigrants into host societies. In Germany, the emergence of a strong anti-immigrant backlash and right-wing anti-

Figure 4.2.   Laissez-Faire and Lazy Foreigners.

The developed world condones the use of cheap labor in developing countries, as companies like GM, Ford, and apparel manufacturers draw upon large pools of inexpensive labor. These same workers, if present in the developed world, may be stereotypically defined as "lazy."

Source: Kirk Anderson, reproduced with permission.

immigration political parties have led to a tightening of the country's asylum law and an imposition of a limit on the number of ethnic Germans allowed to return per year. Germany has made the integration of the foreign-born a priority of successive governments, but such policies have not been successful. Being the poorest and most visible guest-worker population (25 percent) in Germany, Turkish integration poses a special concern. Although displaying less residential segregation than in American cities, Germans regard the Turkish population as the most difficult group to integrate, given their lower education and skill levels. France too has struggled with the integration of its foreign-born populations. Two of its primary concerns, that of religious differences between Christian European countries and Islamic fundamentalism, and of being overwhelmed by immigrants from the developing world, are echoed in other European countries.[59]

Spain's relatively late entrance into the immigration debate has not yet produced the same degree of political isolation as that seen in Germany or France, perhaps reflecting its previous immigration history. Prior to 1985, most foreigners within the country were retirees or wealthy northern or Western Europeans. After 1985, the majority of entrants were workers from Morocco, the Philippines, or elsewhere in the developing world. As recently as the early 1990s, public opinion was tolerant of immigrants, but Spaniards may not be ready to accept the new realities as immigrant numbers increase and they grapple with the cultural leap from labor exporter to importer. All this changed quickly, with increasing violence toward immigrant populations, particularly illegal immigrants and Moroccans who are especially disdained within Spanish society. Still, Spain has still managed to avoid the emergence of anti-immigrant political parties.

Fourth, Western Europe fears the demographic and societal implications of massive immigration from non–European Union countries in the face of changing global trading structures and linkages. Fears of increased immigration from Turkey have led Germany to oppose Turkey's entrance into the European Union, which would allow the free movement of workers across Europe. As the southern door into the European Union, Spain keeps an uneasy watch on the poor and rapidly growing populations of North Africa, who are only twenty kilometers from Spain across the Straights of Gibraltar. At a regional scale, the European Union has moved to harmonize immigration policies, with frontline states like Spain screening arrivals.[60]

EMERGENT THEMES AND ISSUES

The demographic realities of low fertility and an aging population mean that European countries are faced with a labor force crisis. Given the difficulties and limitations associated with fertility policies as discussed in chapter 1, increased immigration may be the only option to meet employment requirements, but it is fraught with political, social, and cultural problems. Increased nativism in Europe and the United States, along with the emergence of anti-immigrant violence and right-wing political parties that have cultivated a fear of foreigners, serves as a warning bell. In response, Europe has moved to limit immigration, but attempts to restrict it have often led to increased "backdoor" immigration, through family reunification policies, illegal immigration, or seasonal worker admission. The failure to control immigration means that European societies must be prepared to transform themselves into immigrant destinations, something that most states are unwilling to do at this time. In part, doing so raises questions regarding the integration of immigrants into the social, economic, and political structure of the host nations. The problem for all of these states is that they must define who "belongs" within their borders. In Europe, immigration has not provided a foundation as it has done in North America, and the cultural shift involved in moving from labor exporter to importer is huge. Consequently, immigration debates are part of the much broader debate of national identity that pervades the economic, social, political, and cultural aspects of a society.

Traditional countries of immigration such as the United States and Canada cannot sit idle and hope that the emergent storms over immigration and national identity will pass them by. Early warning signs that anti-immigrant sentiment is rising within both American and Canadian societies is already present. Welfare reform, Proposition 187, increased nativism, illegal immigration control, and the Balkanization debate provide ample evidence of increasing public concern with legal and illegal immigration alike, fueled by shifts in immigration sources, policies, and rights in the past three decades. Up until the 1960s, immigration to the United States and Canada was shaped by white Anglo-Saxon images of society. Liberalization of immigration policies during the 1960s broadened the scope of immigration, but injected new racial and ethnic tensions into the debate, even as they were defined as white versus black differences. But such debates cannot be cast in a "black versus white" or "us versus them" context. In both Canada and the United States, there is a growing population that identifies with a mixed racial or ethnic heritage, and intermarriage between racial or ethnic groups is increasing. In the 2000 U.S. Census, for example, Americans could choose to identify themselves by more than one race, and responses pointed to an increasingly diverse population. Selling immigration's humanitarian dimension is an alternative option, albeit one that is unlikely to meet with widespread success.

The recent history of European immigration policies and the pressure of domestic and international changes suggest that there is relatively little room for states to maneuver immigration policy. Countries might pursue economic development in origin countries, a policy that the European Union is pursuing in North Africa and is roughly equivalent to the *maquiladoras* that line the Mexico–U.S. border. Over the short term, however, the economic restructuring generated by such policies may actually increase immigration as redundant workers search for employment. As a second option, states are increasingly reliant upon the removal of political rights among immigrants, flying in the face of decades of advances. Most nations, including France, Germany, and the United States, are now advancing a mix of agendas that remove or reduce access to welfare services, including education and health care, reduce employment options, and reduce programs meant to block the integration of immigrants and discourage permanent settlement. Recent policy shifts in the United States highlight this trend. In order to regain control of its borders, the United States has moved to restrict access and, in doing so, has realized that this requires a rollback of civil and human rights for noncitizens. Recent legislation, including welfare reform and Proposition 187, either removed or proposed to remove rights and protections given to U.S. immigrants. An additional example is the policy of interdicting Haitian immigrants on the ocean to prevent them from reaching the United States and initiating the refugee process.[61]

Removal of the right to work is particularly problematic. Unless the right to work is withdrawn, curtailing the rights of immigrants is unlikely to reduce immigration, since there is little evidence that demonstrates that the provision of social services is an important reason for movement. Instead, employment and income are the main determinants. As long as countries demand low-cost labor, immigration will continue. As the native-born shun low-paying, manual-labor positions, there is a growing demand for inexpensive and illegal labor. Moreover, removing the right to work is hardly a deterrent, given the role of the underground economy and illegal immigration in the developed world. It is estimated, for example, that 50 to 80 percent of U.S. farm workers are illegal immigrants, with an annual entry of an estimated 150,000 illegals into the United States.[62]

Given the experiences of the United States and other countries, closing the doors to immigrants is unlikely to stem the flow given the strength of pull and push factors in both origin and destination areas. Realizing that state control over immigration is limited and incomplete, labor unions have recently voiced *support* for more open and moderate immigration policies.[63] Fearing that immigrants would compete with the native-born for employment and reduce wages, unions have traditionally sought to limit immigrant numbers, making the current involvement of unions in the immigration debate a seemingly strange bedfellow. In recent years, however, unions in Europe and America have supported liberalized immigration policies and courted immigrant workers. In the United States, the AFL-CIO withdrew their support for employer sanctions and called for an amnesty of illegal immigrants in February 2000. Similarly, one proposal that would benefit the agricultural sector would increase the number of seasonal workers in the United States from 40,000 to 250,000 per year, a measure that has been supported by some unions, since these workers would be represented by unions.[64] In Los Angeles, unions have focused their organization efforts on immigrant workers, allowing them to add members faster than anywhere else in the United States.[65] Promoting moderate labor immigration is seen as one way to protect workers, ensure a safe work environment, reduce illegal immigration, and maintain union strength at a time of dwindling membership.

Countries are slowly awakening to the realization that immigration policy is truly problematic. Whichever way they turn—either to restrict immigration or promote particular components of immigration—is not guaranteed to achieve the desired results. Attempts to decrease immigrant flows have proven largely unsuccessful in the face of economic restructuring and globalization. Increasing immigration is problematic in its own way, threatening ethnic, racial, or social instability, while creating a cadre of low-paid workers that would reduce wages and compete for positions with the native-born. Opening the doors may represent a slippery slope that governments would not be able to back away from, with immigration further spiraling beyond their control. Both measures carry the risk of mixed messages that condone immigration on the one hand, while reducing it on the other. Ultimately, the future shape of immigration policy is unclear.

NOTES

1. For a discussion of measurement and definition of migration, see David Plane and Peter Rogerson, *The Geographical Analysis of Population* (New York: Wiley, 1994).

2. Following the collapse of the Soviet Union and its satellite states, ethnic Russians who had been relocated to other republics for political and economic control, have been returning to Russia. Interestingly, housing and the provision of employment for returning Russians pose a difficulty for the Russian government at a time of economic restructuring. If the expectations of its citizens are not met, it has the potential to create civil unrest.

3. For summaries of these theories, see Douglas Massey, Joaquin Arango, Graeme Hugo, Ali Kouaouci, Adela Pellegrino, and J. Edward Taylor, "Theories of International Migration: A Review and Appraisal," *Population and Development Review* 19, no. 3 (1993): 431–466; Douglas Massey, Joaquin Arango, Graeme Hugo, Ali Kouaouci, Adela Pellegrino, and J. Edward Taylor, "An Evaluation of International Migration Theory: The North American Case," *Population and Development Review* 20, no. 4 (1994): 699–752.

4. Wayne A. Cornelius, Philip L. Martin, and James F. Hollifield, "Introduction: The Ambivalent Quest for Immigration Control," in *Controlling Immigration: A Global Perspective*, eds. Wayne A. Cornelius, Philip L. Martin, and James F. Hollifield (Stanford, Calif.: Stanford University Press, 1994), 1–22.

5. Cornelius, Martin, and Hollifield, "Introduction," 1.

6. The term was borrowed from the ethnic fragmentation observed in the Balkans. See, for example Mark Ellis and Richard Wright, "The Balkanization Metaphor in the Analysis of U.S. Immigration," *Annals of the Association of American Geographers* 88 (1998): 686–698; William Frey, "Immigrant and Native Magnets," *American Demographics*, 18 (1996): 37–53; James G. Gimpel, *Separate Destinations* (Ann Arbor: University of Michigan Press, 1999).

7. Cornelius, Martin, and Hollifield, "Introduction," 1.

8. Julie R. Watts, *An Unconventional Brotherhood: Union Support for Liberalized Immigration in Europe* (La Jolla, Calif.: Center for Comparative Immigration Studies, 2000).

9. Cornelius, Martin, and Hollifield, "Introduction," 1.

10. Manuel Garcia y Griego, "Canada: Flexibility and Control in Immigration and Refugee Policy," in *Controlling Immigration: A Global Perspective*, eds. Wayne A. Cornelius, Philip

L. Martin, and James F. Hollifield (Stanford, Calif.: Stanford University Press, 1992): 119–142.

11. Recent trends in U.S. opinion can be found in Thomas J. Espenshade and Charles A. Calhoun, "An Analysis of Public Opinion toward Undocumented Immigration," *Population Research and Policy Review* 12 (1993): 189–224; Rita J. Simon and Susan H. Alexander, *The Ambivalent Welcome: Print Media, Public Opinion, and Immigration* (Westport, Conn.: Praeger, 1993).

12. James P. Smith and Barry Edmonston, *The New Americans* (Washington, D.C.: National Academy Press, 1997). In Canada, a similar review of the costs and benefits of immigration was carried out in the late 1980s: Review of Demography, *Charting Canada's Future* (Ottawa: Health and Welfare, 1989).

13. <http://www.census.gov/Press-Release/www/2001/cb01cn61.html> (12 March 2001).

14. John Isbister, *The Immigrant Debate: Remaking America* (West Hartford, Conn.: Kumarian Press, 1996); K. Bruce Newbold, "Immigration: Prospects and Policy," *Policy Options* 15, no. 8 (October 1994): 42–45; Smith and Edmonston, *The New Americans.*

15. Smith and Edmonston, *The New Americans.*

16. Similar conclusions have been found in Canada. See Roderic Beaujot, *Population Change in Canada* (Toronto: McCelland Stewart, 1991).

17. Michael Janofsky, "Illegal Immigration Strains Services in Arizona," *New York Times*, 11 April 2001, 10(A).

18. Stanley Lieberson and Mary C. Waters, "The Location of Ethnic and Racial Groups in the United States," *Sociological Forum* 2, no. 4 (1987): 780–810.

19. For an expanded discussion of the history of U.S. immigration policy, numbers, and origins, see Kitty Calavita, "U.S. Immigration and Policy Responses: The Limits of Legislation," in *Controlling Immigration: A Global Perspective*, eds. Wayne A. Cornelius, Philip L. Martin, and James F. Hollifield (Stanford, Calif.: Stanford University Press, 1994): 55–82; Roger Daniels and Otis L. Graham, *Debating American Immigration, 1882–Present* (Lanham, Md.: Rowman & Littlefield, 2001); John Isbister, *The Immigration Debate* (West Hartford, Conn.: Kumarian Press, 1996); Philip Martin and Elizabeth Midgley, "Immigration to the United States," *Population Bulletin* 50, no. 2 (June 1999).

20. Immigrant flows in 1998 from Canada, which has traditionally been a major exporter of immigrants to the United States, totaled just 1.5 percent. Therefore, the majority of flows from the Americas were from South and Central America and the Caribbean.

21. Calavita, "U.S. Immigration and Policy," 55.

22. Cornelius, Martin, and Hollifield, "Introduction," 1.

23. Calavita, "U.S. Immigration and Policy," 55.

24. Keith Crane, Beth Asch, Joanna Zorn Heilbrunn, and Danielle C. Cullinane, *The Effect of Employer Sanctions on the Flow of Undocumented Immigrants to the United States* (Lanham, Md.: University Press of America, 1990).

25. Philip Martin, "Proposition 187 in California," *International Migration Review* 29, no. 1 (Spring 1995): 255–263; William A. V. Clark, *The California Cauldron* (New York: Guilford Press, 1998).

26. In 1882, anti-Chinese sentiments in California led to the National Exclusion Act. See Alexander Saxton, *The Indispensable Enemy: Labor and the Anti-Chinese Movement in California* (Berkeley: University of California Press, 1971).

27. Clark, *The California Cauldron.*

28. Deborah L. Garvey and Thomas J. Espenshade. "State and Local Fiscal Impacts of New Jersey's Immigrant and Native Households," in *Keys to Successful Immigration: Implications of the New Jersey Experience*, ed. Thomas J. Espenshade (Washington, D.C.: Urban Institute Press, 1997).

29. Clark, *The California Cauldron.*

30. George J. Sanchez, "Face the Nation: Race, Immigration, and the Rise of Nativism in Late-Twentieth Century America," in *The Handbook of International Migration: The American Experience*, eds. Charles Hirschman, Philip Kasinitz, and Josh DeWind (New York: Russell Sage Foundation, 1999): 371–382.

31. Smith and Edmonston, *The New Americans.*

32. TANF replaced AFDC benefits (Aid for Families with Dependent Children).

33. U.S. Border Patrol, Immigration and Naturalization Service. <http://www.ins.usdoj.gov/graphics/lawenfor/bpatrol/strategy.htm#Californi a> (17 March 2001).

34. Understandably, apprehensions are the only measure of the success of Border Patrol operations. They are only a rough approximation for the number of individuals who try to cross the border, and may include multiple attempts by the same persons.

35. Frank D. Bean, "Illegal Mexican Immigration and the United States/Mexico Border: The Effects of Operation Hold-the-Line on El Paso/Juarez," Report Prepared for the U.S. Commission on Immigration Reform (July 1994).

36. James Sterngold, "Devastating Picture of Immigrants Dead in Arizona Desert," *New York Times*, 25 May 2001, 1(A).

37. Sanchez, "Face the Nation," 371.

38. U.S. Census 2000 indicated that white, non-Hispanics were no longer the majority in California.

39. Peter Brimelow, *Alien Nation: Common Sense about America's Immigration Disaster* (New York: Random House, 1995).

40. See Isbister, *The Immigrant Debate*; Smith and Edmonston, *The New Americans.*

41. Joseph P. Ferrie, *Yankeys Now: Immigrants in the Antebellum U.S., 1840–1860* (New York: Oxford University Press, 1999).

42. Mirta Ojito, "Best of Friends, Worlds Apart," *New York Times*, 5 June 2000, 1(A); Emily Skop, "Race and Place in the Adaptation of Mariel Exiles," *International Migration Review* 35, no. 1 (2001): 449–471.

43. Calavita, "U.S. Immigration and Policy Responses," 55.

44. James S. Woodsworth, *Strangers within Our Gates* (Toronto: University of Toronto Press, 1972). (Originally published in 1909.)

45. Citizenship and Immigration Canada, <http://www.cic.gc.ca/english/pub/anrep 01e.html> (10 March 2001).

46. Statistics Canada. 1996. *Canada Year Book* (Ottawa: Statistics Canada, 1997).

47. Manuel Garcia y Griego, "Canada: Flexibility and Control in Immigration and Refugee Policy," in *Controlling Immigration: A Global Perspective*, eds. Wayne A. Cornelius, Philip L. Martin, and James F. Hollifield (Stanford, Calif.: Stanford University Press, 1992): 119–142.

48. See discussions by Beaujot, *Population Change in Canada*; Raymond Breton, "Ethnic Stratification Viewed from Three Theoretical Perspectives," in *Social Stratification in Canada*, eds. James E. Curtis and William G. Scott (Toronto: Prentice Hall, 1979).

49. See articles by Daniel Hiebert, Alan Nash, and Niall Majury in the special focus section of *The Canadian Geographer*, 38 no. 3 (1994): 254–270.

50. Peter Cheney and Colin Freeze, "200,000 May Be in Canada Illegally," *Globe and Mail*, 26 May 2001, 1(A).

51. Tom Fennell, "The Smuggler's Slaves," *Macleans* 113, no. 5 (2000): 14–19.

52. Cornelius, Martin, and Hollifield, "Introduction," 1.

53. Allison Tarmann, "The Flap over Replacement Immigration," *Population Today* (May–June 2001): 7.

54. James F. Hollifield, "Immigration and Republicanism in France: The Hidden Consensus," in *Controlling Immigration: A Global Perspective*, eds. Wayne A. Cornelius, Philip L. Martin, and James F. Hollifield (Stanford, Calif.: Stanford University Press, 1992): 143–176.

55. Philip L. Martin, "Germany: Reluctant Land of Immigration," in *Controlling Immigration: A Global Perspective*, eds. Wayne A. Cornelius, Philip L. Martin, and James F. Hollifield (Stanford, Calif.: Stanford University Press, 1992): 189–226.

56. Estimates place Spain's illegal population at approximately half its legal immigrant population of nearly 700,000, or 1.3 percent of the total population.

57. Roger Cohen, "Europe's Migrant Fears Rend a Spanish Town," *New York Times*, 8 May 2000, A1.

58. Philip Martin, "Europe: A New Immigration Area?" <http://www.prb.org/regions/europe_NIS/EuropeNewImmigrationArea.html> (24 May 2001).

59. Martin, "Germany: Reluctant Land," 189.

60. Stefan Teloken, "Europe: The Debate Over Asylum: It's a Long Way to . . . Harmonization," *Refugees* 113 (1999): 3–7.

61. Cornelius, Martin, and Hollifield, "Introduction," 1.

62. Ginger Thompson and Steven Greenhouse, "Mexican 'Guest Workers': A Project Worth a Try?" *New York Times*, 3 April 2001, 1(B).

63. Watts, *An Unconventional Brotherhood*.

64. Ginger Thompson and Steven Greenhouse, "Mexican 'Guest Workers': A Project Worth a Try?" *New York Times*, 3 April 2001, 1(B).

65. Steven Greenhouse, "Los Angeles Warms to Labor Unions as Immigrants Look to Escape Poverty," *New York Times*, 9 April 2001, 7(A).

5

Refugees, Asylees, and IDPs:
The Growing Crisis

As a subset of migration flows, refugees and other displaced persons represent a growing population. Defined by the United Nations 1951 Convention Relating to the Status of Refugees and the 1967 Protocol Relating to the Status of Refugees,[1] refugees (and **asylees**)[2] are persons outside of their country and are unable to return, owing to fear of persecution for reasons of race, religion, nationality, or membership of a particular social group or political opinion.[3] In 2000, sixty countries produced uprooted populations. Of these, forty-four countries produced over 100,000 displaced people, and twenty-four countries produced over 0.5 million displaced individuals.[4] According to the United Nations High Commissioner for Refugees (UNHCR), the leading coordinator and protector of refugees, estimates placed the total number of refugees at over 11.5 million in 1999 (see table 5.1).[5] Major generators included Afghanistan, Iraq, Burundi, Sierra Leone, Sudan, Somalia, Angola, Congo, and Eritrea.

Despite the legal definition within UN documents, who is or is not a refugee has significant implications with respect to the degree of support and protection an individual receives, along with the priority given to the long-term resolution of his or her status. The fundamental right that refugee status confers is that they will not be returned to their country of origin against their will. Legally, this is **"non-refoulement,"** and nations that ratify the Convention and Protocol are obligated not to expel individuals without due process. Defining individuals as refugees also obligates the host country to provide medical care, schooling, and basic civil rights that are enjoyed by other legal immigrants. In cases of large-scale refugee flows, the international community or agencies such as the UNHCR may fill gaps in the care of refugees.

Given the economic and political obligations associated with refugees, governments may dispute refugee claims to avoid these responsibilities.[6] The United

123

Table 5.1 Refugees and Internally Displaced Persons by Major Source Countries, 1999

	Internally Displaced Persons			Sources of Refugees	
Rank	Country	Number	Rank	Country	Number
1	Sudan	4,000,000[a]	1	Palestine	3,931,000[a]
2	Angola	2,000,000[a]	2	Afghanistan	2,560,000[a]
3	Colombia	1,800,000	3	Iraq	568,000[a]
4	Burma	1,000,000[a]	4	Sierra Leone	460,000[a]
5	Turkey	1,000,000[a]	5	Somalia	425,000[a]
6	Iraq	900,000[a]	6	Sudan	420,000
7	Bosnia and Herzegovina	830,000	7	Yugoslavia	390,000[a]
8	Burundi	800,000[a]	8	Angola	340,000
9	Congo, Democratic Rep.	800,000[a]	9	Croatia	340,000[a]
10	Russian Federation	800,000[a]	10	Eritrea	320,000[a]
11	Afghanistan	750,000[a]	11	Burundi	310,000
12	Rwanda	600,000[a]	12	Bosnia and Herzegovina	300,000[a]
13	Yugoslavia	600,000[a]	13	Vietnam	292,000
14	Azerbaijan	568,000[a]	14	Liberia	250,000[a]
15	Sri Lanka	560,000	15	El Salvador	248,000[b]
16	India	507,000	16	Burma	240,000[a]
17	Congo, Republic of	500,000	17	Congo, Democratic Rep.	240,000
18	Sierra Leone	500,000[a]	18	Azerbaijan	230,000
19	Syria	450,000	19	Armenia	188,000
20	Uganda	450,000[a]	20	Guatemala	141,000[b]

Source: U.S. Committee for Refugees <www.refugees.org/world/statistics> (18 May 2001).
[a]Sources vary widely in number reported.
[b]Includes asylum cases pending in the United States.

Nations and other countries do not, for example, accord refugee status to those who flee for economic reasons, largely out of fear within the developed world that this would open a floodgate of refugees into a system that is already strained by the existing number of political refugees. In essence, for example, recognizing economic refugees would legalize Mexican immigration into the United States, as entrants would simply need to claim economic refugee status to gain legal entry. Proving the legitimacy of a refugee claim is difficult, especially when clouded by ideological, social, or economic concerns. The United States, for example, has been accused of having a double standard. With its acceptance of Mariel Cubans in the early 1980s, most of whom did not meet the international definition of refugee status, the U.S. government was accused of altering its definition of political refugees for political expediency. At roughly the same time, it denied entry to Haitians who claimed political asylum, with the government defining them as voluntary and economic migrants, even in light of evidence of political persecution by the Haitian government. Likewise, the question of what defines "fear" may not, for example, be a sharply defined fear of individual persecution. Instead, it may be fear of being caught in the crossfire, which has little to do with individual traits. This is not meant to belittle the fear of the individual, since this fear is no less real. Consequently, the definition of refugee generally extends beyond persecuted individuals to whole groups of people fleeing danger.

With the end of the cold war, the nature of conflict has changed from large-scale confrontations backed by superpowers to smaller, internal struggles. Old alliances have been disrupted and totalitarian regimes that had kept the social order have been toppled. The former Yugoslavia is a case in point as Serbian leadership struggled to maintain control of Yugoslavia in the face of unilateral declarations of independence by Slovenia and Croatia in 1991. Later, in its wars in Bosnia and Kosovo, it would attempt to carve out a "greater Serbia." In the process, an estimated 863,000 refugees were generated during the Bosnia conflict in the early 1990s, and an additional 900,000 were generated in Kosovo in 1999. Similar situations have evolved or threaten to evolve in the former Soviet Union, including conflict in Soviet Georgia, Chechnya, Armenia, and Azerbaijan. Former republics such as Tajikistan and Uzbekistan also teeter near the brink of civil disorder, while thousands of Afghan refugees fled the country to neighboring Pakistan to avoid conflict between pro- and anti-Taliban forces. In Africa, decades of political turmoil following the end of the colonial era continue to generate a seemingly endless list of conflicts and refugees. The growing number of conflicts and evolving political landscape also increased the number of refugees and created a relatively new and rapidly growing group known as **internally displaced persons (IDPs).** Unlike refugees, IDPs are unable to leave their country of nationality and typically cannot avail themselves of the services of international agencies for protection and assistance, meaning that they face an uncertain future. It is estimated that twenty-five million individuals are displaced, the fallout of civil strife, ethnic unrest, or disasters, found in Bosnia, Sri Lanka, Azerbaijan, Kosovo, East Timor, Russia, Afghanistan, Liberia, and Rwanda. Because they tend to fall through the cracks of current assistance and international recognitions, the United Nations has engaged the debate on who should be responsible for their care, a difficult situation given the importance associated with state sovereignty.

Rather than focusing upon the individual generators of refugees and displaced persons and how or why they were generated, this chapter focuses on the implications and options of displaced populations. The chapter begins by exploring the alternatives available to deal with refugee populations, including their return to the country of nationality, settlement in the country of asylum, or resettlement to a third country. No one option is politically expedient or costless, and the following discussion examines each alternative before considering North American and European responses to refugees. Historically, Canada and the United States have played an active role in the resettlement of refugees. Like issues observed within immigration policy in the previous chapter, recent high-profile events such as the arrival of Chinese refugees have left both countries grappling with rising public concerns over refugee policies and a general consensus that the countries are "too soft" on entrants, leading to abuse of the system. Europe, on the other hand, has not been a major resettlement destination and has, in some cases, actively tried to avoid the resettlement of refugees within its borders. Instead, it has dealt with large numbers of asylum seekers, who are also seen as abusers of the system. European response has been to tighten their refugee and asylum policies as well. The chapter then considers the internally displaced population, the most rapidly growing segment of displaced peoples. It concludes with a discussion of emerging issues and trends with respect to the displaced population.

ALTERNATIVES FOR REFUGEES: NO EASY WAY HOME

Once outside their home country, the international community is faced with three broad alternatives in assisting the refugee population, including voluntary repatriation, settlement in the country of first asylum, or resettlement in a third country.[7] Of these, voluntary return to the home country is the ideal solution, particularly for the refugee. It is perhaps also the most difficult of the three alternatives, since a minimum requirement for return is the resolution of the problem that created the refugee flows in the first place. Additional material and financial support for the refugees may also be needed until they can reestablish their livelihoods after their return. Despite difficulties, voluntary repatriations have succeeded, the most recent being the return of Kosovar Albanians following the end of the war in late spring 2000. However, their return and continued security has depended heavily upon assistance from nongovernmental organizations such as the Red Cross, donations and support from other nations, and the continued presence of peacekeeping forces, which may yet prove to be a long-term requirement.

Permanent settlement outside of the home country, which is typically referred to as country of first asylum, is a poor second alternative but frequently the only practical one. The welcome that a country extends to refugees depends upon a complex set of considerations, including economic strength, political stability of the host government, and compatibility of refugees with the host society. Given that many countries of first asylum are in the developing world, most have difficulties meeting the needs of refugees. Even provision of basic needs including water, sanitation, food, and shelter may prove difficult given poor infrastructure or the lack of financial resources to deal with the refugee population. By necessity, host governments are forced to put their native-born populations first. Any attempts to do otherwise may increase tensions between the native-born populations and the refugees. As such, most countries rely heavily on organizations such as the Red Cross or UNHCR to provide assistance in meeting the basic needs of the refugees in the short term.

Support of refugees is not necessarily a short-term effort. Over the longer term, refugee populations may continue to require external support, and they may or may not be fully incorporated into their host countries, a problem that is exemplified by Palestinian refugees.[8] Spread throughout Jordan, Lebanon, Syria, along with the Israeli-occupied West Bank and Gaza Strip, Palestinians became refugees when they fled Israel in 1948 (when the State of Israel was established) or later during the 1967 Six-Day War. The United Nations, through its Relief and Works Agency (UNRWA) for Palestine refugees in the Near East provides education, health, and relief and social services to Palestinians. With the exception of Jordan, where more than half of its population is Palestinian, the admission and integration of Palestinians by other Arab countries has been less than enthusiastic, largely out of fear by the host governments that removal of the refugee label would destroy chances of re-creating a Palestinian state.

In other cases, the presence of refugees may inflame tensions between countries or ethnic groups. In Lebanon, the delicate balance between Muslims and Christians has prevented Palestinian refugees from naturalization, for fear that the political balance would be upset. In other cases, fighters or militia members often use refugee camps as a base, promoting instability within the refugee camp as well as externally to the camp. As in the case of Rwandan refugee camps in Zaire, they became the base for rebel Hutu fighters who conducted border raids into Tutsi-dominated Rwanda.[9] Complicating matters, soldiers who were often guilty of genocide within Rwanda at the start of the crisis frequently controlled food and other supplies within the camps, and the UNHCR was accused of feeding and protecting those accused of genocide. Their safety within the refugee camps was hardly guaranteed. Later, in the face of a relatively powerless UNHCR, the predominately Hutu refugees became the target of Tutsi rebels within Zaire, who would eventually overthrow the Zairian government of Mobutu Sese Seko and establish the Democratic Republic of Congo, furthering the bloodshed.

Racially or ethnically heterogeneous societies face further pressures, where an influx of refugees may upset the existing delicate balance between groups. In the 1999 Kosovo conflict, for example, approximately one million ethnic Albanians sought refuge in the neighboring countries of Albania, Macedonia, and Montenegro.[10] In an already politically unstable region, the sheer number of refugees endangered the political stability of Kosovo's neighbors and threatened to embroil the region in a larger civil war.[11] Albania, for example, is the poorest country within Europe with a weak political system that was already reeling from internal conflict and anarchy following the collapse of its government in 1997. Refugees were arriving in a remote and economically undeveloped part of the country, and its financial and economic ability to cope with the influx was limited.[12] In Macedonia, where ethnic Albanians represent 25 percent of the population, it was feared that a large influx of Kosovar Albanians, estimated at 239,000, could radicalize Macedonian nationalism and Albanian separatism, upsetting the existing ethnic balance and increasing the likelihood of an expanded regional war. These were not minimal concerns. With an estimated ethnic Albanian population of 506,000, the Macedonian Albanian population was inflated by approximately 50 percent. Since Macedonia's emergence as an independent state in 1992, internal conflict between ethnic Albanians and Macedonians (Slavs) had threatened the state's existence on numerous occasions. Although most refugees eventually returned to Kosovo and the conflict did not expand during 1999, this fear seemed to come to fruition in the spring of 2001 as Kosovar Albanians fought with Macedonian security forces for control of the Albanian-dominated areas in Macedonia.

The strain associated with Kosovar refugees was felt elsewhere in Western Europe.[13] Although Germany, France, and Italy were all concerned with the number and location of refugees, Germany was perhaps the most vocal, openly expressing its belief that refugees should stay in the Balkans and out of northern or Western Europe. This clearly meant that poor neighboring states would have to deal with refugees, but it also demonstrated the ability of the Kosovo conflict to destabilize and politically charge the European continent. However, the fear of Western European countries also reflects European concerns with state identity and the influx of foreigners discussed in the previous chapter, with European countries becoming increasingly concerned with the social, economic, and political implications of large numbers of foreigners.

Symbolized in the late 1970s by Indochinese boat people and Kosovo Albanians in the late 1990s, resettlement to a third country such as Canada, the United States, or Australia is a long-term but the only option for many.[14] According to the UNHCR, the major countries of resettlement in 1999 included the United States, resettling approximately 85,000 individuals. Canada, Australia, and Norway were also major resettlement regions (resettling 17,000, 8,300, and 4,000 refugees in 1999, respectively), but the total number of refugees resettled within any one year is small relative to the total number. In 1999 alone, some seven million individuals were newly uprooted, relocating from countries including Kosovo, East Timor, Congo, Chechnya, Angola, Afghanistan, Sierra Leone, and Colombia.[15] In other words, less than 1.5 percent of this population was relocated to a third country in 1999. If the total displaced population of twenty-five million is counted, less than 0.5 percent was resettled. Remaining refugees were far less fortunate, experiencing life in desolate refugee camps, threatened by violence, and frequently marginalized by the host society. Even among those who are resettled, however, life is not easy. Refugees must adjust to their host country and frequently suffer from depression or post-traumatic stress disorder in the months immediately after arrival.

In contrast to those who legally immigrate for economic opportunities or family reunification, refugees are often the least successful of all entrants, frequently entering the host country with a poor or variable set of skills relative to other legal immigrants. Over the longer term, as has been the case with Marielitos or Southeast Asian refugees, most refugees become legal, permanent residents within their host countries. Although technically no longer labeled as refugees, this raises interesting questions and possibilities. Do, for example, former refugees attain similar benchmarks or levels of adjustment in the host country relative to legal immigrants or other refugees? In what direction do they assimilate? What is the time frame?

Existing evidence suggests that refugees continue to have divergent experiences after arrival, reflecting differences including the endowed human capital that refugees bring with them and their period of arrival (i.e., economic conditions in the resettlement country or whether they were among the first to flee, a group typically characterized by higher socioeconomic status). By definition, the refugee population is characterized by a broader diversity of human capital (i.e., skills or education) than the immigrant population, who self-selects themselves into the immigration process (i.e., the better educated or those with more skills are more likely to immigrate) and who are screened by the host country. Among refugees, the endowed human capital or skills that these groups bring with them will influence the adjustment process, allowing the possibility of more rapid socioeconomic advancement among those with higher skills. Among Southeast Asian refugees, for example, differences in the adaptation of Sino- and ethnic Vietnamese refugees have been noted,[16] with the Vietnamese tending to be more economically integrated than other Southeast Asian refugees despite similar lengths of residency within the United States.[17] An emerging Vietnamese business class contrasts with other Southeast Asian refugees, best reflected by the Laotian population, who continue to have lower rates of business ownership and are more likely to be dependent upon public assistance programs and on minimum wage labor.[18]

Yet, the process of adjustment into the host society is something that is only partially dependent upon the abilities and experiences that refugees bring with them. Instead, broader issues contextualize their opportunities and relative success or failure within the host country. Refugees often lack the networks and ties in the destination that can help with locating jobs or accommodations, making them more likely to require state assistance during the transition period. This poses a fiscal burden to the host country. In recent decades, government policies have played a key role in the admittance of refugees, with public assistance available to refugees that is not available to other, legal immigrants. But, the availability of public aid may interact with other characteristics that potentially lead to different outcomes. Dependence upon government or other sources for assistance may prove beneficial or slow their adaptation into the host society.[19] National and ethnic origin and the level of public and private reception also influence the post-arrival success of refugee groups. Hungarians have successfully adapted to the United States and Canada, but their success was dependent not only on their skills but also the fact that they were white and fleeing a communist country at the height of the cold war. Although Mariel Cubans have fared relatively well, assisted by an already economically and politically strong Cuban community, differences between "white" and "black" Cubans have been noted.[20] Even recent arrivals are forced to conform to American expectations (and stereotypes) of race and its consequences for social mixing, residential location, and employment opportunities. Together, this is suggestive of a complex and unequal process that transforms "refugees" into "immigrants" and ultimately naturalized citizens of the host country.

NORTH AMERICA: WELCOMING REFUGEES?

Although relocation of refugees to a third country is a difficult and less than ideal option, Canada and the United States both have long histories of admitting refugees[21] for permanent resettlement, including the resettlement of European refugees in the immediate post–Second World War years, along with Hungarian refugees in 1956.[22] In 2000, for example, the United States expected to resettle over seventy-five thousand refugees, resettling more refugees than all other countries combined. Similarly, Canada targeted twenty thousand refugees for resettlement, a somewhat higher per-capita rate of resettlement than in the United States.[23] Despite their records of accomplishment, the evolution of refugee policies in both countries was relatively slow, and both adopted ad hoc policies for refugee admission throughout much of the postwar era. The admission of Hungarian refugees came at the height of the cold war, and both countries viewed their admission as a foreign-policy tool to control communism. Later, the absorption of some 132,000 Cuban refugees by the United States following the Cuban revolution in 1959 reflected the same foreign-policy agenda.

In fact, it was not until the 1960s that refugee legislation was codified in both countries.[24] The 1965 Immigration and Nationality Act formalized U.S. refugee policy by establishing that 6 percent of all immigrants (the so-called seventh preference category) could enter as refugees *if* they satisfied certain conditions. These included: (1) departure from a communist country or the Middle East; (2) that their departure was caused by fear of persecution on account of race, religion, or opinion; (3) they had departed in flight; and (4) that they were unwilling or unable to return. In essence, the United States had adopted the UN definition of a refugee, but attached geographical and ideological caveats. It finally recognized the UN Convention in 1968, but did not amend its immigration and refugee statutes to reflect its new obligations. Canada ratified the UN Convention and its Protocol in 1969.

Only in 1980 did the United States pass the Refugee Act and fully ratify the UN Convention, regularizing refugee admissions and institutionalizing resettlement assistance. Still, the act failed to change the political considerations underlying refugee admission and selection, and the refugee system remains highly politicized even now. Each year, the president and Congress determine the number of authorized admissions (the 1998 ceiling was eighty-three thousand) broken down by origin region. The president and Congress also define who is of special humanitarian concern to the United States, which may be manipulated to bar entry to those from countries friendly to the United States, even in the face of observed persecution, as has been the case with Haitian entrants. Some critics have gone as far as suggesting that refugee flows from the former Soviet Union and its satellite states were more about family reunification in the 1990s than they were about being true refugees. At the same time, needy refugees in Africa were overlooked.[25] Although there has been improvement, with refugees sourcing from several African countries including Sudan, Somalia, and Liberia in 1999, these numbers remain small (less than ten thousand entrants) in comparison to other origins and the scale of the displacement. Major origins in 1999 included nearly 13,000 from the former USSR, almost 10,000 from Vietnam, 2,018 from Cuba, and 38,213 from the former Yugoslavia (Croatia, Bosnia, and Kosovo), showing the continued domination of former communist countries, *or* an ongoing failure to recognize the refugee crisis in Africa (table 5.2).[26]

Although following a similar timeline, Canada's refugee policy has differed in important respects from American policy, following a more liberal and humanitarian interpretation of the 1951 UN Convention.[27] Over the past thirty years, for example, Canada resettled large numbers of refugees from Chile, Uganda, El Salvador, and Guatemala, groups that the United States did not welcome for various (largely political) reasons (table 5.3). Canada also led the United States in incorporating the principles of the UN Convention into Canadian statutory law in 1976, four years before the United States did. The 1976 act also defined two classes of refugees. First, "convention refugees" follow UN guidelines. Individuals seeking resettlement must be Convention refugees and are subject to medical, security, and criminality screening. Approximately twenty thousand UN Convention refugees were received in 2000, the major sources included Kosovo, Bosnia, Afghanistan, Croatia, along with African countries including Sudan, Somalia, Ethiopia, Burundi, and the Congo.[28] Second, Canadian refugee law recognizes persons in "designated classes," including those who do not entirely qualify for entrance as refugees but need protection and are admitted with private sponsorship.

While both countries accepted refugees specifically chosen for resettlement in the post–Second World War era, neither dealt with large numbers of asylum seekers until the last two decades of the twentieth century, pressuring them to reform their refugee systems. In the United States, the 1980 Refugee Act provided a statutory asylum policy. Importantly, the asylum provision did not establish a limit on the number of aliens who could apply or be granted asylum in a year, meaning that any alien who arrives in the United States could request asylum, allowing the individual to remain within the country until the review is completed and entitling them to benefits.

The number of asylum cases ranged from over 160,000 in 1995 to slightly less than 42,000 in 1999, with the major origins including China, Somalia, Haiti, Indonesia, Mexico, and El Salvador. Asylum cases are heard before an asylum officer who determines the validity of the claim.[29] Like the resettlement of refugees, political considerations appear to influence the granting of asylum, emphasizing control of the border rather than protection of individual rights, even though State Department involvement in asylum cases was supposedly reduced in the 1990 revisions to the Refuge Act,[30] with regional variations in approval rates remaining in 1998. On average, 23 percent of asylum cases were approved in 1998, which is roughly representative of the preceding five years, but approval rates were below average for many Latin American countries.[31] For example, the 1998 approval rate was 17 percent for Nicaragua, 9 percent for Guatemala, 13 percent for Haiti, and 7 percent for El Salvador. In contrast, approval rates were generally higher among many Asian, North African, and Eastern European states. Refusal of asylum could result in detention and deportation.

United States law also provides for a number of "refugee-like" situations, giving

Table 5.2   U.S. Refugee Arrivals by Top Ten Origins, Fiscal Years 1996–1998

	1996			1997			1998		
Rank	Country	Number	Percent	Country	Number	Percent	Country	Number	Percent
—	All Countries	74,791	100.0	All Countries	69,276	100.0	All Countries	76,181	100.0
1	Soviet Union, former	29,536	39.5	Soviet Union, former	27,072	39.1	Yugoslavia, former	30,906	40.6
2	Vietnam	16,130	21.6	Yugoslavia, former	21,360	30.8	Soviet Union, former	23,349	30.6
3	Yugoslavia, former	12,030	16.1	Vietnam	6,660	9.6	Vietnam	10,288	13.5
4	Somalia	6,436	8.6	Somalia	4,974	7.2	Somalia	2,951	3.9
5	Cuba	3,498	4.7	Cuba	2,911	4.2	Iran	1,699	2.2
6	Iraq	2,528	3.4	Iraq	2,679	3.9	Cuba	1,587	2.1
7	Laos	2,201	2.9	Iran	1,305	1.9	Liberia	1,494	2.0
8	Iran	1,256	1.7	Laos	939	1.4	Iraq	1,407	1.8
9	Sudan	575	0.8	Sudan	277	0.4	Sudan	1,252	1.6
10	Ethiopia	194	0.3	Liberia	231	0.3	Ethiopia	152	0.2

Source: U.S. Immigration and Naturalization Service, *Statistical Yearbook 1996–1998.*

Table 5.3 Canadian Refugee Arrivals by Top Ten Origins, 1997–1999

Rank	1997			1998			1999		
	Country	Number	Percent	Country	Number	Percent	Country	Number	Percent
—	All Countries	24,130	100.0	All Countries	22,700	100.0	All Countries	24,367	100.0
1	Bosnia-Herzegovina	3,677	15.2	Bosnia-Herzegovina	3,590	15.8	Bosnia-Herzegovina	2,692	11.1
2	Sri Lanka	2,564	10.6	Sri Lanka	2,130	9.4	Sri Lanka	2,606	10.7
3	Afghanistan	1,674	6.9	Iran	1,472	6.5	Afghanistan	1,814	7.4
4	Iran	1,665	6.9	Croatia	1,285	5.7	Iran	1,440	5.9
5	Iraq	1,346	5.6	Afghanistan	1,278	5.6	Somalia	1,376	5.7
6	Croatia	996	4.1	Somalia	1,195	5.3	Croatia	1,187	4.9
7	Bangladesh	795	3.3	Iraq	947	4.2	Pakistan	1,088	4.5
8	India	770	3.2	India	829	3.7	Iraq	915	3.8
9	Pakistan	752	3.1	Pakistan	723	3.2	Algeria	743	3.1
10	Somalia	729	3.0	Sudan	614	2.7	India	694	2.9

Source: Citizenship and Immigration Canada.

the government and president latitude for allowing entry or residency in a number of situations, but also underscoring the differential and ambiguous responses by the government to Haitian and Cuban entrants (see figure 5.1). Haitians, most of whom arrived by sea, claimed political asylum, but were defined by the government to be economic migrants searching for a way to leave the poorest country in the Western Hemisphere.[32] Yet, despite ample evidence of persecution by the Haitian government, the U.S. government refused entry to most Haitians so as not to undermine the Haitian regime. Fearing a large and uncontrollable influx of Haitian refugees should the door appear to be opened, the U.S. government has also vigorously pursued a policy of **interdiction** on the high seas, with detainees returned to Haiti. Differentiating between political and economic refugees is often difficult, and the situation is compounded when ideological considerations cloud definitions.

Arriving shortly after the 1980 Refugee Act was signed, the reception of Mariel Cubans was decidedly different, and only a minority met the conventional requirements of asylum.[33] Rather than processing the Marielitos under the new system, the U.S. government bypassed the Refugee Act and "paroled" Cubans directly into the

Figure 5.1. "Elian" and "Alien."

The disparities in the reception of Cubans and Haitians are illustrated. In 1999, Elian Gonzalez was rescued from the Caribbean after a failed attempt to reach the United States, becoming the object of a months long tug-of-war between American Cubans, the U.S. government, and Cuba. In contrast, Haitians attempting to enter the United States are turned away, despite oppression by the Haitian government.

Source: Kirk Anderson, reproduced with permission.

United States. Eventually, the government regularized their status, allowing them to become immigrants in 1986.[34] The United States has also used a number of devices, including EVD (extended voluntary departure) and TPS (temporary protected status) to grant "safe haven" to groups in the United States in situations where a return to their countries of nationality would be dangerous owing to political or other reasons, including natural disasters. The TPS statute provides aliens with employment authorization, but does not convey residency status. Decisions to provide these measures have typically been based upon humanitarian grounds, as had been extended to the Chinese following the Tiananmen Square massacre in 1989 and more recently to Hondurans and Salvadorans following the devastating earthquakes in those countries.[35]

Canada has also dealt with an increasing number of asylum claims, with an average of twenty-five thousand to thirty thousand asylum claims made each year in the late 1990s, sourcing largely from China, Sri Lanka, Pakistan, Hungary, India, and Mexico.[36] In Canada, asylum claims are heard before the Immigration Review Board **(IRB),** an independent administrative tribunal that is charged with determining the veracity of the refugee claims. In the recent past, approximately 45 percent of cases were approved, although this number is lower than that just a few years ago.[37] While waiting for the hearing, refugees are eligible to apply for employment authorization (if it can be shown that they could not subsist on public assistance) and are eligible to apply for student authorization so that they can go to school. Emergency and essential health services are also provided.

While Canada has not experienced widespread abuse of its immigration system in general, its refugee system has been problematic, forcing the government to adjust refugee policy on a number of occasions and in response to specific concerns.[38] Most recently, the arrival of boatloads of Chinese from Fujian Province during the summers of 1999 and 2000, en route to the United States or Canada, reignited a long-running debate over Canada's immigration and refugee laws. Those apprehended immediately claimed refugee status, raising public concerns over backdoor, illegal immigration and the abuse of the refugee system. Their arrival also contrasted markedly with the warm reception given to Kosovar refugees just months earlier, underlining the ambiguity of refugee policy, public opinion, and the definition of who is or is not a refugee.

Reforms tabled in the Canadian House of Commons in February 2001 were meant to close this backdoor by increased screening of potential refugees in their origin country, detention, interdiction, and increased penalties for smugglers.[39] New measures to screen refugees (and immigrants) were also introduced following the September 11th terrorist attacks in the United States, and both Canada and the United States have also moved to harmonize immigration and refugee requirements.

The United States has also moved to tighten its refugee and asylees process and insulate itself from becoming the primary destination for asylum applicants. The 1980 Refugee Act did not limit the number of aliens who could apply for or be granted asylum in any year, making it an unknown quantity in immigration. Although it has long used measures such as interdiction and detention to deter the arrival of asylum seekers, the Illegal Immigration Reform and Immigrant Responsibility Act of 1996 directly responded to the perceived abuse of the asylum system.[40] Persons entering the United States without documentation or false identification were subject to immediate detention and could be deported. If asylum was requested, a screening process determines the credibility of their claim and whether the full asylum process should be initiated. Nor has the act been without its critics. Pointing to the policy of interdiction and detainment, the system has been accused of mistreating those it is meant to protect. Finally, both the United Sates and Canada have moved to adopt policies of "safe third country," allowing them to return would-be asylees to a previous country of transit if that country was deemed safe and they could have applied for asylum there.

EUROPE: A LUKEWARM RECEPTION

Most European countries have not been resettlement destinations, although Norway, Sweden, Denmark, and Finland have accepted limited numbers of refugees through the 1990s. With little opportunity to immigrate legally to Western Europe, would-be immigrants have sought entry through asylum. Until the early 1980s, the number of asylum seekers arriving in Western Europe was approximately 100,000 per year, with most arriving from Eastern Europe. By the mid-1980s, the number of refugees had grown rapidly, and their influx fueled anti-foreigner violence that threatened the political stability of European governments as they dealt with rising nationalism, part of the larger unease with immigration that was discussed in the previous chapter. Rather than being viewed as legitimate refugees fleeing persecution, entrants from north Africa, Turkey, or Eastern Europe are frequently viewed as illegitimate economic refugees. Interestingly, the growth of nationalism coincided with Western Europe's move toward a common currency and market, surrendering a portion of their sovereignty and allowing the free movement of European Union members throughout the community. This apparent paradox is explained by anti-foreigner sentiments—anyone outside the European Union was foreign and a threat. Discussions of asylum are consequently cast in terms of national security, with implications for the shape and outlook of European society.

Although the pressure to deal with refugees was felt throughout Western Europe, the pressure has been particularly acute in Germany, where its generous asylum laws were associated with an upsurge in the number of asylum seekers from approximately 100,000 per year in the mid-1980s to over 430,000 by 1992. Most would-be asylees arrived from Turkey, Yugoslavia, Poland, Bulgaria, and Romania.[41] Although Germany's approval of asylum applicants was less than 5 percent, many of those denied legal status either slipped into the underground or moved elsewhere. Germany's attempt to deal with the rush of asylum seekers was ad hoc and limited. To discourage asylum seekers from traveling to Germany, the government moved to deny work permits. The response was immediate and predictable: idle refugees made for highly visible targets, fanning anti-foreigner sentiments that were already high because of the cost to local taxpayers to support arrivals. Numerous examples of violence and attacks upon foreigners were reported in the early 1990s, leading to questions regarding the integration of foreigners and asylum laws. In response, Germany reformed its asylum laws in 1993, allowing it to turn back asylum seekers without a hearing if they had transited through a safe third country that also offered asylum, unilaterally declaring all immediate neighbors as "safe" countries. For those who illegally slipped into the country, Germany followed a complex system for determining asylum.

Germany's move to reform its asylum laws was later reflected throughout the European Union. In light of a growing numbers of asylees seeking residency within Europe, governments were faced with the difficult task of interpreting who was a legitimate refugee. Building upon the Dublin Convention of 1990, which marked the first attempt to coordinate asylum policies, the Amsterdam Treaty of 1997 moved the European Union toward a harmonization of policies.[42] The treaty introduced a variety of measures to limit asylee flows, including the detention of asylum seekers and reduced social benefits, which were meant to reduce the differences in facilities and benefits between northern Europe, where benefits have been traditionally better, and the south.[43] Europe has also imposed a narrow interpretation of the UN Convention on refugees. Germany's courts, for instance, ruled that persons fleeing Afghanistan's Taliban regime do not qualify for refugee status since the Taliban is not a recognized government. This allows countries to recognize persons persecuted by a government or its agents but not, for example, at the hands of a rebel movement. Even if a state's authority has completely broken down in the origin, a request for protection could be refused.[44] Bosnian Muslims, Somalis, and others have run into this legalistic barrier as well, but there is nothing in the UN Convention that would exclude refugee status for persons persecuted by nonstate agents. Finally, the European Union has followed the principle that a would-be refugee must seek asylum in the first country that she or he is able to do so. The so-called safe third country policy is legally binding, designed to prevent asylum seekers from "shopping" for the best place for refuge.

INTERNALLY DISPLACED PERSONS: A GROWING CONCERN

While the number of refugees has declined in recent years, the number of IDPs has moved in the opposite direction. Similar to refugees, in that they have been forced to flee their homes for fear of persecution, conflict, or human rights abuses, IDPs differ from refugees in that they do not reside outside of their countries of nationality. Many are trapped in war zones, unable to cross international borders into safer areas. By 1999, IDPs represented over twenty-five million individuals, the result of multiple wars and conflicts. In Sudan alone, two decades of war between the Islamic government of the north and the Christian south has produced over four million displaced individuals.[45] Other major populations at the end of 1999 were found in Afghanistan, Indonesia, Angola, Sri Lanka, Indonesia, Azerbaijan, Sierra Leone, and Yugoslavia. Indonesia has recently joined this group, becoming home to an internally displaced population exceeding one million persons from virtually every province (excluding an estimated 125,000 East Timorese refugees who remain in Indonesia). In many cases, a large percentage of the displaced were originally **"transmigrants,"** products of a long-standing government program that relocated Indonesians from the island of Java to less populated areas by offering economic and land incentives. But the cause of recent, forced displacements were deep and spatially variant across the island state. In some locations, displacement was caused by conflict between the government and rebels. In others, religious conflicts between the country's majority Muslim population (90 percent) and Christians grabbed headlines, but were underlain by economic control and power, transmigration, and the control of resources.

Internally displaced persons are often faced with an insecure future. They may be confronted with an ongoing internal conflict or without a safe place to stay, and domestic governments may view them as enemies of the state or as enemy sympathizers. Internally displaced persons are not protected by international refugee laws and have little access to international assistance, typically falling between the cracks of current humanitarian laws. In part, this reflects Western interests and the ability of certain conflicts to "grab the headlines," including conflicts that threaten the national security of developed countries or are defined as "interesting." In other cases, there is only indifference toward long-running disputes. Three of the world's most protracted conflicts—Sudan, Angola, and Colombia—are largely internal conflicts that are ignored by the Western media.

The failure to protect internally displaced persons is much more than just Western awareness of the events, but reflects the current viewpoint that state sovereignty is sacrosanct, making it extremely difficult to work with a displaced population in the country that was responsible for its displacement. Can the United Nations and international law, for instance, override issues of state sovereignty to provide humanitarian assistance? This issue was grappled with in both Bosnia and Kosovo long before NATO became involved. Although assistance was ultimately provided in these cases, many other low-profile or long-term crises do not have this benefit, with donor money or assistance instead directed toward visible refugee crises. Nongovernmental organizations and other aid groups have had some success, but still reach only a small segment of the total displaced population. The UNHCR has increasingly become involved by assisting IDPs, but still deals with only a small proportion of the total displaced population, including in Chechnya, Yugoslavia, and Indonesia, and it will only intervene when asked by the UN secretary general and given consent by the state or parties involved.

Changing political circumstances, independent and sovereign states versus a rebel army, and control of territory complicate the provision of assistance. In response to the growing numbers of internally displaced persons, the United Nations has established a set of guiding principles to protect displaced populations.[46] These guiding principles call for the protection of a person's basic rights, outline the responsibilities of the state, and provide the individual with the right to leave a state. Although ignored by most governments with displaced populations, the principles have gained some acceptance, paving the way for increased involvement by organizations such as the UNHCR and the United States Committee for Refugees **(USCR).**

EMERGENT THEMES AND ISSUES

In the United States, Canada, and other countries of resettlement, the overseas admission of refugees has been built upon a humanitarian basis. Currently, receiving countries such as Canada or the United States are able to control the intake and flow of refugees from overseas. Post September 11th, however, means that many countries will revisit refugee policies, restricting refugee admissions and tightening the screening of refugee claimants, meaning that refugee policies are likely to change over the short-term. However, the tightening of entrance requirements will come at a cost. With an increasing world population, conflict will become increasingly common, spurred by ideology, land, and the control of resources, ultimately leading to population displacement. Widespread poverty also provides a fertile breeding ground for tensions that can erupt in violence. Together, the ongoing potential for political instability means that it is unlikely that the total number of displaced persons (refugees, asylees, and IPDs) will decrease soon. In response to increasing the relatively unrestricted flow of asylum seekers, countries will increasingly move to close their borders at a time when greater access is needed.

In Europe, the asylum crisis in the 1990s led to a streamlining and harmonization of procedures and policies across the European Union, reflecting an increasing reluctance to offer refugee status. The reduction of benefits given to asylees, the imposition of a narrow definition of UN Convention refugees, and binding third-country policies have ultimately lead to a partial closing of the doors. While the European Union has mounted a response to asylum seekers that maintains the spirit of the 1951 UN Convention, each country wants to take as few refugees as possible while attempting to shift the problem elsewhere. The poor recognition of refugee claims raises troubling questions, highlighted by Western Europe's fear of being the destination for Kosovar refugees. First, low rates of recognition (i.e., a recognition rate in 1998 of just 13 percent throughout Europe)[47] could further erode public support for refugees. Rather that being viewed with compassion, public opinion could perceive all asylum applicants as abusers of the system. In North America, both Canada and the United States have moved to tighten asylum laws through a variety of measures. Second, the implementation of safe-third-country policies by the European Union, Canada, and the United States is one technique to slow the flow of asylum seekers. Yet, there is no clear consensus on what constitutes a "safe" country. Should countries such as Romania be declared "safe" when their democracies are young and still fragile?

Third, if Europe, Canada, and the United States are unable to implement generous asylum practices, how can poorer countries be expected to allow large numbers of refugees entry? Many smaller states have refused to acknowledge refugees, fearful of the economic, political, and social implications of doing so. At the height of the Kosovo crisis, Macedonia closed its doors to refugees and physically removed others. In short, in backing away from refugee resettlement, the developed world is setting a dangerous and shortsighted precedent, one that the developing world has simply followed. Instead, governments have increasingly relied upon aid organizations and nongovernmental organizations (NGOs) to safeguard the rights of refugees and IPDs. Rather than providing their fair share of assistance, it is incumbent upon the richer, developed world to do more. The challenge lies in states finding the balance between protecting their own interests while allowing for the legitimate claims of refugees, something in itself that is difficult.

The reluctance of developing countries to accept refugees must be partially attributed to the failure of the developed world to accept greater numbers of refugees, along with a hesitancy to become involved in humanitarian issues. Fears associated with a large influx of asylum seekers have host countries concerned with the control of their national borders, as they have grown fearful of the economic, political, and social instability that frequently accompanies large refugee flows. Compassion for refugee claimants has turned to fatigue, underlain by a feeling that refugees are simply abusing the system. The difficulty of distinguishing bona fide refugees from economic, voluntary migrants, superimposed upon national political, social, and economic concerns, clouds the picture. Refugee flows have therefore been redefined as a national security threat to the receiving country, with many countries looking to impose greater restrictions on asylum seekers and tighter refugee policies that include detention and interdiction.

Attempts to restrict asylum may, of course, be only partially successful. Like the attempts to restrict legal immigration discussed in the previous chapter, closing the doors to refugee movements may only serve to increase illegal entry. Already, European governments have a poor record of removing individuals who were not granted asylum. Instead, they slip into the underground economy. Refugees may also increasingly turn to smugglers as a means of reaching safety. Reports of refugees trying to get into England via the Channel Tunnel (smuggling themselves onto trucks or under trains, risking death by crushing, electrocution, or exposure) or travel by sea to Canada and the United States in boats that are barely ocean-worthy point to the desperation of these people. Once reaching a safe haven, their ordeal is hardly over, with most struggling for years in poor working conditions to repay smugglers under threats of violence to themselves or family members. Others are lured into prostitution. One estimate places human smuggling at a $7 billion(U.S.) annual business, linked to the arms trade, drugs, prostitution, and child abuse.[48] Most governments in the developed world are trying to address problems associated with human smuggling, a growing phenomenon that preys upon the impoverished and desperate in the developing world. Both Canada and the United States are considering new legislation to slow the flow, including stiff penalties and life in prison for traffickers.[49] But these policies, including Canada's proposed reforms to the Immigration and Refugee Act, also victimize the victims. Policies allowing detention mean that many would-be asylees are held for months pending a refugee hearing. In the case of illegal immigrants from China, most have been deported at the end of the process to face an uncertain future, policies the UNHCR and other human rights groups have criticized.

Closing the doors to refugee movements may also simply shift the refugee problem to one of dealing with an internally displaced population. If settlement in a second or third country is barred, then the number of internally displaced people must increase. So, while it may appear that the number of refugees has decreased (as the evidence to date would suggest), individuals are simply redefined as internally displaced. Their lack of protection under international law and lack of access to resources magnifies the problem.

The forced displacement of individuals is not only the result of political instability, but it can perpetuate instability as well. As is the case of Kosovo Albanians in Albania and Macedonia or Palestinian refugees in Lebanon and other Arab countries, the presence of refugees may upset the political and ethnic balance within a state, or strain a state's abilities to meet the obligations of a refugee population. Radicalism caused by population imbalances may result in members calling for the separation of the state or increased nationalism that further oppresses the minority group. In Israel, the peace process is complicated by Palestinian and Jewish demographics as noted in chapter 1. The Palestinian population, which at 3.7 million is the world's largest refugee population, is characterized by high fertility in contrast to the relatively low rates of fertility and population growth among Israeli Jews.[50] The scattered Palestinian population and its right to return complicates the peace process. Israel opposes the Palestinian's return because of the demographic implications, while the existing infrastructure in Gaza and the West Bank would be heavily taxed if Palestinian refugees were to return.

On a different theme, the actual demography of displaced populations is an inexact science, one that needs to be refined.[51] UNHCR and USCR figures illustrate this problem, with the UNHCR estimating the refugee population at some 14 million, while the UNHCR estimate is 11.5 million. Estimation of the size of the displaced population is difficult, hampered by the conditions that events generating flows occur in. Further, refugees may not stop in designated camps, but filter into the larger population. Yet, demographic data and estimates of the size of the displaced population are relied upon by aid organizations to determine the amount and type of food, shelter, or other assistance needed. Detailed estimates of the age and sex distribution of the population would provide detailed information relating to the need, for example, for immunization or prenatal care. Regardless of the perspective, much more can and must be done to assist refugees and IDPs.

NOTES

1. The 1951 UN Convention was meant only to deal with European refugees associated with pre-1951 events at the end of the Second World War. The 1967 Protocol removed the provisions associated with geography and the requirement that only victims of pre-1951 events could be defined as refugees.

2. Asylees are individuals forced out of their country of origin who are seeking refuge in the new country in which they are living.

3. <http://www.unhcr.ch/un&ref/who/whois.htm> (15 April 2001).

4. <http://www.refugees.org/world/statistics/wrs00_tableindex.htm> (15 April 2001).

5. The spring 2001 (vol. 35) issue of *International Migration Review* is a special issue that deals with the UNHCR: "UNHCR at 50: Past, Present and Future of Refugee Assistance."

6. Kathleen Newland, "Refugees: The New International Politics of Displacement," in *Perspectives on Population*, eds. Scott W. Menard and Elizabeth W. Moen (New York: Oxford University Press, 1987), 314–321.

7. Newland, "Refugees," 314.

8. Farzaneh Roudi, "Final Peace in the Middle East Hinges on Refugee Population," *Population Today* 29, no. 3 (April 2001): 1. Readers can also find information applicable to Palestinian refugees through the UN Relief and Works Agency (UNRWA) for Palestine Refugees in the Near East, <http://www.un.org/unrwa/> (30 April 2001).

9. Ray Wilkinson, "The Heart of Darkness," *Refugees* 110 (Winter 1997): 3–8.

10. Holly Reed, "Kosovo and the Demography of Forced Migration," *Population Today* 27, no. 6 (June 1999): 4–5.

11. Carlotta Gall, "Crisis in the Balkans: In Macedonia; At Wit's End, a Neighbor Turns Back the Refugees," *New York Times*, 31 March 1999, 1(A).

12. Misha Glenny, "When Victims Become a Threat," *New York Times*, 6 April 1999, 2(A); Anthony DePalma, "Crisis in the Balkans: Neighbor; Kosovo Crisis Strains Already Struggling Albania," *New York Times*, 26 May 1999, 4(A).

13. Roger Cohen, "Crisis in the Balkans: The Europeans; Already Burdened, Western Europe Is Reluctant to Take in Kosovo's Outcasts," *New York Times*, 2 April 1999, 3(A).

14. Following the resolution of the war in Kosovo, many refugees who had been resettled to North America chose to return home. Many others stayed.

15. <http://www.refugees.org/world/statistics/wrs00_tableindex.htm> (15 April 2001).

16. Jacqualine Desbarats, "Ethnic Differences in Adaptation: Sino-Vietnamese Refugees in the United States, *International Migration Review* 20, no. 2 (1986): 405–427.

17. David W. Haines, *Refugees as Immigrants* (Totowa, N.J.: Rowman & Littlefield, 1986).

18. Alejendro Portes and Reuben Rumbaut, *Immigrant America: A Portrait* (Berkeley: University of California Press, 1996).

19. Sara Corbett, "The Long Road from Sudan to America," *New York Times Magazine*, 1 April 2001, 1–6. For an academic discussion of the adjustment of refugees to the host

society, see Reginald P. Baker and David S. North, *The 1975 Refugees: Their First Five Years in America* (Washington, D.C.: New TransCentury Foundation, 1984); Haines, *Refugees*; Alejendro Portes, "Economic Sociology and the Sociology of Immigration: A Conceptual Overview," in *The Economic Sociology of Immigration,* ed. Alejendro Portes (New York: Russell Sage, 1995), 1–41.

20. Emily Skop, "Race and Place in the Adaptation of Mariel Exiles," *International Migration Review* 35, no. 1 (2001): 449–471.

21. I use this term with caution. Both the United States and Canada have resettled large numbers of refugees in the past from a variety of sources. However, U.S. refugee policy has frequently been a tool of foreign policy, as discussed later in this section. Moreover, while both countries have resettled refugees, there is much more that they could do.

22. Not all groups have shared equally in the generosity of Canada and the United States, with both countries blocking the admission of European Jews during the 1930s and 1940s. See, for example, Irving Abella and Harold Troper, *None Is Too Many: Canada and the Jews of Europe 1933–1948* (Toronto: Lester and Orpen Dennys, 1983).

23. Larry Yungk, "From Sudan to North Dakota," *Refugees* 119, no. 2 (Summer 2000): 8.

24. Hania Zlotnik, "Policies and Migration Trends in the North American System," in *International Migration, Refugee Flows and Human Rights in North America*, ed. Alan B. Simmons (New York: Center for Migration Studies, 1996), 81–103.

25. Ray Wilkinson, "Give Me . . . Your Huddled," *Refugees* 119, no. 2 (Summer 2000): 5–21.

26. <http://www.ins.usdoj.gov/graphics/aboutins/statistics/refasy98.htm> (16 April 2001).

27. This should not be interpreted that Canada has always followed a strict humanitarian agenda. At the beginning of the Indochinese refugee crisis in the 1970s, Canada was initially slow to offer resettlement to refugees.

28. <http://www.cic.gc.ca> (April 2001).

29. Each year, the number of applications for asylum exceeds the number granted, following the determination of the veracity of the refugee claim. Calculating an average approval rate would be misleading, since approval rates vary significantly by country, being higher in the 1980s and 1990s for aliens from the former Soviet Union and lower for Central Americans.

30. T. Alexander Aleinikoff, "United States Refugee Law and Policy: Past, Present and Future," in *International Migration, Refugee Flows and Human Rights in North America*, ed. Alan B. Simmons (New York: Center for Migration Studies, 1996), 245–257.

31. <http://www.ins.usdoj.gov/graphics/aboutins/statistics/refasy98.htm> (16 April 2001). See *Refugees, Asylees, Fiscal Year 1998.* (Washington, D.C.: Immigration and Naturalization Service, 1998).

32. Lucas Guttentag, "Haitian Refugees and U.S. Policy," in *International Migration, Refugee Flows and Human Rights in North America*, ed. Alan B. Simmons (New York: Center for Migration Studies, 1996), 272–289.

33. Newland, "Refugees," 314.

34. Aleinikoff, "United States Refugee Law and Policy," 245.

35. Aleinikoff, "United States Refugee Law and Policy," 245.

36. <http://www.cic.gc.ca/english/pub/anrep01e.html#app-b> (April 2001).

37. Wilkinson, "Give Me," 5.

38. Manuel Garcia y Griego, "Canada: Flexibility and Control in Immigration and Refu-

gee Policy," in *Controlling Immigration: A Global Perspective*, eds. Wayne A. Cornelius, Philip L. Martin, and James F. Hollifield (Stanford, Calif.: Stanford University Press, 1992), 119–142.

39. <http://www.cic.gc.ca/english/about/policy/imm-act.html> (3 April 2001).

40. <http://www.ins.usdoj.gov/graphics/index.htm> (16 April 2001). See also Wilkinson, "Give Me," 5.

41. Philip L. Martin, "Germany: Reluctant Land of Immigration, in *Controlling Immigration: A Global Perspective*, eds. Wayne A. Cornelius, Philip L. Martin, and James F. Hollifield (Stanford, Calif.: Stanford University Press, 1992), 189–226.

42. Stefan Teloken, "Europe: The Debate over Asylum: It's a Long Way to . . . Harmonization," *Refugees* 113 (1999): 3–7.

43. Judith Kumin, "Europe: The Debate over Asylum: An Uncertain Direction," *Refugees* 113 (1999): 8–13.

44. Teloken, "It's a Long Way," 3.

45. <http://www.unhcr.ch> (April 2001).

46. Ray Wilkinson, "IDPs: The Hot Issue for a New Millennium: Who's Looking After These People?" *Refugees* 117 (1999): 3–8.

47. Kumin, "An Uncertain Direction," 8.

48. Judith Kumin, "A Multi-Billion Dollar Trade in Humans," *Refugees* 119 (2000): 18–19.

49. <http://www.cic.gc.ca/english/about/policy/imm-act.html> (3 April 2001).

50. Farzaneh Roudi, "Final Peace in the Middle East Hinges on Refugee Population," *Population Today* 29, no. 3 (April 2001): 1.

51. Reed, "Kosovo," 4.

6

Population, Economic Growth, Resources, and the Environment

Early on in this book, it was established that the continued growth of the human population is inevitable. Even if the demographic transition results in lower fertility and growth rates, population momentum and above replacement fertility rates will ensure that the population reaches 7.5 or 8 billion by 2025, bringing with it potentially significant societal and economic consequences. The question that remains, however, is whether a growing population has had positive or negative implications for resources, food production, and economic growth. The debate has a long history, dating to Thomas Malthus's "Essay on the Principle of Population," written in 1798 and later writings by Karl Marx and Friedrich Engels. Writing during a period of poor harvests and food shortages, Malthus[1] argued that food supply would increase in a linear fashion (1, 2, 3 . . .), while population would increase exponentially (2, 4, 16 . . .). Ultimately, population would exceed agricultural output, unless population growth was somehow "checked." Historically, Malthus argued that so-called positive checks, including famine, plague, and war, decreased the population. Alternatively, population growth could be controlled through "preventative checks," with individuals imposing their own limits on reproduction. With Malthus holding out little hope that humanity would be able to control their sexual and reproductive needs, he forecast a dismal future of population decline and widespread poverty. In opposition to Malthus, Marx and Engels argued that people were poor because economies and societies were organized in such a way that they did not have the opportunity to be anything else but poor. Influenced by the social and economic conditions of Europe during the Industrial Revolution, they promoted social and political change (often through revolution), and believed that a just and equitable distribution of resources aided by technology would allow unlimited population growth.

Time has proven the basic perspectives of **Malthusian** and Marxian theories both right and wrong—our mere presence on this planet points to the failings of Malthus's ideas. While fertility has been reduced largely through personal choices as standards of living rose and new ideas filtered through society, technology, the **green revolution,** and biotechnology have allowed the world to accommodate a population far larger than Malthus ever saw possible. Agricultural production has grown tremendously, allowing per capita food supplies to increase despite population growth. Marx's position, on the other hand, seems vindicated in China. With a population in excess of 1.2 billion, China has proven that it can provide the basic needs of a large and rapidly growing population. At the same time, China has recognized that there are limits to growth, moving to reduce fertility through its one-child policy.

Even now, however, over 800 million people are malnourished worldwide. Approximately 43 percent of these are found in sub-Saharan Africa, and 22 percent of the South Asian population is malnourished.[2] Millions more consume sufficient calories but fail to get the necessary proteins. Consequently, the world continues to grapple with the basic question of whether it can feed itself in the years to come. At the same time as agricultural production has increased, degradation of cropland through erosion, desertification, salinization, and urbanization have reduced the amount of land available for agriculture.[3] Erosion, for example, created by poor farming practices, deforestation, and use of ecologically marginal land, can decrease average yields by reducing the soil's ability to retain moisture, by carrying away nutrients and by degrading its physical qualities. The unequal distribution of food owing to distributional difficulties, conflicts, or politics within and among countries compounds the problem.[4] With the world's population growing at a rate of 1.3 percent per year, and with over eighty million new souls each year requiring food and clothing and other resources, questions as to whether the earth can feed and sustain such a large population continue to be raised.[5]

While Malthus's dire predictions remain a focal point of the debate over population growth, and the ability to feed the world's population remains an important question,[6] the debate has expanded from the original correlation between population and food to include linkages between population, resources, environmental degradation, and economic development and to encompass three competing perspectives. The debate, currently defined by **neo-Malthusians** (accepting of the Malthusian position), distributionists **(Marxist),** and economic optimists (those who believe that population growth stimulates economic development) has splintered, generating two lines of arguments, with one focusing on population—resource linkages (i.e., food, water, cropland)—and the other considering the potential connections between population and economic growth. Such a division creates an artificial divide within the population debate, when the reality is that resources, economic growth, and population are all tightly related. First, neo-Malthusian, economic optimist, or distributionist perspectives underpin both divisions. Second, the degradation, depletion, or denial (i.e., through legislation or conflict) of resources will have a direct impact upon economic growth and the livelihood of populations. Conversely, economic growth or population growth directly influences the level, type, and quantity of resources consumed within a society.

In the coming decades, population growth, rising per capita resource consumption of food and resources, and inequalities in resource access guarantee that scarcities of **renewable resources** will become an issue. The need for resource substitution and conservation will be urgent and complex, increasing the need for political and scientific leadership that is able to find solutions without aggravating existing problems and group conflicts. The following chapter focuses upon the linkages between population growth, resource scarcity, and economic opportunities. The intent is to draw upon ideas developed in previous chapters and to evaluate their relationship relative to broader issues of resources and economic development. Doing so, however, requires an understanding of alternative approaches that link population growth with resource and economic development issues. These opposing approaches, including their merits and problems, are discussed, along with current perspectives and how the differences between each may be reconciled. The chapter moves on to discuss linkages between population growth, economic development, and resource scarcity, considering whether renewable resources are truly renewable, and it concludes by looking at emerging issues.

SETTING THE STAGE: THE DEBATE AND CURRENT PERSPECTIVES

Growing from the initial Malthusian–Marxian distinctions within the literature, three perspectives underline the current debate and influence public policy and commentary.[7] Pointing to growing carbon dioxide concentrations, the declining health of oceans, reductions in biodiversity, and degradation of land, *neo-Malthusians* argue that finite resources place strict limits on the growth of the human population and consumption.[8] If limits are exceeded, social breakdown occurs.[9] Writing in the 1960s, Paul Ehrlich's *The Population Bomb*[10] alerted the public to the population crisis, bringing with it a sense of urgency. *Economic optimists*, characterized by Julian Simon, see few limits to population growth and prosperity, provided the economic system and market mechanisms work correctly.[11] Following their reasoning, few societies face strict limits to growth or consumption, with optimists pointing to improvements in human health, life expectancy, and increasing food production to support their position. Finally, the *distributionist* viewpoint, which is favored by Marxists, focuses upon inequalities in the distribution of wealth and power within a society. The viewpoint argues that the poor distribution of resources, poverty, and inequality are the causes, not consequences, of population growth and resource depletion.

While the neo-Malthusian, economic optimist, and distributionist perspectives are still identifiable within the literature, the debate has essentially become two-sided, with neo-Malthusians on one side and optimists on the other. Each argument contains grains of truth, but neither conveys the entire story. So, what went wrong and where do we currently stand? First, returning to the neo-Malthusian perspective, empirical and anecdotal evidence has failed to support the assumption that population growth is limited by resource barriers. In very general terms, the human population has grown beyond most of the barriers that were assumed by neo-Malthusians. Over the past two centuries, agricultural technology and capital have increased agricultural productivity tremendously, allowing agricultural output to increase. Similarly, neo-Malthusians forecasted energy shortfalls, predicting that energy prices would grow over fivefold between 1973 (the first oil crisis) and 2000. Today, however, energy and other **nonrenewable resources** arguably remain as abundant and inexpensive as they were thirty years ago.

Economic optimists have been much better in explaining the ability of the world to adapt to these apparent barriers. For them, the operation of economic institutions, and particularly free markets, is key. Properly functioning institutions can facilitate conservation, substitution, innovation, and global trade of goods. Induced innovation theory[12] argues that changes in endowments of land or labor, for example, are reflected in market price signals. Through its ability to generate profit, markets induce innovations and stimulate technological innovation that loosen or remove constraints to population growth, and price changes encourage people to tap new resources or to substitute. Ester Boserup, for example, shows that scarcity of cropland stimulates greater labor specialization, increased productivity, and changes in agricultural practices.[13] Likewise, new lands may be opened to agriculture, conservation may be stimulated, or resource substitution may promote the increased use of fertilizers to increase agricultural output. Similarly, scarcities of nonrenewable resources can be overcome through resource substitution, conservation, improved production efficiencies, and enhanced resource extraction technologies. Economic optimists also argue that population growth has a key advantage in that it produces more geniuses, providing society with the means to resolve scarcities. For Julian Simon, resources are only limited by humanities' ability to invent. Thus, innovation and technical fixes allow societies to move beyond constraints to growth. Resource scarcity and degradation are therefore not due to population growth or increased consumption, but are instead due to market failure.

Like the neo-Malthusian perspective, however, the optimist framework is also flawed. A larger population does not, for instance, necessarily mean more discoveries or more Einsteins, but perhaps only that more people make the same discovery. Instead, the supply of scientists and other thinkers is constrained by the level and accessibility of education, the brain drain out of many countries in the developed world, limited capital, poor and incompetent bureaucracies, corruption and weak states. The brain drain from developing countries and into the developed world may have an especially pernicious effect. As was discussed in chapter 4, much of the developed world has tailored its immigration policies to accept the educated or those with skills. This institutionalized brain drain poses further and long-term difficulties for the developing world in terms of maintaining social capital and its ability to generate, retain, and utilize the highly educated members of its populations, which will be necessary to solve impending problems.

Moreover, optimist's arguments rest on the free operation of the market, an assumption that is stretched in many cases. Free markets are far from universal. Even in America, the quintessential free-market economy, regulations at various government levels (state, national, and international) interfere with its free operation. In the developing world, the markets frequently become murkier. Institutional limitations, including market failure associated with unclear common property rights and inappropriate pricing for scarce resources (i.e., undervalued) limits the creation or substitution of alternatives. In addition, institutional biases may be present within markets, such that there is a tendency for institutions to favor some actors over others, leading to the marginalization of segments of the population. Consequently, a key caveat of the optimist viewpoint is the *quality* of institutions, policies, and technologies that is inherent within a society. Together, these effects, which are in turn modified by cultural, historical, and ecological factors, have direct bearing upon the ability to respond to resource scarcity. If markets are not able to identify or effectively incorporate the costs of scarcity so that resources or goods are undervalued, resources will be exploited and solutions to scarcity will not be forthcoming. Relatedly, it is unlikely that population growth can promote increases in agricultural output that will keep pace with population growth rates in Africa and parts of Asia.

For the most part, the debate between these three groups has stopped here, a debate that Homer-Dixon characterizes as sterile and with relatively little advancement.[14] Science, however, has better revealed the complexity and interconnectivity of ecological systems with implications for the population. In the past, the earth's environmental systems were regarded as stable and resilient to our tampering. Instead, there is mounting evidence drawn from observation of ocean currents, ozone depletion, and fish stocks that environmental systems are not stable given human actions. What was previously considered slow or incremental changes to systems might be better described as nonlinear, changing their character when some threshold is exceeded, making chaos and anarchy better descriptors of environmental systems.[15] Humanity is taxing the earth's resources to such a degree that complete ecosystems are disappearing. Global warming and the loss of biodiversity may, at some point, cascade to produce dramatic changes that humanity is ill prepared to deal with.

Extreme events, interdependency, and the interactivity of environmental systems further complicate our understanding of ecosystems, with implications for the ability to manage scarce resources. Even if global environmental systems change only slowly, the frequency of extreme events, such as flooding, drought, and so forth, will increase. Interdependency and interactivity of environmental systems means that degradation or damage to one resource produces effects that reach throughout

neighboring systems. Clear-cut logging, for example, removes habitats in the immediate area and the ability to sequester carbon dioxide, a greenhouse gas. But the
effects are much more widespread. The reduced or altered ability of the land to
absorb rain water alters drainage patterns and increases soil erosion. In turn, this
may lead to siltation of streams and rivers, destroying fish habitats and local fisheries,
and reducing the ability to manage river flows for the purposes of irrigation, naviga-
tion, or generation of hydroelectric power. Moreover, multiple human impacts upon
environmental systems could produce damaging outcomes that are far greater than
the sum of their individual effects, so that agricultural output could be stressed by
local deforestation, erosion, and changing rainfall patterns associated with climate
change.

Given threshold effects, interdependence, and interaction, societies will be forced
to deal with these problems and resource scarcity through increased ingenuity and
innovation. As argued by Homer-Dixon,[16] one of the key questions is, however,
whether societies will be able to provide the necessary ingenuity to tackle new and
emergent problems. Countries will respond differentially to scarcities and will, as a
result, provide various qualities and quantities of ingenuity. Innovation or ingenuity
is more likely to come from those with the resources, including time, capital, and
properly functioning institutions that allow the development of new concepts or
technology. Julian Simon, for instance, argued that if population growth was to be
beneficial, it must occur within a democratic, capitalist system.[17] Yet, democracy
may be just what the doctor *didn't* order. If a democracy exists in a society where it
does not have a history or foundation, the appropriate checks and balances that are
essential within the democratic system are unlikely to be in place. Under conditions
where corruption maintains power and wealth within a small circle of elites, existing
scarcities and ethnic or religious differences could aggravate problems and produce
further societal discord. Obviously, such a line of reasoning would be a difficult sell
in Washington, which has long triumphed the power of democracy.[18] Unfortunately, democracy is no better at ensuring equality of resource distribution or
income within a population than any other form of government. In fact, it may only
institutionalize inequality between groups, particularly in countries where corruption is rampant. The evidence is widely available in countries such as Chad, Angola,
Iraq, Kazakhstan, Nigeria, and Angola, where the wealth provided by booming oil
prices has failed to lift them out of poverty, but instead has enriched the pockets of
the elite within corrupt societies that are mired in conflict. In addition, it is already
apparent that poorly functioning markets and other institutions may limit the ability
of a society to respond to resource scarcity.

If the ability to generate ingenuity is missing or its supply is insufficient, it is
reasonable to assume that the ability of countries to respond to resource scarcity will
be diminished. The "ingenuity gap,"[19] or the difference between the need for ingenuity and societies' ability to supply it, becomes an important variable in the ability
of societies to deal with resource scarcity. If a society can supply the needed ingenuity, limits to growth can be overcome. But societies may lack the infrastructure, or

economic and political institutions may block the ability of a country to overcome resource scarcities and limits. For those societies that lack the ability to generate ingenuity, they will be increasingly unable to deal with rising scarcities and their implications. Instead, a gap between the supply and required amount of ingenuity will develop, and societies may be faced with increasing resource scarcity, with implications for social organization, social dissatisfaction, and violence. Resource scarcity may, for example, stimulate competition to protect and secure existing resources, a process known as resource capture, which is further examined in the coming pages. Social friction between groups, engendered by ethnic, ideological, or religious differences, also reduces the ability of societies to adapt by diminishing the capacity to supply ingenuity needed to resolve resource scarcity. In other words, rather than creating technological change, as optimists would argue, the lack of ingenuity and social capital may exacerbate resource scarcity. Resource scarcity may also force actors, such as state governments, to secure resources through legislative or military means. Doing so places severe pressures upon marginalized groups and fails to resolve the long-run difficulties of resource scarcity.

Given the advances on the scientific side of the debate, Homer-Dixon argues that the concepts of ingenuity supply and adaptation allow the various perspectives of population growth to be bridged.[20] Improved markets and greater equality in the distribution of wealth, ideas that are agued by both optimists and distributionists, will assist in reducing the negative effects of a scarcity. The ability of a society, however, to make improvements will be partially determined by the scarcity itself, which is also determined by its physical context, including economic resources. The neo-Malthusian perspective can also be addressed by focusing on the supply and need for ingenuity. Rather than focusing on strict limits to population, which neo-Malthusian perspectives do, Homer-Dixon argues that it is better to consider the ability of a society to supply ingenuity in the face of increasing requirements. If a society can supply the needed ingenuity, limits can be overcome. If not, a gap between the supply and required amount of ingenuity will develop, and societies may be faced with increasing resource scarcity, with implications for social organization, social dissatisfaction, and violence.

POPULATION AND ECONOMIC DEVELOPMENT

As the economies of the developing world, and particularly the poorest sub-Saharan countries, started to stagnate in the 1980s, social scientists scrambled to unearth the linkages between rapid growth and economic development.[21] After all, foreign investment and aid had poured into the developing world for years, and yet there was little to show for it. Instead, per capita incomes had declined and an increasing proportion of the population lived in poverty. At the heart of the debate is the question of whether population growth favors economic development or hinders it, with the available data supporting a number of interpretations.[22] On the surface, it is readily apparent that the richest countries are also those with slow population growth characterized by low rates of fertility and low mortality levels, while some of the poorest countries have high rates of population growth. The relationship is, however, not perfect, with, for example, the oil-producing countries in the Middle East having high population growth (the rate of increase in Saudi Arabia and other gulf states remains at over 3 percent per year) as well as strong economic growth. The opposite is also true, with low population and economic growth rates.

Muddying the waters are countering arguments that population growth promotes economic development. Recalling Boserup's[23] argument (first presented in chapter 1), optimists have long asserted that population growth promotes economic development, assuming that it is a motivating force in the adaptation of societies, including the uptake or innovation of new technologies and techniques or economic reforms. The notion that population growth is in fact good for economic growth is well grounded. In Europe and North America, population growth and declining mortality levels are thought to have stimulated economic development and the Industrial Revolution. However, a different perspective is seen in the developing world. Building upon a much lower standard of living than Europe or the Americas at similar stages in their economic development, and having far greater rates of population growth, this group of countries is not, on average, following the lead of developed countries. In fact, enhanced by the HIV/AIDS epidemic and its social and economic ramifications, they may be slipping further into economic crisis.

Although the linkage between population and economic development is complex, emerging evidence reinforces the *negative* linkage between rapid population growth and economic development. The U.S. National Research Council reinforced population's negative effect on economic growth, concluding that rapid population growth damages economic growth.[24] For economic development to occur, capital must be invested in such things as education, health, or infrastructure, a difficult proposition in much of the world where poverty impedes the ability for governments and individuals to invest. For economies to grow, the level of capital investment must also grow, with higher rates of population growth necessitating higher rates of capital investment. Following a Malthusian line of reasoning, if the population growth rate exceeds the investment rate, countries will be trapped in poverty, unable to invest in themselves and provide the needed infrastructure. Although economic growth would occur under these situations, population growth is so high that economic growth is distributed throughout a larger population, meaning that individuals will receive a smaller proportional share.

This negative linkage can be viewed through a number of relationships linking rapid population growth and high fertility to economic growth.[25] First, rapid population growth tends to dampen the growth of per capita gross domestic product (GDP, the total value of goods and services produced in a country), a relationship that first appeared in the 1980s and appears strongest among the poorest countries.[26] The growth of GDP can be limited by high young dependency rates (where the proportion of youth aged zero to fourteen is high relative to the size of the labor force), a result of high fertility rates. With a young population profile, the attendant costs associated with health and education for children is high, reducing household savings and increasing government expenditures. In turn, the growth of GDP is reduced, with the investment providing only long-term economic payoffs.[27] The impact on economic growth is also seen in the creation of new jobs. In countries with rapid population growth, labor markets are frequently unable to provide sufficient employment opportunities for the young, leading to underemployment or unemployment. This negative relationship continued into the 1990s, ensuring that inequalities between the developed and developing world remain and providing little hope for their rapid amelioration.

Second, population growth and high fertility tend to aggravate poverty and promote its institutionalization from one generation to the next. In particular, population growth will likely reduce or slow wage growth among the least skilled and lowest income groups. India, for example, has accommodated high population growth, but economic development policies have favored or improved the status of only 15 to 20 percent of the population. The poor in India have paid the highest price. Much of India's public education system, which is predominantly attended by lower socioeconomic classes, is underfunded and inadequate. The poor are progressively marginalized and are increasingly unable to participate in the economy because of poor health, lack of nutrition, or illiteracy.[28] In addition, a cadre of low-skilled, low-wage workers may slow the adoption of more efficient technologies.

Third, high fertility inhibits household savings, instead forcing household expenditure on basic goods and services for a larger number of people, while savings or expenditures upon education are postponed or neglected. Conversely, declining population growth and fewer children mean that households are able to invest in education and place more of their earnings in savings, a necessary condition for economic growth. The economic literature has, for example, largely attributed the growth of Asian economies such as South Korea during the 1980s to increased household saving rates as fertility dropped and incomes grew.[29] As families saved more, domestic savings increased and were invested both within the country as well as exported elsewhere.

Fourth, higher fertility rates mean that parents have less to invest in each child than those with smaller families. Similarly, children from larger families have less schooling on average than their counterparts from smaller families. In countries with rapid population growth, there is increased pressure placed on education and health care facilities, requiring increased financial commitments. Unless rapid growth of government revenues is also occurring, or governments are willing to shift spending priorities, expenditures on education and health are depressed.[30] Again, evidence in support of this can be drawn from Asia. In South Korea, decreasing fertility levels and young dependency rates meant that the government was able to quadruple real per-student educational expenditure between 1970 and 1989, even as it spent an approximately equivalent proportion of its national budget on education. If South

Korea's share of school-age children had grown as fast as Kenya's during the same period, it would have needed to spend more than double what it did.[31]

Finally, population growth threatens resources by placing increased pressure upon them, whether resource use is associated with increased per capita consumption (i.e., through increasing incomes and demand), or through increasing demand generated by a growing population, even if per capita demand remains the same. Forest products, fisheries, cropland, and fresh water resources, along with the services they provide, are all vulnerable to human-induced pressures.

Rapid population growth and high fertility seemingly have the greatest negative impact in the poorest countries where national institutions are weak.[32] In these cases, population growth reinforces a downward economic spiral, reflective of several sub-Saharan countries with high fertility rates and lower average per capita incomes today than two decades ago.[33] Poorly developed markets and/or ineffectual government programs and leadership fail to protect, invest in, or build the basic infrastructure that is needed. Without strong institutions to assist national programs associated with education, fertility and family planning, or infrastructure development, rapid population growth will decrease the supply of ingenuity, exacerbating resource scarcity and environmental degradation. In turn, failure to invest in infrastructure and the degradation of assets can cripple institutions and markets. Moreover, governments in developing countries often lack the financial or political ability to invest in institutions that will promote labor force development.

POPULATION AND RESOURCE SCARCITY

The debate over the relationship between population growth and resources parallels that of population and economic development, pitting neo-Malthusians against economic optimists, with both groups claiming evidence to support their position. One point seems intuitive: the collective impact of six billion people on the earth's ecosystems, measured through resource use, consumption, or pollution, is tremendous. Whether the current rate of resource consumption is sustainable is unknown, but it is suspected that current consumption patterns and human impacts are not sustainable over the long run. Already, many regions are faced with environmental scarcity, including scarcities of cropland, water, and forests.

In his 1999 book, Homer-Dixon identified three sources of resource scarcity: supply-induced, demand-induced, and structural scarcity. Supply-induced scarcities occur when resources are depleted in quantity or have become degraded, perhaps through overexploitation or pollution. Demand-induced scarcity occurs when population growth and changes in consumption patterns boost the demand for a resource. Such scarcities occur only when a resource is **rivalrous**, meaning that its use by one economic actor reduces its availability for others, with examples including fisheries, water, or forests. Structural scarcity occurs when there is an imbalance in the distribution of the resource or in power and wealth within a society, such that certain groups get a proportionately larger share of the resource. If a resource is excludable (i.e., cropland), such that its use can be restricted or blocked through property rights or other institutions, some groups may be prevented from accessing the resource.

Not surprisingly, population growth is a key factor driving all three types of resource scarcity. Rather than operating independently, each of these sources of scarcity may interact and reinforce one another, either through **resource capture** or **ecological marginalization.**[34] Resource capture occurs when a scarce resource forces actors (i.e., governments or ethnic groups) to assert control over resources through legislation or other means. Land scarcities in Chiapas, Mexico, encouraged wealthy landowners and ranchers to seize lands from the indigenous population by exploiting weak land laws. The marginalized peasants were forced deeper into poverty and off their traditional lands, a process that eventually resulted in violence as they rebelled against the Mexican government. The indigenous population of Chiapas was also ecologically marginalized, the outcome of population growth and a maldistribution of resources (structural scarcities) that forces individuals into ecologically marginal areas such as rain forests and steep hillsides, increasing the risk of resource degradation through erosion, siltation, or desertification.[35] Poverty, desperation, and a lack of environmental knowledge to protect resources magnify the problem.

It is questionable whether some countries, such as China, Egypt, and India, have the resources and economic ability to sustain their populations indefinitely, even if population growth was to cease immediately. Writing for the World Watch Institute in 1995, Lester Brown questioned the ability of China to feed itself in the coming decades.[36] Drawing from the experiences of other Asian countries, Brown forecasted that a combination of rising standards of living, which tend to move people "up the food chain" from staples to more complex diets, increased consumption, loss of cropland, and declining water resources, among other factors, would mean that China would not be able to feed itself. The inability to domestically grow a sufficient food supply would force China to turn to world markets to purchase the necessary grains and other foodstuffs. The problem lies in its expected demand for grains, which Brown projected to exceed total world output, driving up prices globally and weakening the ability of smaller, poorer countries to purchase their requirements.

Whether the discussion is global or national, it is not just a question of feeding a large population, but also the tasks of providing health care, education, and infrastructure while finding employment and increasing the standard of living over the longer term in a sustainable fashion. Population growth also influences such diverse issues as increased energy consumption, global warming, ozone depletion, deforestation, loss of cropland, loss of biodiversity, and shrinking fresh water resources. Together, the requirements of a growing population may only be met by extracting a huge toll upon limited resources, which may only cripple future sustainability, a situation that is compounded by unequal access to resources and the marginalization of populations.

The Fallacy of Renewable Resources

When the well's dry, we know the worth of water.

—Benjamin Franklin

When discussing resources, most authors distinguish between nonrenewable (finite) resources such as oil and gas reserves, and renewable resources, such as timber, fish stocks, and water. Renewable resources can be harvested and used up to some threshold without threatening their long-term viability. Provided this is achieved, long-term use of the resource can be ensured. The question is, however, whether our use of renewable resources is sustainable over the long term? In many places where people rely on renewables, they are being degraded or depleted faster than they can be renewed. Population growth amplifies many of the effects of human activity upon renewable resources simply through increased demand (demand-induced scarcity). Renewable resources can also be directly or indirectly depleted or degraded by direct consumption or harm to that resource (i.e., pollution), which in essence makes them nonrenewable. Likewise, thresholds are not always known or acknowledged, inadvertently leading to the degradation of a resource. Although a useful distinction, it is therefore arguable whether renewable and nonrenewable resources should be seen as necessarily exclusive categories. Much of the world is in danger of learning this the hard way, as renewable resources are wasted, mismanaged, or overused.

A number of brief examples serve to highlight the point that resources are not necessarily renewable. Water, for example, is an abundant resource but one that is unevenly distributed. Despite being renewed through the hydrological cycle, significant shortages loom on the horizon. From 1900 to 1995, global water consumption increased six times, more than double the rate of population growth, and over 500 million people live in countries that have water shortages, a number that is expected to grow dramatically to three billion in the next two decades.[37] Many areas, including the southwest United States, the Middle East, and northern Africa, are already faced with insufficient water resources at the same time as an increasing population, urbanization, and industrialization increases demand. This means, therefore, that per capita supplies drop as population increases. Israel faces an annual deficit of water (i.e., more water is used than is supplied through renewable sources on a yearly basis), a deficit that is covered by the overwithdrawal of aquifers, including those under the West Bank. Consequently, aquifer levels have dropped, some wells have been exhausted, and others have been infiltrated by seawater, limiting their use in the future. The situation is only expected to worsen with the continued growth of Israel's population.[38]

Water scarcity in Israel and elsewhere has implications for violence, especially since many water resources (especially rivers) are transnational, meaning that a scarce resource is shared by many states with potentially differing claims and needs for water. Israel, for example, moved to protect its water resources by limiting water use by Jewish settlers and Arabs alike on the West Bank (figure 6.1). With Arabs receiving far less water than their Jewish counterparts, the limits were far from equitable. The number and depth of new Arab wells was also limited, resulting in a reduction of the amount of irrigated agricultural land by Arab farmers. Abandoning the land for lack of water, Arab farmers were instead forced to rely upon day labor or move into crowded cities within the West Bank or Gaza. Although the links and processes that have generated unrest within the occupied territories are complex and reflect multiple social, religious, political, and economic factors, it seems reasonable to assume that water scarcity and its economic implications contributed to violence in these areas. In other cases, critics have asserted that water has been a cornerstone of the Israeli political and military agenda. While moving to create a security zone to protect northern Israel, Israel's invasion of southern Lebanon in 1982 placed the waters of the Litani River within Israel's borders for the duration of the occupation. Nor is this so far-fetched, since there have been repeated calls, with some dating from as early as 1919, that the Litani should be the border of a new Jewish state.[39] In short, while water is a renewable resource, its increasing scarcity threatens the livelihood and ultimately the security of groups and states within the region.

Cropland scarcity is another issue, with scarcities already found in diverse locations such as Chiapas, Haiti, the Philippines, and Bangladesh. When first colonized, Haiti was heavily forested. Since then, logging for commercial activities as well as fuel wood has dramatically reduced forest cover, with less than 2 percent of the forest remaining,[40] a process that has been perpetuated by poor economic institutions and slow economic growth. With the loss of the protective forest cover, soil erosion has increased, and United Nations estimates show that a majority of the farmland is now permanently lost or degraded. In the poorest country in the Western Hemisphere, deforestation and erosion have been reinforced by poor land management policies, farming of hillsides, along with fragmented and small landholdings. Peasants have tried to augment their small incomes by using wood for charcoal production, and the army, who has benefited from high fuel wood prices, has ripped up seedlings, further contributing to deforestation. The government has also played a key role through its failure to provide capital for agricultural improvement.

Canada's Atlantic cod fishery provides another example of the depletion of a renewable resource to a point where its future is questionable. Once dominated by small, individual fishers and so plentiful that all fishers had to do was drop a bucket in the water, the fishery was self-sustaining. Improved technology, including the introduction of offshore trawlers and factory ships, allowed increased catches of cod beyond that which the fishery could support. While the cod fishery was a victim of overfishing, it also represented a lack of awareness of the threshold or sustainability of the industry, including a lack of knowledge regarding the reproductive cycle of the codfish and an inability to correctly forecast stock sizes. Although the Canadian government has continuously (and perhaps optimistically) argued that the cod fishery will be reopened, fish stocks have not recovered since the moratorium was first

Figure 6.1.   Israel.

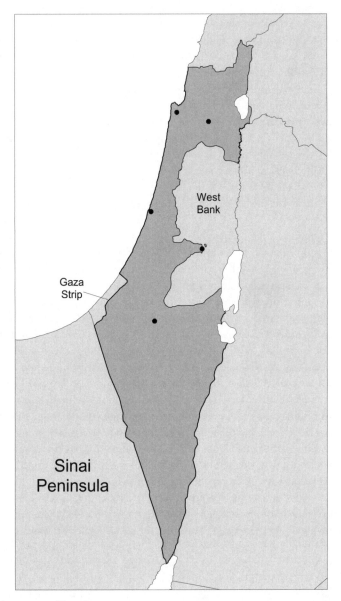

Source: Map courtesy of Roger Stump.

imposed in 1992, and there is speculation that it is irreparably damaged and will never again support the same level of catches and employment as it did in the past.[41]

The Atlantic cod fishery is not unique, with depletion or degradation of fishing stocks occurring at a variety of spatial scales due to exploitation, eutrophication, pollution, or the destruction of nursery grounds. On the local scale, dams, the discharge of pollutants, or siltation has reduced the potential of fisheries. The construction of a dam on India's Naramda River will likely eliminate coastal fisheries by the mouth of the river, not to mention upstream damage due to the permanent loss of forests, cropland, and biodiversity.[42] Globally, the United Nations Food and Agricultural Organization (**FAO**) notes that a majority of the world's fishing stocks are depleted, exploited, or overexploited, with over 69 percent of stocks in need of urgent management.[43] Over both the short and long term, the situation is not sustainable and will extract ecologic and economic damage if not corrected.

It is now generally acknowledged that population growth has a deleterious effect upon renewable resources. Therefore, while resources such as fish stocks, soil, and water are all technically renewable resources, humanity has often removed the renewable label through degradation or the overtaxation of resources in light of increasing human population and per capita consumption. In many parts of the world, scarcities of these resources are appearing. With approximately half of the world's population relying on local renewable resources for some aspect of day-to-day living; these scarcities have an immediate impact upon the well-being of a large number of people. Millions are already directly affected by the depletion and degradation of cropland, water, fuel wood, and fishing stocks. Optimists would argue that these issues could be corrected through technology, input substitution, properly functioning markets, or democracy. Input substitution does not necessary offer alternatives. In the case of water, it is a difficult (if not impossible) resource to substitute, meaning that technology must be relied upon to "fix" the problem. This is perhaps true, and can be accomplished through appropriate wastewater treatment, desalinization, or efficient irrigation technologies, but implementing these fixes is often prohibitively costly. Desalinization, for example, is an expensive and energy intensive option. Capturing and treating polluted water (including surface runoff, industrial and domestic water sources) are also expensive. Other tactics such as market reform, improved irrigation technology, and conservation techniques are available, but may not remove the underlying problem of resource scarcity in the face of a growing population. Instead, such technologies may merely postpone resource scarcity. As discussed earlier in this chapter, it is also important to realize that the ability to generate solutions and overcome problems may not be available in many cases.

EMERGENT THEMES AND ISSUES

The ongoing debate between neo-Malthusians, who have been euphemistically referred to as **"doomsters,"** contrasts with that of economic optimists or **"booms-**

ters." Intuitively, we can find relationships between population growth, resource use, and environmental scarcity. For example, in regions where population growth is high, resources such as food, fuel, and water are often scarce and the risk of environmental degradation is increased, and we need not look further than Haiti to reinforce this. But this is not a perfect relationship. In fact, understanding the linkages between population growth, the environment, and resources is sketchy at best. However, even if the most alarmist predictions are discounted, most commentators now believe that population growth slows economic growth and multiplies the damage created by other problems. That is, it is difficult not to conclude that population growth exacerbates land degradation; resource depletion promotes violence and conflict and places pressure upon institutions and governments. This is not to say that population growth is solely responsible for these problems. Environmental degradation, for example, is not just a function of the number of people, but how much and what they consume and how that consumption damages the environment. Nevertheless, population growth is an issue.

The not-so-trivial question that both neo-Malthusians and economic optimists consider is whether the world can provide sufficient food, water, and other resources to the existing population in addition to the eighty million that are born each year at the same time that the standard of living is increased, necessarily raising consumption and use of resources. Given the record of increasing agricultural production over the past fifty years, a number of commentators have proclaimed that food shortages have been largely solved.[44] A recently released FAO report,[45] for example, concludes that agricultural output will continue to grow faster than the world population over the next two to three decades. Even as the report cautioned that there are several areas in the world, including portions of Asia, where the potential for further agriculture is exhausted, it concluded that a population of 8.9 billion could be fed. Most of the increase in food production would come from multicropping, improvements in inputs and technology (i.e., irrigation, aquaculture, application of pesticides and herbicides), particularly in the developing world, along with the addition of some cultivatable cropland.[46] Assuming some modest increase in agricultural output through biotechnology and genetic engineering and that future population predictions are reasonably correct (the Population Reference Bureau estimates a continued slowing of population growth in the next five decades, with a total population of 9.1 billion by 2050), the world might just squeak through. Additional improvements in storage and distribution would also help to alleviate the problem.

Yet it remains unclear whether the world *can* feed its growing population, both now and in the future, and the rosy speculation of the FAO may be premature.[47] Food production might continue to grow faster than the population, and the world will likely be able to feed a much larger population, but it may yet have difficulty feeding its population. At the risk of invoking neo-Malthusian responses, which were criticized earlier, it must be realized that critical resources, including "renewable" resources, such as land and water, are finite. Their degradation or depletion has lead to continued uncertainty about the ability to provide for both the current and future population, particularly if society wishes to improve the standard of living of the majority of the world's population. At some point, it is likely that humanity will simply exhaust earth's capacity to produce, particularly as the world's standard of living is improved. The geographer Vaclav Smil, for example, estimates that the **carrying capacity** of the earth has already been exceeded, if all six billion were fed a diet similar to that of an average American.[48] Fortunately, Americans tend to be overfed, the American diet is wasteful, and there are global inefficiencies in the way food is produced, distributed, and consumed. Correcting these inefficiencies and altering the diet, for example by decreasing or removing animal protein (which tend to be less efficient users of agricultural resources), Smil estimated that a population of 8.4 billion could be supported, with no new land required for cultivation or no new technologies that dramatically increase agricultural output.

While dietary changes are possible, they are unlikely, meaning that the world must look to remove inefficiencies in storage and distribution, as well as increase crop yields to ensure an adequate food supply in the future. Such expectations are also problematic. Despite the green revolution, it is unrealistic to expect future increases in crop yields and agricultural output similar to those observed during its peak. In fact, declining rates of growth in agricultural output and increasingly marginal returns to the application of additional inputs such as fertilizers have recently been observed: the green revolution is ending. Concerns are also being raised that new patent restrictions in agriculture and biotechnology are limiting the free exchange of seeds and technology.[49] The implication is that research on crop improvements has been delayed or abandoned, and new developments may not be introduced into widespread use quickly because of patent restrictions. If biotechnology or gene research ultimately yields advances, their large-scale application could be decades away. At the same time as private investment is increasing, growth in government spending on agricultural research, which has traditionally provided a large proportion of agricultural advances, has slowed. Worldwide, the amount of arable land has decreased 42 percent from 0.45 hectares per person in 1961–63 to 0.26 hectares in 1995–97,[50] with increasing amounts of cropland lost to nonagricultural uses through urbanization or industrialization.[51] While an erosion of the amount of cropland per capita does not mean decreasing output or decreasing ability to coax food out of the ground, there are long-term problems. Average figures of the amount of cropland or food resources, for example, are misleading, since inequalities frequently mean weaker or marginal groups will be subjected to greater scarcities than revealed by averages. Similarly, there may be long-term problems of maintaining the productivity of irrigated cropland as water becomes scarce or soils become saline. Loss of topsoil through erosion and the movement of people up the food chain cast further doubt on the long-term ability to feed the world's population, while the effects of global warming remain unknown. More generally, the problems of feeding, providing shelter and employment, and improved standards of living would have just begun. Importantly, however, the ability to support a population in excess of eight billion does not imply sustainability over longer terms.

What of the broader resource and economic issues? Can the same logic be extended to include the impact of a growing population and increasing consumption upon other resources? Are current levels of resource consumption sustainable? The emerging consensus is that rapid population growth and high young **dependency ratios** relative to the labor force reduce economic growth by increasing poverty and underemployment, weakening investment in human and physical assets (i.e., education, institutions, family planning, household savings), decreasing ingenuity, and degrading resources. Worse, rapid population growth and poor economic growth appear to be self-reinforcing, making it exceedingly difficult for countries to pull themselves out of this downward spiral given the lack of well-developed institutions in many of the poorest countries. Despite decades of global economic growth and development aid, the number of countries that the United Nations defines as **"least developed"**—those with incomes less than $900(U.S.) per year and little investment in health, nutrition, and education—has nearly doubled from twenty-five to forty-nine since 1971.[52] More than half of the population of 630 million in these countries, predominantly found in sub-Saharan Africa and Asia, but also including Haiti, live on less than a dollar (U.S.) a day, and aid money to these countries has dropped by 45 percent since 1990. With rapid population growth and average per capita incomes less than they were two decades ago, sub-Saharan Africa is hit particularly hard.

Expressing hope for the future of sub-Saharan Africa, Cincotta and Engleman note that the region is remarkably similar in terms of health and economic indicators to those observed in Southeast Asian countries in the 1950s just prior to the boom that transformed their economies.[53] In Asia, slower population growth created opportunities for sustained economic growth. Applying this same logic to sub-Saharan Africa is problematic, given the lack of investment, poor institutions, unstable governments, poor health, and the HIV/AIDS epidemic. Slowing population growth in sub-Saharan Africa cannot solve all the problems related to economic growth, resource scarcity, environmental degradation, or violence, but it can contribute to their solution. The best hope for solving many of these problems lies in early intervention—act early and act quickly. Programs targeting the prevention of resource scarcities, population growth, or economic development will be more effective now than after-the-fact. In other words, the world should not be forced to adapt to a scarcity, but rather prepare for it. For sub-Saharan Africa and other regions, this means that attention is required on a number of fronts. This includes market reform to remove institutional biases or limitations, externally generated public and private investment, increased education and literacy (particularly among women), and continued investments in family planning services.[54] Perhaps then, countries will be able to generate the necessary ingenuity and inertia to overcome barriers to growth and to extract themselves from economic stagnation. Pinning hopes on just one or two options is not sufficient. Indeed, there is no "magic bullet" solution to the problems of population growth, economic stagnation, or resource scarcity.

Many of the potential solutions are also problematic. Slowing population growth is difficult, but a worthwhile long-term pursuit. Technology, ingenuity, resource substitution, and free markets offer solutions commonly espoused by economic optimists. Yet, the value or applicability of such concepts may be limited. Input substitution does not necessarily offer alternatives, particularly if the alternative is scarce itself or prohibitively expensive. Ingenuity and technical fixes that allow populations or countries to overcome Malthusian limits are also possible. However, as argued by Homer-Dixon, ingenuity is not a costless or ubiquitous good itself. Instead, ingenuity is fostered in locations where resources such as time and capital are abundant, a tangible concept that may be missing from many poor developing countries and that cannot simply be provided through free markets or democracy. Markets and other institutions may be poorly developed, and resources may not be correctly priced to reflect their scarcity. If the ability to generate ingenuity is missing, countries may be faced with an ingenuity gap, and their ability to respond to resource limits or other threats will be diminished.

Discussed in detail in the following chapter, the available evidence also suggests that population growth and its impact upon resource scarcities, especially of critical resources such as cropland or water, contribute to violence. This should not be taken that they are the cause of wars or violence, but rather that they contribute to social stress and stimulate ethnic violence within populations. For countries faced with a gap between the requirement for ingenuity and their ability to generate it, social disruption and environmental degradation is likely to occur. Although marginalized groups will tend to be the most affected, gaps may result in an undermining of agricultural or economic productivity and mass population migrations. There is a potential then, for the ability and legitimacy of governments to be questioned or undermined, leading to increased conflict. In turn, conflict or civil disobedience further erodes the ability for societies to supply ingenuity and solve resource issues as human and financial capital will flee and the crisis is reinforced.[55] Rather than a "have" and "have-not" or "developed" and "developing" world, it may therefore be possible, as Homer-Dixon argues, that there will be an increasing division between societies that can generate ingenuity and those that cannot. Resource scarcities will therefore be local and regional, occurring within countries that are unable to generate sufficient ingenuity to adapt to changing environments.

Complicating matters is that scarcity of resources will affect the world with greater severity, speed, and scale, meaning that effects will not be confined to a spatially small area. Instead, effects will be regional (i.e., water scarcity), or perhaps even global. Violence and civil unrest are not issues that will be felt within the developing world alone. Instead, their consequences will ripple across the globe, promoting (among other things) international migration and the displacement of populations, the destabilization of governments, threatening trade relations or economic development, and inducing further environmental degradation. While many scarcities and environmental problems are observable now, the effects of global warming or ozone depletion are long term, large scale, and not completely understood, becoming a wild card in the population debate. Although a growing consensus now agrees that global warming is occurring and will result in an increased temperature between 1 and 3 degrees Celsius over the next hundred years, the implications of warming are relatively unknown. There is the very real possibility that global warming will exacerbate environmental scarcities by shifting precipitation patterns, altering growing seasons, coastal flooding, and/or more extreme weather events. These changes are likely to affect agricultural production worldwide, effects that may be multiplied if other resources such as cropland or water supplies are degraded or depleted.

Finally, this chapter has argued that scarce resources either prompt actors to secure scarce resources, or that scarce resources prompt ingenuity that allows a society to adapt. A third possibility, and one that Homer-Dixon does not really consider, is that scarce resources may also become a bargaining chip within peace processes, equal to or greater than land and territory that have frequently underlain previous peace agreements. Indeed, water has figured within recent peace treaties within the Middle East. With the signing of the peace accord between Israel and the Palestine Liberation Organization (PLO) in 1995, Israel pledged to increase the Palestinian share of West Bank water as well as search for new sources.[56] In an earlier (1994) agreement with Jordan, Israel was to increase the diversion of water from the Jordan River to benefit Jordan. Previously, the water that Jordan was receiving from the river was far below its allocation. In addition, both sides agreed to build dams on the Yarmouk and Jordan Rivers to boost water supplies. As of 2001, the anticipated benefits and payoffs of these peace agreements remain a distant hope. Indeed, the peace agreement between Israel and the PLO has largely broken down, and restrictions on water supplies remain. Nevertheless, water or other scarce resources have the potential to become a source of cooperation rather than antagonism and conflict.

NOTES

1. Thomas Robert Malthus, *An Essay on the Principle of Population*, in *Perspectives on Population*, eds. Scott W. Menard and Elizabeth W. Moen (New York: Oxford University Press, 1987).

2. William Bender and Margaret Smith, "Population, Food, and Nutrition," *Population Bulletin* 51, no. 4 (February 1997). See also the United Nations Food and Agricultural Organization Web site: <http://www.fao.org/news/2001/010401-e.htm> (2 May 2001).

3. Bender and Smith, "Population, Food, and Nutrition"; Paul Ehrlich, Anne Ehrlich, and Gretchen Daily, "Food Security, Population, and Environment," *Population and Development Review* 19, no. 1 (1993): 1–32; Robert Livernash and Eric Rodenburg, "Population Change, Resources, and the Environment," *Population Bulletin* 53, no. 1 (March 1998).

4. Frances Lappe and Joseph Collins, *Food First* (Boston: Houghton Mifflin, 1977).

5. Digby J. McLaren, "Population and the Utopian Myth," *Ecodecision* 21 (June 1993): 59–63.

6. See, for example, Ehrlich, Ehrlich, and Daily, "Food Security."

7. In particular, the popular press and green movement have adopted neo-Malthusian perspectives, while the viewpoints of economic optimists inform the governments of most developed nations and are found in the policies of the World Bank.

8. In his original writings, Malthus did not believe in birth control. Neo-Malthusians are distinguished from true Malthusians in their belief that birth control can be used as a check against population growth.

9. Numerous authors have contributed to this debate. One of the most famous is Paul Ehrlich and Anne Ehrlich, *The Population Explosion* (New York: Touchstone, 1991).

10. Paul Ehrlich, *The Population Bomb* (New York: Ballantine Books, 1968).

11. Julian L. Simon, *The Ultimate Resource* (Princeton, N.J.: Princeton University Press, 1981).

12. John Richard Hicks, *The Theory of Wages* (London: Macmillan, 1932).

13. Ester Boserup, *The Conditions of Agricultural Growth: The Economics of Agrarian Change under Population Pressure* (Chicago: Aldine, 1965).

14. Thomas Homer-Dixon, *Environment, Scarcity, and Violence* (Princeton, N.J.: Princeton University Press, 1999). Much of the following discussion is derived from his writing.

15. See, for example, Wallace Broecker, "Unpleasant Surprises in the Greenhouse?" *Nature* 328, no. 6126 (9 July 1987): 123–126; William Clark, *On The Practical Implications of the Carbon Dioxide Question* (Laxenburg, Austria: International Institute of Applied Systems Analysis, 1985).

16. Thomas F. Homer-Dixon, *The Ingenuity Gap* (Toronto: Alfred Knopf, 2000).

17. Simon, *The Ultimate Resource.*

18. Homer-Dixon, *Environment, Scarcity, and Violence.* See also Lynda Hurst, "The Global Guru," *Toronto Star*, 19 July 1995, 1(C).

19. Homer-Dixon, *The Ingenuity Gap.*

20. Homer-Dixon, *Environment.*

21. Jane Menken, "Demographic-Economic Relationships and Development," in *Population—the Complex Reality: A Report of the Population Summit of the World's Scientific Academies*, ed. Francis Graham-Smith (Golden, Colo.: North American Press, 1994).

22. John R. Weeks, *Population: An Introduction to Concepts and Issues*, 7th edition (Belmont, Calif.: Wadsworth, 1999).

23. Ester Boserup, *Population and Technological Change: A Study of Long-Term Trends* (Chicago: University of Chicago Press, 1981); Ester Boserup, *The Conditions of Agricultural Growth* (Chicago: Aldine, 1965).

24. National Research Council, Committee on Population, *Population Growth and Economic Development: Policy Questions* (Washington, D.C.: National Academy Press, 1986).

25. Richard P. Cincotta and Robert Engelman, *Economics and Rapid Change: The Influence of Population Growth* (Washington, D.C.: Population Action International, 1997).

26. Allen C. Kelley and Robert M. Schmidt, *Population and Income Change: Recent Evidence* (Washington, D.C.: World Bank, 1994).

27. Edward M. Crenshaw, Ansari Z. Ameen, and Matthew Christenson, "Population Dynamics and Economic Development: Age-Specific Population Growth Rates and Eco-

nomic Growth in Developing Countries, 1965 to 1990," *American Sociological Review* 62, no. 6 (1997): 974–984.

28. Cincotta and Engelman, *Economics and Rapid Change*.

29. See, for example: Kenneth H. Kang, "Why Did Koreans Save So 'Little' and Why Do They Now Save So 'Much,'" *International Economic Journal* 8, no. 4 (1994): 99–111. See also World Bank, *The East Asian Miracle* (Oxford: University of Oxford Press, 1993).

30. Allen C. Kelley, "The Consequences of Rapid Population Growth on Human Resource Development: The Case of Education," in *The Impact of Population Growth on Well-Being in Developing Countries*, eds. Dennis Ahlburg, Allen C. Kelley, and Karen Oppenheim Mason (New York: Springer, 1996): 67–137; T. Paul Schultz, "School Expenditures and Enrollments, 1960–1980: The Effects of Incomes, Prices and Population Growth," in *Population Growth and Economic Development: Issues and Evidence*, eds. D. Gale Johnson and Ronald D. Lee (Madison: University of Wisconsin Press, 1985): 413–436.

31. Cincotta and Engelman, *Economics and Rapid Change*.

32. Cincotta and Engelman, *Economics and Rapid Change*.

33. United Nations Development Programme (UNDP), *Human Development Report 2000* (New York: UNDP, 2000).

34. Homer-Dixon, *Environment*.

35. While supporting lush rain forests, the soils themselves are poor and thin. The transformation of forests to agricultural uses for crops or grazing is not sustainable over the long term and may only support a family for a few years before they are forced to relocate and repeat the process, pushing deeper into the rainforest.

36. Lester R. Brown, *Who Will Feed China? Wake-up Call for a Small Planet* (New York: W. W. Norton, 1995). See also Lester Brown, "Averting a Global Food Crisis," *Technology Review* (November–December 1995): 44–53.

37. Alanna Mitchell, "The World's 'Single Biggest Threat,'" *Globe and Mail*, 4 June 2001, 8–9(A).

38. Hussein Amery and Aaron T. Wolf, *Water in the Middle East: A Geography of Conflict* (Austin: University of Texas Press, 2000).

39. Terje Tvedt, "The Struggle for Water in the Middle East," *Canadian Journal of Development Studies* 13, no. 1 (1992): 13–33.

40. Laurence Lewis and William Coffey, "The Continuing Deforestation of Haiti," *Ambio* 14, no. 3 (1985): 158–160.

41. <http://cbc.ca/cgi-bin/templates/view.cgi?category = Canada&story = /new s/2001/04/10/cod_stocks010410> (1 May 2001). The Canadian Fisheries Resource Conservation Council (FRCC) has been charged with oversight of the cod stocks. See <http://www.dfo-mpo.gc.ca/frcc/> (1 May 2001).

42. Bradford W. Morse and Thomas R. Berger, executive summary of "Sardar Sarovar Projects: Independent Review," *STEPS Quarterly* 2, nos. 3–4 (1992): 28–34.

43. UN FAO. <http://www.fao.org/fi/publ/circular/c920/intro.asp#INTRO> (2 May 2001).

44. The FAO has essentially proclaimed that food shortages are no longer of concern. See also Andrew Pollack, "The Green Revolution Yields to the Bottom Line," *New York Times*, 15 May 2001, 1(D); Andrew Pollack, "Changing Times Challenge World Hunger Organization," *New York Times*, 15 May 2001, 2(D).

45. FAO, *Agriculture: Towards 2015/2030, Technical Interim Report* (April 2000). Excerpts

from this report can be found at <http://www.fao.org/ag/magazine/0012sp1.htm> (7 May 2001). The full report can be found at <http://www.fao.org/es/ESD/at2015/toc-e.htm> (7 May 2001).

46. The report used a generous definition of the potential for cultivation. Already, the most productive agricultural land is under production. For the remaining "cultivatable" land, portions were defined as marginal or ecologically sensitive. Expansion runs the risk of accelerating land degradation. Land availability in South America and Africa, the two regions with the largest potential for increased cropland, are far from markets. Developing this land requires infrastructure.

47. John Bongaarts, "Can the Growing Human Population Feed Itself?" *Scientific American* (March 1994): 36–42.

48. Vaclav Smil, "How Many People Can the Earth Feed?" *Population and Development Review* 20, no. 2 (1994): 225–292.

49. Pollack, "The Green Revolution Yields," 1(D); Pollack, "Changing Times" 2(D).

50. <http://www.fao.org/es/ESD/at2015/toc-e.htm> (7 May 2001).

51. One U.S. estimate placed the loss of cropland equal to the size of Connecticut each year. Between 1970 and 1990, the population of the Chicago CMSA grew by just over 4 percent, but the amount of land consumed by the urban region grew by over 50 percent, with most lost to low-density urban sprawl, including transportation routes and growth along the periphery in "edge cities." Once it is lost or "paved over," it is very difficult to reverse.

52. Constant Brand, "Poor Countries Demand More Help, Trade from Rich," *Globe and Mail*, 15 May 2001, 12(A).

53. United Nations Development Programme (UNDP), *Human Development Report 2000* (New York: UNDP, 2000).

54. Cincotta and Engelman, *Economics and Rapid Change*.

55. Although violence and decreasing capital investment may provide a sufficiently strong impetus to leave, the departure of the countries' best and brightest does not only occur under these conditions. Instead, the best and brightest are wooed to other countries by promises of higher pay and higher standards of living.

56. Serge Schmemann, "Israel and PLO Reach Accord to Transfer West Bank Areas," *New York Times*, 25 September 1995, 1(A).

7

=ᗡᗢᗢᕢ=

The Potential for Conflict

In his 1994 article "The Coming Anarchy," journalist Robert Kaplan paints a dire prediction of the world's future.[1] Robbed of their economic power by globalization, poor leadership, and environmental decay, peripheral states would disintegrate into smaller units defined by ethnicity or culture and ruled by warlords and private armies. Kaplan held out Africa and its seemingly endless list of war-ravaged countries including Rwanda, Burundi, Sierra Leone, Angola, Sudan, and Ethiopia as already symbolizing the decay of the current world order, having already succumbed to environmental and demographic distress, leading to the breakdown of traditional civil government. Violence and conflict have become the norm.

While perhaps sensationalized, the basic question within Kaplan's article is whether resource scarcity can prompt conflict. A short answer would be yes, with conflict potentially arising from scarcities and disputes over cropland, water, forests, or other resources, all of which are underlain by population issues. Resource scarcity may lead to harmful social effects, including constrained economic or agricultural production, migration, segmentation of society along ethnic or religious lines, and the disintegration of societal institutions, all of which can lead to conflict.[2] Effects are often causally linked, oftentimes with some feedback measure that tends to reinforce the initial negative consequences, such that resource capture arising from scarcity may induce further environmental degradation or greater scarcity of the resource.

Previous chapters have discussed demographic events such as fertility, mortality, migration, and their outcomes. It is understood, for instance, that below-replacement fertility leads to an aging population. Likewise, it is relatively simple to forecast the demographic implications of HIV/AIDS in sub-Saharan Africa. Indeed, projections of decreased life expectancies and slowing economic growth are already visible in many countries in the region. While this chapter highlights how and why population growth could lead to conflict, forecasting the implications of population growth is, however, a bit like gazing into a crystal ball. Resource scarcities generally do not cause conflict, but they can stimulate conflict through underlying ethnic unrest, by creating societal stress, and/or by interacting with other contextual effects, including the physical setting and political and social structures. Although the predictions are becoming clearer as greater interest is placed on the subject, the best we can do is learn from existing conflicts, recognize the problems created by a growing population, and project what this might mean in the coming years.

POPULATION, RESOURCE SCARCITY, AND CONFLICT

Although the effects of resource scarcity are still poorly understood, there is a strong possibility and a growing body of evidence that they will affect social stability and ultimately underlie conflict. While this is an intuitive assumption, questions remain as to what the exact relationship is and how it works. How, for example, does resource scarcity contribute to conflict? Most likely, it is through a complex of interactions. Given that population growth will continue in the coming decades, and that scarcities of renewable resources caused by depletion or degradation are relatively certain, it is reasonable to assume that supply, demand, or structural scarcities could result in negative social effects, including reduced agricultural and economic output, migration and displacement, **social segmentation,** and institutional disruption. In turn, each of these could independently or collaboratively induce conflict.[3] In addition, resource scarcity can produce resource capture when actors seek to change the distribution of resources in their favor, owing to a decline in the quality or quantity of a resource, leading to the ecological marginalization of weak groups. Both processes further environmental degradation, reinforce poverty, and increase the potential for conflict as groups seek to control resources or address imbalances in the distribution of resources. Resource scarcity is particularly problematic in the developing world, which is heavily reliant upon local resources for day-to-day survival. Even now, many developing countries face a bleak future resulting from large-scale demographic, environmental, economic, and societal stresses.

Resource Scarcity and Negative Social Effects

On their own, population growth and resource scarcity are unlikely to trigger conflict directly. Instead, a series of mediating social effects, including reduced agricultural and economic output, migration and displacement, social segmentation, and the disruption of institutions, independently or in tandem, have the potential to induce social stress and conflict. Of these five effects, reduced agricultural output associated with resource scarcity may be the most problematic. Despite the impact of the green revolution and agricultural advances observed over the last decades of the twentieth century, per capita agricultural output has dropped in many African, Latin American, and Asian countries. At the same time, growth rates of agricultural yields have been declining, having reached the limit of benefits derived from the green revolution, and foreshadowing a declining potential for dramatic increases in agricultural output. Likewise, advances through biotechnology or genetic engineering are likely decades away, if they ever reach the market. Poor food distribution networks, insufficient knowledge of sustainable agricultural techniques, poor institutions, inequitable distribution of land, conflict, and poverty compound wide disparities in food availability. Ultimately, for those faced with scarcities of land and water and poor institutions, agricultural output will decrease. The poor and marginalized, who derive much of their income from the land or have relatively little to spend on foodstuffs, will be affected the most.

Increased resource scarcities can also reduce economic productivity, with declines in economic productivity closely aligned with agricultural productivity since many developing countries are highly dependent upon agriculture for income generation, economic growth, and stability. A number of resource scarcities could affect economic production, including a shortage of water, limiting not only agricultural productivity but also industrial production. In Gaza, Israel, the overpumping of coastal aquifers has resulted in their increased salinization, which in turn is associated with adverse health effects and declining quality and yields associated with agricultural production as cropland becomes increasingly saline. While resource scarcity will generally constrain local or national economic development, constraints will also result in an increasing gap between the elite of a society, who are able to take advantage of the opportunities created by resource scarcity, and the marginalized portion of society through resource capture and ecological marginalization.

Economic or ecological marginalization may prompt migration or population displacement, including the forced relocation of populations, creating what some authors have defined as "environmental refugees," a label that implies that resource scarcity was directly responsible for their relocation.[4] Rather than being a direct cause of displacement, however, resource scarcity is only a partial motivator. Instead, population relocation is a function of both "push" and "pull" factors.[5] Migrants, including Haitians and Bangladeshis (see the later discussion in this chapter), are motivated by income opportunities in potential destinations, with resource scarcities or lack of economic opportunities contributing to the decision to move. If large-scale population displacement occurs, migration may aggravate divisions within a society among religious, ethnic, or linguistic groups. This social segmentation encourages competition among groups for control of resources and sharpens the distinction between winners and losers. Scarcity also produces insularity as groups work to protect their own interests, reducing social interaction. Ultimately, social segmentation erodes civil society and the network of nongovernmental organizations and associations that mediate between the state and individuals, making the society less able to function cooperatively by reducing the availability of protective social capital within a society.

Together, these effects are able to disrupt the state and its legislative, judicial, military, and banking institutions in a complex process that is frequently self-reinforcing. Mass migrations, for example, can disrupt local power structures and labor markets along with altering the relationship between ethnic or other groups. Likewise, social segmentation can result in competition between groups over scarce resources, prevent new institutions from developing, or limit the ability of institutions to respond to changing needs. By weakening the state and its institutions, resource scarcities limit the ability of the state to generate and deliver social and technological ingenuity. It reduces the national and international autonomy of the state, engenders competition among elites over resources, and produces social segmentation as groups struggle for dominance and power. While complex, the process raises the possibility of conflict as power is shifted from the state to challenger groups.

Egypt provides a useful example of the linkages among these processes.[6] Confined to less than 3 percent of the country's territory, the country's population of sixty-eight million is strung out along the Nile River. Heavily dependent upon its waters, Egypt is a country that has been economically taxed by population growth (the TFR is seemingly stuck at 3.5 and the country's population will double in thirty-three years), contributing to low-level but ongoing conflict between Muslim fundamentalists and the more secular government. Egypt's weak economic position, along with local scarcities of land and water,[7] has reduced its ability to pursue economic and agricultural development, making it unable to generate and provide institutions and services including health care, education, and other social services for its population, reducing the reach and legitimacy of the state. In its absence, the fundamentalist Muslim brotherhood has stepped in, a group that has openly and violently challenged the authority of the Egyptian government.[8] Opposing Egypt's secular government, it has cultivated grassroots support by operating social institutions such as schools, clinics, hospitals, and charities, providing services to the poor that are otherwise not available from the government. Simultaneously, fundamentalist groups have sought to weaken Egypt's government by attacking tourist operations, a key income-generating industry. Finally, differences in religious viewpoints have also promoted social segmentation, as some of the more radical fundamentalist groups have isolated themselves from mainstream social and religious institutions. The development of fundamentalist views has placed increasing pressure upon Coptic Christians who, representing approximately 10 percent of the population, face discrimination.

The Nature of Resource Conflict

In the past, national and international conflicts have frequently been predicated upon the territorial ambitions of governments and the concept of nation-state.[9] In the twenty-first century, the nature of conflict is likely to represent the new realities of resource scarcity and population growth, a potential that is greatest where local institutions are weak, population growth is the greatest, and resources are the scarcest. Consequently, the number of conflicts linked to resource scarcity is likely to increase in the coming decades, with the developing world being at greatest risk. Having greater dependency upon local resources for economic and agricultural production and prosperity, frequently lacking the financial resources to buffer themselves from the negative effects of resource scarcity, and having fragile institutions, they are also less able to adapt.

If the emergence of resource scarcity potentially leads to conflict, what types of conflict are most likely to occur? Homer-Dixon[10] identified five potential types of conflict, including:

- Disputes directly related to environmental degradation;
- Ethnic conflicts due to migration and population displacement caused by environmental scarcities;
- Civil disorder and conflict caused by environmental scarcity that affects economic productivity and livelihood, and in turn, people's economic livelihoods and the ability of governments to meet new demands;
- Resource scarcity induced by wars between states;
- Conflicts between the developed and developing world over resources and environmental issues.

Distillation of these five points, regardless of their spatial scale, means that population or resource scarcity issues will increasingly underlie conflicts in the coming years. Of these five, Homer-Dixon discounted resource scarcity conflicts between the developed and developing world as being relatively unlikely, limited by the military, technological, and financial advantages of the developed world. Likewise, he argued that disputes related *directly* to environmental degradation would produce little more than local, small-scale violence. Rather, the disputes that would be relatively more likely to occur—resource scarcity, group identity, and civil strife/insurgency—would occur in the developing world where environmental scarcities would interact and be contextualized by existing economic, cultural, political, or social factors, perhaps even reinforcing conflict and the decline of institutions.

In their simplest case, resource conflicts are easily understood within the traditional paradigms of territory, power, and interstate relations, as states or other actors have commonly moved to secure nonrenewable resources such as oil. Conflicts related to oil include the civil wars in Sudan and Angola and Iraq's invasion of Kuwait in 1990, which was partially based upon Iraq's desire to control major oil fields in the region.[11] With projections that known world oil supplies are likely to peak within the next twenty years, oil is likely to remain the "prize," a resource that is fought over in the coming years.[12] This form of resource capture, whereby the decreasing quality or quantity of a resource interacts with population growth and increasing consumption and encourages groups to control a resource through trade or military conquest, can also be extended to renewable resources such as cropland, forests, or fresh water.[13] Scarcities of some of these resources are increasing rapidly in places, leading to their potential seizure through military or other means, marginalizing groups and increasing resource scarcity or degradation.

The distinction between conflicts related to renewable and nonrenewable resources is important. While several conflicts, including the Gulf War, can be attributed to the need to access oil or mineral resources, there is, in fact, relatively little evidence to support the notion that scarce *renewable* resources have caused interstate conflict. In part, the long payoff time to incorporate resources such as forests or cropland does not quickly or easily translate into increased state power and influence. In contrast, states can quickly utilize resources such as oil or diamonds to finance military operations or to expand industry, trade, and commerce. In addition, countries that depend heavily upon renewables tend to be poor, and the very ones that could not support or do not have the military ability to attack their neighbors.

The exception to this might be fresh water resources, a resource that is critical for both the survival of individuals as well as the state. While water is a renewable resource, its increasing scarcity, reduced not only through consumption but degraded through pollution and salinization, threatens the livelihood and security of states, with the shortage defined as "water vulnerability."[14] But, rather than directly causing conflict, water scarcity tends to limit economic development, promote resource capture, or lead to social segmentation, which in turn produces violence. Moreover, its transnational character, with rivers or underground aquifers crossing state borders, means that the use and actions of one country affects neighboring states. Various observers have not missed the strategic importance of water. In 1995, the World Bank cautioned that wars in the coming century would be fought over water,[15] a statement that echoed an earlier prediction by Jordan's King Hussein in 1990, who declared that only water issues could incite a war between Jordan and Israel. Years earlier, Egypt's former president Anwar Sadat indicated that he was prepared to use force if Ethiopia blocked or reduced Egypt's access to waters from the Nile, while Ethiopia chided Egypt for placing water from the Nile on the negotiating table during peace negotiations between Egypt and Israel in 1976.[16] At other times, water in the Middle East has been described as being more valuable than the oil pumped out of the ground. Still, conflict over scarce water resources is only valid in a limited number of circumstances where the downstream country is dependent on the water and the upstream country restricts its flow. Similarly, conflict is only likely to occur when the water supply is essentially finite (i.e., limited renewal), as it is in many Middle East countries, so that an increasing population means a decreasing per capita supply.

Despite the constraints of downstream and upstream geography, there are multiple examples of water's ability to induce conflict. When water resources and the relationship between states are contextualized by differences in religion and historical animosities, such as between Israel and its Arab neighbors or between Turkey and Syria, the potential for conflict between states is further increased (figure 7.1). As discussed in the previous chapter, water resources may have promoted Israel's military campaigns in south Lebanon. Likewise, water has colored relations between Egypt, which is dependent upon the Nile River for fresh water, and its upstream

Figure 7.1.   The Middle East.

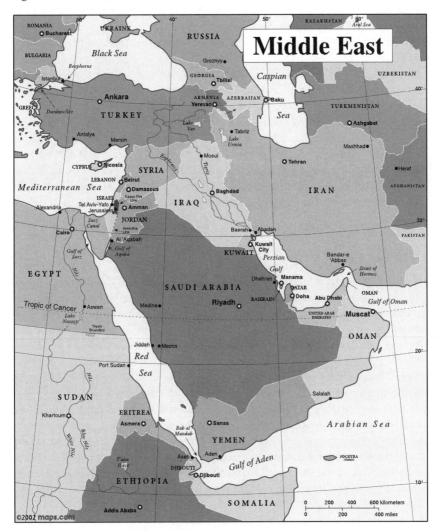

Source: Maps.com.

neighbor Ethiopia. Relations between Turkey, Syria, and Iraq have also been strained over control and access to the Euphrates and Tigris Rivers, with Turkey's Great Anatolia project, a massive complex of dams and irrigation systems in east Turkey, promising to significantly reduce the flow of the Euphrates when it is completed. What water does reach Syria will be contaminated with runoff laden with fertilizer, pesticides, and salts. Syria is already short of water, and its population growth (2.6 percent, doubling in approximately twenty-seven years) complicates its need for water. Although Syria is weak relative to Turkey and therefore does not pose a likely military threat as a provoked downstream neighbor, these two countries have already exchanged threats over water resources. However, Syria allegedly sanctions Kurdish guerrillas fighting the Turkish government over control of eastern Turkey for the creation of a Kurdish state.[17]

In Africa, South Africa's support of a coup in Lesotho in 1986 has been linked to its desire to divert water out of Lesotho and into South Africa.[18] Elsewhere in Africa, the Senegal, Zambezi, and Niger Rivers all flow through several countries, with the Senegal River the focus of conflict between Mauritania and Senegal. In the Lake Chad basin in north Africa, geophysicists have warned of the shrinkage of Lake Chad.[19] Since the 1960s, it has shrunk by 95 percent, with irrigation and drought the major causes. The loss of water in a region with a population of over 750,000 that continues to grow, even as the diminished water supply threatens fish stocks and crops, could result in increased tensions between the four countries (Nigeria, Niger, Cameroon, and Chad) that utilize the lake's water.

Group Identity Conflict

Of the five potential sources for conflict identified by Homer-Dixon, group identity conflicts involving religion, ethnicity, or nationalism[20] may be the most common because of large-scale population movements caused by resource scarcity. Discrimination, group status, access to limited resources, or other issues promotes group identity at the same time as it results in social segmentation and cleavages within the society as leaders look to exploit these differences to increase their own political power. Two examples serve to illustrate group identity conflict. First, the breakup of the former Republic of Yugoslavia can largely be attributed to the efforts of Slobodan Milosevic, the former leader of Yugoslavia, who mobilized Serb identity and nationalism by defending Serb ethnic and political interests. His actions, along with the general decline of the Yugoslav economy through the 1980s, largely shaped the disintegration of the federation, spawning multiple group identity conflicts at various spatial scales between Serbs, Croats, Albanians, and Muslims. The movement of Kosovar Albanian refugees into Macedonia during the Kosovo war in 1999 (see chapter 5) raised tensions between Macedonians and ethnic Albanians and elevated the potential for armed conflict between the two groups. These fears were realized in the spring of 2001 when Albanian insurgents, operating out of Kosovo, sought to carve out an ethnic Albanian state by securing territory dominated by ethnic Albanians within Macedonia. The insurgency pressured the Macedonian government, placed the country on the brink of civil war, and strained the already fragile peace between Serbs and Albanians.[21]

The situation in India, where the migration of an estimated twelve to seventeen million Bangladeshis into the Indian states of Assam, Tripura, and West Bengal has generated social segmentation and conflict, is also a good example.[22] Population growth in Bangladesh has contributed to increased land scarcity (demand-induced),[23] pushing migrants out of the country. At the same time, better income potential and living conditions in India, along with a welcoming political environment that empowered the immigrants, attracted large numbers of cross-border migrants. Their arrival produced significant changes in land distribution, with Bangladeshi immigrants accused of taking the best cropland, co-opting local politics, and altering economic relations in the destination states. Further contextualized by a history of colonialism and its vestiges, which altered the balance of political power in India and sensitized locals to the loss of political control, their arrival ultimately triggered violence between the groups.

Insurgencies and Civil Strife

On smaller spatial scales, insurgencies and civil strife within states pose additional challenges to national security. Rooted in group-identity or resource scarcity issues, rebellion and guerrilla wars may be explained through traditional theories of grievance, deprivation, and the opportunity presented to groups to act upon their grievances.[24] If, for example, resource scarcities result in deprivation, perhaps by reducing a group's economic opportunities, then the level of grievance will also increase. Given the opportunity to challenge the state and the current status quo, groups may resort to violence and confrontation to rectify the situation. The likelihood of civil strife is greatest when multiple pressures interact, advancing grievances and opportunity together by increasing social segmentation, weakening state institutions, and contributing to economic problems. As before, contextual factors, including leadership, degree of social segmentation (grievances will find a larger audience when shared by groups organized by identity), local concepts of justice, power structures (is the deprived group speaking from a position of strength or weakness?), and the pervasiveness of the problem, will alter the outcome.

Examples of the linkages between environmental scarcity and violence include the events in Chiapas, Mexico, and the New Peoples Army (NPA) in the Philippines. In the Philippines, violence flared in the 1980s and early 1990s in response to ecological marginalization and long-standing grievances against landowners and the government.[25] Desperation with the lack of economic opportunities in lowland agricultural areas or urban areas forced peasants into ecologically marginal upland areas to earn a living. There, soils were easily degraded and lost through erosion associated with poor agricultural practices (i.e., slash and burn), lack of knowledge of appropriate practices, and uncertain land-tenure systems, which meant that they did not care for the land. Strict economic policies in the early 1980s further depressed incomes, increased unemployment, and encouraged migration into marginal areas as peasants sought to make a living. Their desperation eventually led to the peasants finding a voice in the NPA.

Urbanization and Conflict

The worldwide growth of the urban population means that the potential for conflict arising from resource scarcity is also an urban problem, with large, dense, and poverty-stricken populations escalating the potential. With the urban population expected to grow dramatically in the coming decades, the implications associated with the growth of large urban areas are enormous. Problems, including poverty, pollution, crime, class tensions, and transportation, will be on a scale never before seen. The situation is frequently worse in cities that have been strained by rapid population growth, little investment, and government ineptitude. Infrastructure systems, such as water, roads, or electricity, have decayed as governments have been unable to keep up with the demand posed by continued in-migration from rural areas and smaller centers. The magnitude of urban growth in the developing world has generated an intense ongoing debate about whether the developing world can accommodate the anticipated growth of cities and whether there is a potential for conflict in areas with few resources and slow economic growth,[26] echoing the earlier limits to growth discussion. Optimists claim good governance, proper management, and investment can overcome population constraints. Others, following neo-Malthusian reasoning, are more concerned. Higher mortality, low standards of living, the poor living environment, depletion of resources, and increasing poverty and inequality are symptomatic of urban problems, all of which could weaken the state.

In the developing world, urban migrants are typically from rural areas, driven by the large gap in the standard of living along with poor rural conditions caused by environmental degradation and a skewed distribution of resources favoring the elite. With rural to urban migration fueling much of the growth of urban areas in the developing world, the migration flow could prompt conflict through a number of channels. Based on the assumption that urbanization and poverty could lead to conflict, the relationship between urban population, poverty, and political change is of growing concern. For example, with poverty remaining one of the most pressing issues in urban areas, migration could breed economic frustration given insufficient employment opportunities and unfulfilled expectations. Perhaps as many as 42 percent (if not more) of the world's urban population can currently be classified as living below the poverty level, with urban poverty increasing in much of the developing world. In 1970, for example, urban areas contained just 36 percent of Latin America's poor. By 1990, the proportion had jumped to 60 percent. By 2025, the World Bank estimates that majority of the world's population will be living in poverty.[27] Migrants may also have problems adjusting to urban areas. Seeking entry into groups for support and friendship in their new surroundings, they could easily be recruited into groups that espouse violence. Since many of the migrants are young men, generating a much larger demand for education and jobs, they are easily mobilized for political ends.

Deficiencies in public and reproductive health are reinforced by poverty, compounding the challenges faced by urban areas and their populations. Although levels of mortality and infectious diseases are generally lower in urban areas relative to rural areas within the developing world, large variations within urban areas remain. The urban poor tend to have far worse health indicators than their wealthy counterparts, reflecting unequal access to health care, cost of care and an inability to afford it, and generally poor or underdeveloped health systems. Infectious diseases related to poverty and malnutrition may be increasing in urban areas, and the transmission of diseases such as cholera and tuberculosis benefits from large, dense, and poor populations living in unsanitary conditions.[28] As noted earlier, HIV/AIDS is a major issue as well, with prevalence rates tending to be higher in urban areas in the developing world where traditional social patterns and sexual values have broken down.

Despite the plausibility of these interrelations, history reveals relatively few linkages between urbanization and political unrest, although the 1979 Iranian revolution is frequently cited as one example. Before the revolution, urban growth rates were higher than in rural areas, and despite increasing education among urban residents, they remained poor, leading to frustration and the eventual overthrew of the shah. Likewise, poor economic opportunities within developing cities in the 1970s and 1980s and austerity measures, which removed price controls or subsidies from key goods such as bread or fuel and were imposed by debt-ridden governments in the early 1980s under guidance from the World Bank, are thought to have contributed to urban violence. The urban poor were particularly disadvantaged, and the removal of subsidies provoked strikes and riots throughout the developing world.[29]

Urban violence, whether it is directed toward the state, intergroup (i.e., ethnic or religious violence, based on perceived differences between groups), or criminal violence, is likely to become increasingly common. The current relative quiet of urban populations in the developing world may not last given trends of increasing poverty, deteriorating economic conditions, and increased strength and reach of organized crime in cities throughout the developing world. While the risk of conflict could prompt democratization and institutional reform, states frequently respond to crises and unrest with increased repression, which only serves to amplify the likelihood of conflict. The poor, underemployed or unemployed young provide ready fodder for uprisings, at the same time as the balance of power shifts from the government to other groups, including crime gangs and religious fundamentalist movements.

Whether or not conflict occurs depends partly on the character of the society and the strength of its institutions. Societies that share a history of cooperation are likely better able to resist conflict. However, in societies that are socially segmented because of ethnic, political, or religious rivalries, the likelihood of violence is increased. Numerous examples illustrate this point. Jerusalem, for example, is a city that is divided between Christians, Muslims, and Jews. The site of frequent and violent clashes between Muslims and Jews, control of the city figures prominently in any peace negotiations between the Israeli state and Palestinians. Similarly, Karachi, Pakistan, is a city that is deeply divided along ethnic, religious, political, and economic lines, and conflict between groups is frequent.[30] Anti-government sentiments have simmered near the surface in the Philippine capital and elsewhere in the geographically fragmented country over the past decade, usually motivated by political or economic issues, including widespread poverty, but is also related to environmental degradation.[31] Egypt's Muslim Brotherhood has found their greatest strength among the poor in Cairo and other urban areas,[32] illustrating the fact that governments who are unable to ensure basic services may find themselves increasingly isolated from their electorate, as other more conservative or anti-government groups step in to "fill the void." Ultimately, divisions between secular and fundamentalist

groups may undermine the legitimacy of the state and government, leading to instability and conflict.

Avoiding urban violence may prove to be difficult given the complexity and absolute size of the problem. Policies that slow urban growth or address urban problems,
for example, have been promoted, including attempts to limit the growth of urban
areas by restricting internal migration. China has, for example, vigorously attempted
to control internal migration, but it has not succeeded at curbing rural to urban
migration. Instead, corruption and economic necessity drives the "illegal" internal
migration, despite a degree of social control that is unknown in most societies.
Moreover, migrants are not necessarily the poorest of urban residents, and policies
that restrict rural to urban migration are typically ineffective and hurt the poor.[33]
Similarly, Indonesia's transmigration policy encouraged relocation from Java, the
most inhabited island. This program too has come with its own problems, engendering social segmentation along religious lines and the violence that erupted between
Christians and Muslims in 2000 and 2001.[34] National and international governments have also invested in the development of strong urban networks that are inter-
connected, deflecting some of the development away from largest or primate cities
and reducing the negative consequences on local resources.

If demographic control is not an option, then urban problems may be addressed
through other policy routes. Most important, economic reform, improved governance, and policies aimed at reducing urban poverty and enhancing the livelihoods
of the poor by promoting political and economic equity between groups can build
a foundation of cooperation and security. Removal of policies that explicitly favor
urban areas and indirectly generate in-migration through the promotion of rural
development may also be successful. None will be easy and all will carry a high price.

EMERGENT THEMES AND ISSUES: GAZING
DEEPER INTO THE CRYSTAL BALL

Over the coming decades, the world is likely to witness an increase in conflict at
various spatial scales, including interstate conflict, internal civil war or violence, and
ethnic violence, many of which will be underlain by issues pertaining to resource
scarcity and population growth. It is quite possible that humanity has underesti-
mated the dependency of its institutions upon the environment and natural systems,
with population growth straining these systems, including renewable and nonrenewable resources in the coming decades. The how and why of conflict are not simple
questions to answer. Assigning fault or attaching significance to specific issues such
as the environment, group dynamics, elitism, or economic and political power is
frequently too simplistic, with the roots of most conflicts deep and tangled.
Although other forces will mediate and contextualize its effect, the environment and
resources will be *the* national security issues of the twenty-first century, fusing with
old ethnic and historical divisions. The combined impacts of an increasing popula-

tion and increasing consumption of resources will have dire consequences upon desertification, deforestation, soil erosion, water depletion, air pollution, and loss of biodiversity. The effect is magnified in societies that cannot generate or supply sufficient ingenuity or financial resources to moderate or alleviate scarcities. The full impact, however, may not be observable until well into the current century.

In deriding the linkage between population, environmental scarcity, and conflict, critics have argued that environmentally based conflicts are not new. This is true, but the speed and regularity with which they will occur will increase in the future as resources become increasingly scarce and as populations grow. Developing countries dependent upon local resources but lacking the ability to mitigate scarcities are likely to be affected sooner, facing more regular, more complex, and more severe problems arising from environmental scarcities. If they do not have the abilities, measured by ingenuity or finances, to overcome these problems, scarcities can overwhelm the country and further erode its ability to overcome the scarcity.

The rewriting of "how" and "why" conflicts occur has broad implications. First, while the traditional concepts of state and national borders and territory will remain important, they are also likely to mean relatively less in the near future. The Western idea of the "state," along with its role and identity, is an inflexible and artificial construct that is increasingly tenuous in an age of globalization.[35] Imposed upon the earth irrespective of geography, language, religion, or culture, the period of the nation-state may be ending. Instead, globalization of markets and commerce, transportation and communications, and the political order will dramatically reshape the globe and reduce the role and ability of the state in world affairs as flows of capital and information cross the globe, siphoning power from the state and placing it within the corporate boardroom. Although globalization has the potential to unite groups, it also comes with the potential to further separate the haves and have-nots as groups or countries are left behind.

Already, globalization has created winners and losers within the existing world order. Portions of the developing world have been left behind, victims of poor resources, poor government, or investments that have simply passed them by.[36] The gap between developed and developing countries, whether measured by investment, capital, level of education, income, or productivity, is widening and is expected to continue to grow. World Bank projections indicate that sub-Saharan Africa and other peripheral areas will be left even further behind in the coming decade.[37] Perhaps Homer-Dixon was too quick to dismiss the potential for conflict between the developed and developing world.[38] If pivotal countries such as China or India, countries that are economically strong but that may yet be hobbled by population growth and environmental scarcity, fall on the wrong side of the divide, the result will invariably be increased political instability at a global scale. Although the developing world may not have the military means and technology to fight the developed world, they have the population. In a world that promotes democracy, numbers count, and technology and advanced military abilities are not always sufficient. Vietnam, Afghanistan, and Somalia are lessons: if rebel fighters could defeat the Soviets in

Afghanistan, or ragtag, poorly trained, and poorly equipped fighters could defeat U.S. troops in Somalia, it can happen elsewhere and it could happen again.

Second, while large-scale conflict is possible, environmental scarcity will generate chronic, diffuse violence, with conflicts increasingly at local or sub-national scales. As a consequence of globalization, governments may be helpless in the face of environmental stress, escalating poverty, and disease and social friction. Conflict will instead reflect ideological or cultural/ethnic issues. For peripheral countries, which are already faced with few economic prospects, population growth, disease, and environmental stress, the future is bleak, and conflict will undoubtedly arise between groups over access to scarce resources. Weakened by globalization that has tended to bypass many of the poorest countries, the increased power of warlords, crime gangs, drug cartels, or guerrilla groups, future conflict may be "borderless," failing to conform to existing notions of interstate or intrastate conflict, with influence exerted not by a state (if they continue to exist), but instead by ethnic groups or clans.[39] At the extreme, territory will not be marked by traditional state borders but will instead be defined by shared ethnicity or some similar construct such as clan or tribe, resulting in a shifting map as power or allegiances change.[40] Maps may have to be redrawn without clear divisions between groups. While the breakup of the former Republic of Yugoslavia in the 1990s did not result in complete anarchy and new states (i.e., Slovenia, Croatia) emerged from the old, the region may yet disintegrate into intractable violence and a fractured series of mini- or city-states,[41] driven by centuries of ethnic and religious rivalries. Bosnia, Kosovo, and Macedonia remain tinderboxes of ethnic violence, with their governments having little control as rival groups struggle for power.[42] Worse off are portions of sub-Saharan Africa, a region described by Knox and Marston as "wild zones,"[43] where tribal warfare, banditry, or political insurrection has already meant that some countries, including Sierra Leone, Liberia, and Somalia, have lost control of their population or territory. Somalia, for example, is a country that technically no longer exists. After Somalia's military leader fled in 1991, the country disintegrated into a violent and chaotic struggle between clans and warlords who now control shifting areas. The resulting famine killed 400,000 people, with U.S. troops intervening in 1992 to provide humanitarian assistance. Just two years later, the U.S. troops had been withdrawn, having been forced out by low-level, low-tech guerrilla warfare.[44]

Central Asia, including Afghanistan and the former Soviet Republics of Uzbekistan and Tajikistan, is politically unstable and threatens to cleave along ethnic lines.[45] It is a patchwork region of ethnic groups that do not neatly correspond to existing state boundaries and who are groping for identity in a post-Soviet, post–cold war world. Again, the potential for conflict does not lie between states but between ethnic groups, although the battle between the Taliban and anti-Taliban forces was facilitated by the United States.[46] Already, Afghanistan is less and less a true state, split along ethnic lines and weakened by two decades of civil war, first with the former Soviet Union, later between rival ethnic groups, and most recently divided by religious ideals. The fundamentalist Taliban movement, which controlled much of the country including the capital prior to October 2001 when the United States and its allies intervened, is composed of ethnic Pathans, and has been heavily influenced by Islamic fundamentalists in Pakistan. Resisting the Taliban, the Northern Alliance is composed of ethnic Tajiks and Uzbeks, both of whom have been strengthened by ties to ethnic groups in Tajikistan and Uzbekistan, former Soviet Republics that are also politically unstable. Despite moves by the United Nations to craft a new government following the defeat of the Taliban, it is unclear whether any agreement on the form of government will hold, raising the possibility that Afghanistan could continue to disintegrate as a meaningful state, with a distinct possibility that the country could be partitioned along ethnic lines. Doing so would threaten Pakistan's territorial integrity because of its minority Pathan population, not to mention threatening to draw in other states.[47]

Third, internal conflict or the disintegration of most any country would most likely produce large flows of displaced persons and migrants, potentially leading toward a downward spiral that reinforces environmental degradation and social segmentation as discussed earlier. Over the past decade, the world has counted an increasing number of displaced persons, a number that can only be assumed to grow as new conflicts emerge and as old conflicts in Sierra Leone, Somalia, or Angola continue uninterrupted. Regardless, conflicts create humanitarian emergencies that frequently involve other countries in peacemaking or peacekeeping duties. The United Nations has frequently stepped into this role, but may find its reach limited or usurped in the future as regional militaries such as that being contemplated by the European Union step in to fill the role, or the United Nations lacks the funds to meet all the potential needs.[48] Despite calls for a full-time peacekeeping unit under the UN flag, member countries are either unwilling to fund the unit or are not prepared to convert traditional militaries (which are not designed for such missions) to permanent, peacekeeping roles, fearing that doing so would mean surrendering power to the United Nations.[49] Moreover, sub-national conflicts will limit the ability of humanitarian organizations such as UNHCR to provide humanitarian assistance, unless specifically requested to do so.

Finally, the developed world is not immune to the consequences of environmental scarcity. In the southwestern United States, states may increasingly compete for scarce water resources in order to sustain the region's population, which has placed a premium on water. In Texas, the state population is nearly twenty-one million, a number that is expected to double within fifty years. El Paso is already experiencing water shortages, and water in the Rio Grande River, which is a primary source of water in the area, is nearly all accounted for, with only a trickle reaching the ocean. In other areas, the Ogallala Aquifer, which stretches north from Texas to South Dakota, is overpumped and stressed.[50] Privatization of underground water rights and "water farms" in Texas, where surface water resources are public but underground water is private, allow water to be pumped without regard for neighbors—a form of resource capture. Indeed, Texas law recognizes it as the "rule of capture." Sold to the highest bidder (i.e., cities or industry), widespread public concerns have been generated that pumping water for profit could threaten supply in some areas, marginalizing those who cannot afford it and potentially disrupting or destroying irrigated agriculture in the Southwest,[51] reminiscent of the great Dust Bowl migration in the John Steinbeck's *The Grapes of Wrath*.[52] On a continental scale, the need to quench the thirst of America's southwestern states has several entrepreneurs and Canadian provinces, including Newfoundland, exploring the idea of bulk water shipments.[53] Home to some 9 percent of the world's fresh water supplies,[54] Canada is unsure where it stands on the idea of exporting bulk water, although it has refused (to date) to sell bulk water shipments, citing safeguards within the North American Free Trade Agreement (NAFTA). Under NAFTA, water is exempted from trade rules that require two-way trade in commodities. If Canada were to start exporting bulk water, however, free trade provisions would be invoked, requiring the trade to continue and restricting the ability of the government to limit its flow, allowing provincial and state governments to challenge the federal position.

The developed world also feels the impact of induced migration from developing countries. Much of the migration from rural Mexico or Haiti into the United States, Chinese immigration into North America, and migrations from North Africa into Europe can be attributed to resource scarcity in a broadly defined way. Many of these undocumented migrants are poor who are leaving behind economically or ecologically marginal areas. With few options in their homelands, they seek a new future elsewhere. For receiving countries, immigration alters the ethnic balance of the receiving country, with immigrants most likely settling in urban areas. As discussed in chapter 4, governments are forced to react, limiting immigration or quelling anti-immigrant sentiments within the larger society. Similarly, the disintegration or political/economic destabilization of states would surely have implications for regional security and trade patterns, and ultimately for the developed world. Countries and their governments may be precluded from effectively negotiating agreements or may be completely excluded by the international community.

NOTES

1. Robert D. Kaplan, "The Coming Anarchy," *Atlantic Monthly* (February 1994): 44–76. Much of Kaplan's article was based on Thomas Homer-Dixon's work, albeit reinterpreted in a very pessimistic and journalistic manner. While pointing out the potential for conflict, Homer-Dixon also provided an important "out" for humanity by pointing out potential interventions to alleviate scarcities and reduce the potential for conflict.

2. Much of the discussion in this chapter is derived from Thomas Homer-Dixon, *Environment, Scarcity, and Violence* (Princeton, N.J.: Princeton University Press, 1999). For additional insights into population and resource scarcity, see also Nicholas Polunin, *Population and Global Security* (Cambridge: Cambridge University Press, 1998).

3. Homer-Dixon, *Environment*.

4. Some authors refer to the generation of "environmental refugees." They include Jodi Jacobson, *Environmental Refugees: A Yardstick of Habitability*, Worldwatch Paper 86 (Wash-

ington, D.C.: Worldwatch Institute, 1988); Arthur H. Westing, "Environmental Refugees: A Growing Category of Displaced Persons," *Environmental Conservation* 19, no. 3 (1992): 201–207. However, the name implies that resource scarcity directly caused their displacement within a short time span, which is rarely the case. Instead, as the text discusses, the reasons for movement tend to be subtler, and environmental scarcity is more likely to produce migrants rather than refugees.

5. See Douglas Massey, Joaquin Arango, Graeme Hugo, Ali Kouaouci, Adela Pellegrino, and J. Edward Taylor, "Theories of International Migration: A Review and Appraisal," *Population and Development Review* 19, no. 3 (1993): 431–466; Douglas Massey, Joaquin Arango, Graeme Hugo, Ali Kouaouci, Adela Pellegrino and J. Edward Taylor, "An Evaluation of International Migration Theory: The North American Case," *Population and Development Review* 20, no. 4 (1994): 699–752.

6. Indonesia and Chiapas, Mexico, provide alternate examples of how these processes operate to produce conflict.

7. The amount of land per capita within Egypt is considered to be below a level suitable for sustainability of food production. See Homer-Dixon, *Environment*. I refrain from reporting the amount of land per capita as many authors do, since these measures tend to be relatively misleading owing to inequalities in the distribution of land and resources.

8. Roger W. Stump, *Boundaries of Faith* (Lanham, Md.: Rowman & Littlefield, 2000).

9. Martin Ira Glassner, *Political Geography,* 2nd edition (New York: John Wiley, 1996).

10. Homer-Dixon, *Environment*.

11. In addition, other significant factors, including Iraq's claim to Kuwait based upon the former Ottoman Empire and access to the Persian Gulf, were used to "justify" the invasion.

12. Clayton Jones, "Paradise Islands or an Asian Powder Keg," *Christian Science Monitor,* 1 December 1993, 14; Daniel Yergin, "Oil: The Strategic Prize," in *The Gulf War Reader,* eds. Micah L. Sifry and Christopher Serf (New York: Times Books, 1991).

13. In fact, Homer-Dixon was interested solely in the role of renewable resources as generators of conflict. It should be noted, however, that states will be just as eager to capture scarce nonrenewable resources through a variety of means, including military options.

14. Alanna Mitchell, "The World's 'Single Biggest Threat,' " *Globe and Mail,* 4 June 2001, 8–9(A).

15. Ismail Serageldin, "Earth Faces Water Crisis," *Press Release,* 6 August 1995 (Washington, D.C.: World Bank).

16. Terje Tvedt, "The Struggle for Water in the Middle East," *Canadian Journal of Development Studies* 13, no. 1 (1992): 13–33. Egypt ultimately backed away from its offer to provide Israel with water from the Nile, realizing its own tenuous supply.

17. See John Kolars and William Mitchell, *The Euphrates River and the Southeast Anatolia Development Project* (Carbondale: Southern Illinois University Press, 1991); Nurit Kliot, *Water Resources and Conflict in the Middle East* (London: Routledge, 1994).

18. Patrick Laurence, "Pretoria Has Its Way in Lesotho," *Africa Report* 31, no. 2 (1986): 50–51.

19. Michael T. Coe and Jonathan A. Foley, "Human and Natural Impacts on the Water Resources of the Lake Chad Basin," *Journal of Geophysical Research* 106, no. D4 (2001): 3349–3356.

20. For a discussion of nationalism and its role in the present-day world, see John Hutchinson and Anthony D. Smith, *Nationalism* (Oxford: Oxford University Press, 1994).

21. Associated Press, "Macedonia to Ask for War Declaration," *New York Times,* 5 May 2001, 5(A); Reuters, "Macedonia Attacks Albanian Guerillas," *New York Times,* 9 May 2001, 4(A).

22. Sanjib Baruah, *India against Itself: Assam and the Politics of Nationality* (Philadelphia: University of Pennsylvania Press, 1999); Myron Weiner, *Sons of the Soil: Migration and Ethnic Conflict in India* (Delhi: Oxford University Press, 1978).

23. Inheritance practices result in the division of land into smaller plots with each generation. Water control institutions have also limited agricultural output.

24. Homer-Dixon, *Environment.*

25. Gary Hawes, "Theories of Peasant Revolution: A Critique and Contribution for the Philippines," *World Politics* 42, no. 2 (1990): 261–298; Gregg Jones, *Red Revolution: Inside the Philippine Guerrilla Movement* (Boulder, Colo.: Westview Press, 1989).

26. See, for example, Richard E. Bilsborrow, *Migration, Urbanization, and Development: New Directions and Issues* (New York: United Nations Population Fund and Kluwer Academic Publishers, 1998); Martin P. Brockerhoff, "An Urbanizing World," *Population Bulletin* 55, no. 3 (September 2000); Gavin W. Jones and Pravin M. Visaria, *Urbanization in Large Developing Countries: China, Indonesia, Brazil and India* (Oxford: Clarendon Press, 1997); Josef Gugler, *The Urban Transformation of the Developing World* (Oxford: Oxford University Press, 1996); Eugene Linden, "Megacities," *Time,* 11 January 1993, 28–38.

27. Brockerhoff, "An Urbanizing World."

28. S. Jay Olshansky, Bruce Carnes, Richard G. Rogers, and Len Smith, "Infection Diseases—New and Ancient Threats to World Health," *Population Bulletin* 52, no. 2 (July 1997).

29. John Walton and Charles Ragin, "Global and National Sources of Political Protest: Third World Responses to the Debt Crisis," *American Sociological Review* 55, no. 6 (1999): 876–890.

30. Arif Hasan, "Karachi and the Global Nature of Urban Violence," *Urban Age* 1, no. 4 (1993): 4–12; Farida Shaheed, "The Pathan-Mhuajir Conflicts, 1985–6: A National Perspective," in *Mirrors of Violence: Communities, Riots and Survivors in South Asia,* ed. Veena Das (New York: Oxford University Press, 1990): 205–223.

31. Historical insight into conflict and uprising in the Philippines can be found in: Richard Kessler, *Rebellion and Repression in the Philippines* (New Haven, Conn.: Yale University Press, 1989). For insight into some of the most recent uprisings, see Mark Landler, "Manila Moves Incite Talk of 'Dark Side of People Power,' " *New York Times,* 3 May 2001, 3(A); Mark Landler, " 'State of Rebellion' Declared after Siege at Manila Palace," *New York Times,* 2 May 2001, 1(A).

32. Roger W. Stump, *Boundaries of Faith* (Lanham, Md.: Rowman & Littlefield, 2000).

33. <http://www.worldbank.org/html/fpd/urban/> (9 May 2001). See also Arjan de Haan, "Livelihoods and Poverty: The Role of Migration—a Critical Review of the Migration Literature," *Journal of Development Studies* 36, no. 2 (2000): 1–23.

34. Jana Mason, *Shadow Plays: The Crisis of Refugees and IDPs in Indonesia* (Washington, D.C.: United States Committee for Refugees, 2001).

35. See Thomas M. Poulson, *Nations and States: A Geographic Background to World Affairs* (Englewood Cliffs, N.J.: Prentice Hall, 1995).

36. Paul Kennedy, *Preparing for the Twenty-First Century* (New York: Random House, 1993). An abridged version of this book can be found in Paul Kennedy, "Preparing for the 21st Century: Winners and Losers," *New York Review of Books,* 11 February 1993, 32–44.

37. World Bank, "Workers in an Integrating World," *World Development Report* (Washington, D.C.: World Bank, 1995).

38. Although the United States intervened, the conflict in Afghanistan is largely an outcome of the terrorist attacks on September 11, 2001, and cannot be described as a conflict between haves and have-nots or between the developed and developing world, despite its geographical focus (the Middle East) and its origins. Instead, it is a new form of war that is based on ethnic and religious differences, with the United States facilitating conflict between groups.

39. See, for example, Robert D. Kaplan, "Countries without Borders," *New York Times*, 23 October 1996, 8(A); Paul L. Knox and Sallie A. Marston, *Human Geography: Places and Regions in Global Context,* 2nd edition (Upper Saddle River, N.J.: Prentice Hall, 2001).

40. I hesitate to use "tribe" as a descriptor because of its negative connotations in North America. However, it still fits social constructs of Africa.

41. See, for example, Kenichi Ohmae, "The Rise of the Region State," *Foreign Affairs*, (Spring 1993): 78–87.

42. Steven L. Burg, "Why Yugoslavia Fell Apart," *Current History* (November 1993): 357–363. For a broader discussion of state disintegration, see Robert K. Schaeffer, *Severed States* (Lanham, Md.: Rowman & Littlefield, 1999).

43. Knox and Marston, *Human Geography.*

44. The United Nations also sent troops to Somalia in 1993. They were withdrawn in 1995 when they too were no longer able to effectively fulfill their role.

45. Boris Rumer and Eugene Rumer, "Who'll Stop the Next 'Yugoslavia'?" *World Monitor* 44 (November 1992): 36–42.

46. It is important to note that the conflict in Afghanistan is not one based upon resource scarcity, but one that has roots in ethnic (and religious) divisions.

47. During the initial campaign against the Taliban and al Qaida in Afghanistan, the Pakistani government was lukewarm to the involvement of America and the use of military force within the region, fearing its own hold on power given the high level of support for the Taliban within Pakistan. Later, as the Taliban and al Qaida were defeated, Pakistani support for the Taliban diminished.

48. The United States, for instance, has lagged in the payment of its United Nations dues.

49. Tad Daley, "Can the U.N. Stretch to Fit Its Future?" *Bulletin of the Atomic Scientists* (April 1992): 38–42; Michael T. Klare, "The New Challenges to Global Security," *Current History* (April 1993):155–161.

50. David E. Kromm, "Low Water in the American High Plains," *The World & I* (February 1992): 312–319.

51. Jim Yardley, "For Texas Now, Water and Not Oil Is Liquid Gold," *New York Times*, 16 April 2001, 2(C).

52. John Steinbeck, *The Grapes of Wrath* (New York: Penguin Press, 1993).

53. Mark MacKinnon and Campbell Clark, "Chretien Lands in Hot Water," *Globe and Mail*, 15 May 2001, 5(A).

54. Statistics Canada, *Canada Year Book 1988* (Ottawa: Minister of Supply and Services, 1987).

Conclusion

❧❦❧

Five Demographic Forces That Will Shape the World

With a population exceeding six billion and a growth rate of 1.3 percent allowing the world's population to double in just fifty-one years, the world's demographic situation is now more critical than ever before by almost any measure. In the preceding chapters, this book has explored the major demographic issues that the world now faces. It has discussed current knowledge and emerging themes and issues and how they are interrelated: how population affects resources and environmental degradation; how population growth may be related to conflict; the implications of low fertility and an aging society; the impact of HIV/AIDS; and fertility questions. Distilling these ideas down to their component parts, the five most compelling demographic forces that the world must still grapple with include population growth, population decline, the HIV/AIDS epidemic, international migration, and refugees and internally displaced persons.

POPULATION GROWTH

Despite declines in fertility rates and slowing population growth rates since the 1960s, the optimistic outlook that the population crisis has passed is premature. Instead, population growth will continue into the near future before leveling off later this century. The certainty of continued growth is grounded in three assumptions. First, improvements in life expectancy (reduced mortality) will contribute to population growth, as individuals survive longer and complete their reproductive years. Second, with a large proportion of the world's population less than reproductive age or just entering it, population momentum will ensure continued growth, regardless of the future fertility decisions of this group of young women. Third, fertility rates remain well above replacement in many regions of the world for the foreseeable future. Although it is reasonable to assume that fertility rates will decline further, the extent of the decline is uncertain, reflecting the complex personal, social, and economic environment that surrounds decisions regarding family size. Given the apparent "stickiness" of fertility rates in Egypt, Bangladesh, and Argentina, it cannot be assumed that all societies will eventually move to a situation where fertility rates will equal or be less than the replacement level.

With the majority of population growth occurring in the developing world, the greatest challenge may be in Africa, where fertility rates remain stubbornly high and there has been relatively little progress toward fertility transition. Moreover, it is unclear when a sustained reduction in fertility levels will occur and how far fertility will drop. Despite improvements, the structures that maintain high fertility, including high mortality, high infant mortality, gender inequality, and poor health care systems remain firmly in place. Various family planning programs have been implemented, but have met with limited success owing to insufficient funding (both domestically and internationally), inappropriate goals, or a population that was not yet ready to reduce fertility. More important, continued population growth poses deep problems for many African nations. Here, where governments are already fiscally strained, state institutions are weak, and health and educational systems are poor, the strain of population growth is already showing, as governments are unable to maintain investment in public infrastructure. Population growth, and ultimately the absolute size of the population, will continue to pose challenges to societies and their governments as they deal with growing scarcities of land and water, the provision of infrastructure, and the provision of social services including education and health care. The potential for conflict is strong as groups or states seek to capture resources.

POPULATION DECLINE

Paradoxically, the decline of fertility rates to below replacement levels in the developed world has meant population decline and aging. Linked to deep societal and economic changes including gender equity and rising consumer aspirations, low fertility (the average for the developed world is just 1.6) has reduced growth to just 0.1 percent per year in the developed world, meaning it will take 809 years to double under current conditions. For the developed world, slowing population growth or decline brings its own problems. In the game of democracy, shrinking populations are associated with declining international political influence and a feared loss of national identity, reflecting the concerns and realities of Quebec's francophone population or the difference in birthrates between Palestinians and Israeli Jews. Domestically, politics are likely to reflect the increasing political power of an aging population and their political agenda as low fertility rates increase the proportional size of the elderly population. Low fertility rates are expected to slow economic growth, and the large baby boom generation threatens to overwhelm medical and social security programs, the costs of which will consume an increasing portion of national budgets at the same time as the labor force and economically active population is shrinking.

Fearing the potential demographic and economic problems of low fertility, the developed world has searched for ways to diminish its impact. Several countries have promoted pronatalist policies including tax incentives, cash bonuses, and preferred access to day care. Most, including Quebec's pro-fertility incentives, have had only modest success. Alternatively, immigration can be used to support population growth, but it too engages thorny issues of national identity and ethnic relations. These issues are particularly relevant in Europe, which has experienced strong anti-immigrant sentiments in the past decade. Although Canada and the United States have been historically more receptive to immigration, with both countries billing themselves as "nations of immigrants," anti-immigrant sentiments have also appeared in legislation including welfare reform and Proposition 187, which may be indicative of emerging ethnic and national tensions.

THE HIV/AIDS EPIDEMIC

With a death toll of nearly twenty-two million individuals to date, and an additional 36.1 million infected, the human immunodeficiency virus (HIV), which causes AIDS, has created a global epidemic far more severe than anyone guessed just ten years ago. Now into its third decade, the HIV/AIDS epidemic is having a significant demographic impact in the developing world where 95 percent of cases are found, and the epidemic continues to grow. Haiti's prevalence rate, for example, is the highest national rate outside of sub-Saharan Africa. In the Russian Federation, more new cases were diagnosed in 2000 than in all previous years. Growth of the epidemic is also possible in Asia, where transmission is aided by high rates of injected-drug use, a known and significant transmission route. In sub-Saharan Africa, where the epidemic is most severe, adult prevalence rates approach 9 percent. In countries such as Botswana, Zimbabwe, and South Africa, this rate exceeds 20 percent and reaches as high as 35.8 percent in Botswana. In these and other countries in the region, death rates are higher, life expectancies have been reduced, population growth has slowed, and infant mortality rates have increased, reversing hard-won improvements in health that occurred in earlier decades. The economic implications of the epidemic are just as severe: reduced economic growth, lower productivity, loss of labor force members, and increased medical costs. Socially, the epidemic is responsible for a swelling number of orphans and personal fear and denial in countries where HIV/AIDS is still seen as a curse and may yet promote conflict as economic growth and institutions are eroded.

Some hope is visible. Reductions in infection rates in a handful of countries have recently been noted, but these examples remain rare. Likewise, the decision by the major drug companies to reduce drastically prices associated with antiretrovirals and to allow production of generic drugs is significant, meaning that millions who have until recently been denied treatment simply because they could not afford it will have new opportunities. While it is obviously far too early to ascertain what effect this decision will have, the decision offers the hope of long-term survival and a productive life, reducing the human and economic costs of the disease. Before the first drugs are distributed, however, governments and other groups must overcome problems associated with the distribution, financing, and compliance associated with any new programs. With the exception of Brazil, no other developing country has such a large-scale HIV/AIDS drug program. The application of new drug programs may be especially daunting in sub-Saharan Africa where the number of cases is greater and distribution is more difficult.

The developed world has obviously not been immune from the effect of HIV/ AIDS. First diagnosed in the United States in 1981, it was initially concentrated in the male homosexual and injected drug user communities. Adult prevalence rates have remained low (less than 1 percent), but it has seeped into the larger heterosexual community where it poses a greater risk. Able to marshal more resources to educate their populations and fund medical research into new anti-AIDS drugs, the developed world has seemingly controlled the epidemic, but vigilance cannot be reduced. The greater prevalence of the disease among African Americans and increased high-risk behavior and correspondingly higher infection rates among young gay men indicate the need for ongoing control efforts over both the short and long term.

INTERNATIONAL MIGRATION

Over the past hundred years, most states in the developed world have moved to control immigration, limiting the type of immigrant (i.e., family reunification and economic), origin, and overall number allowed entry. Despite their efforts through both legislation as well as active enforcement of borders, most countries have found it increasingly difficult to control the entry of immigrants, creating an immigration crisis reflective in what has been described as the "gap" between immigration control policies and their outcomes. The emerging reality is that governments are less able to control immigration now than fifteen or twenty years ago. Globalization and the increasing flow of labor and capital, the emergence of civil rights and liberalism, and the domestic need for inexpensive labor, which legitimized immigration flows, have contributed to this inability to control legal migration flows.

While not denying past immigration policies that were openly racist and exclusionary, both the United States and Canada have historically been receptive to immigration. South of the 49th parallel, this history may be in danger, illustrated by the fear of demographic "Balkanization," welfare reform, and the debate over Proposition 187 in California. Anti-immigrant sentiments are especially visible in Europe, coloring national political debates and economic opportunities. European countries have only recently shifted from being labor exporters to importers of labor, a shift that is difficult to digest. Yet, the demographic realities of low fertility and an aging population mean that European countries are faced with a crisis in their labor force. Increased immigration may be the only option to meet employment requirements, but it remains an option that carries significant political, social, and cultural problems since most Europeans continue to associate the foreign-born with unskilled work and unemployment. Most likely, Europe will ultimately need to address its new role as a receiver of immigrants. In addition, both North America and Europe are grappling with increasing flows of illegal immigrants, imposing burdens upon local service providers at the same time as illegals sustain the economy by working or low pay and in positions or conditions that few others are willing to tolerate.

It is increasingly apparent that there is relatively little room for states to maneuver with their immigration policies. Attempts to restrict immigration often end up increasing the foreign-born population through loopholes and "backdoor" immigration or illegal entry. Moving to overtly increase immigration flows would mean political suicide, particularly in Europe where political parties promoting reduced immigration are enjoying greater support. Reduced fertility coupled with economic globalization will mean that developed countries will become increasingly dependent upon foreign labor to fill job vacancies. At the same time, globalization and high fertility will produce a surplus labor force in the developing world. In other words, international migration into the developed world will continue. Restricting entry will not solve the problem, but only shift it to one of illegal immigration, as the demand for and the supply of labor will remain. The reality may create strange bedfellows as trade unions, who have traditionally resisted immigration, move to embrace immigration as one way of protecting their viability in the new world order.

REFUGEES AND INTERNALLY DISPLACED PERSONS

As the developed world grapples with legal and illegal immigration, refugees and internally displaced persons pose a significant humanitarian challenge around the globe. Already representing a population of over thirty-five million people, it is likely that the new millennium will witness a continued increase in the number of displaced persons. With the end of the cold war, the nature of conflict has changed from large-scale confrontations backed by superpowers to smaller, internal struggles. Population growth only compounds the problem, with new conflicts spurred by ideology, land, and scarce resources, ultimately leading to population displacement. The human and economic costs associated with displacement are incalculable. What is measurable is the size of the displaced population. While the actual number of refugees has declined over the preceding years, the number of internally displaced persons has increased. Uprooted but unable to leave their state, they are caught in civil war, criminalized by the state or other groups, and are typically not eligible for humanitarian assistance, posing additional challenges to the international relief community.

At the same time as the number of displaced people are increasing, states are moving to restrict entry, fearing the fiscal and social responsibilities mandated under the UN Convention, along with the political fallout as refugees clash with the native-born in the host country over ideology or ethnic differences. Even the developed world has become increasingly uneasy with large-scale refugee resettlement. Refugee policy in the United States has frequently been a tool of foreign policy. Moreover, while Canada and the United States have resettled refugees from a variety of origins, there is much more they could do, including increasing the number of refugees that are resettled each year and/or increasing financial assistance and support to agencies such as the UNHCR. Likewise, Europe has moved to close its borders to refugees. The actions of the developed countries have rippled around the world, with smaller and poorer states refusing to protect refugees.

In light of the events of September 11, 2001, and the terrorist attacks on America, it is likely that much of the developed world will revisit immigration and refugee policies, further restricting resettlement. Immigrants and refugees alike will be more carefully screened for security issues, operating under the fear that terrorists may be included in legal immigrant and refugee flows. Countries with more liberal policies, such as Canada, may be forced to place greater restrictions on the movement of individuals into the country. Doing so would probably mean some loss of Canadian sovereignty as Canada and the United States adopt common entry controls and strengthen perimeter control while making it easier to move between the two countries.

INTERACTIONS AND OTHER EFFECTS

Independently or together, these five main demographic forces will drive a series of related demographic processes that will shape the global environment in the decades to come. While the debate between neo-Malthusians, distributionists, and economic optimists drags on, the emerging consensus is that population growth slows economic growth. In the process, population growth may exacerbate land degradation and resource depletion, promote violence and conflict, and place pressure upon institutions and governments. In effect, there is a causal linkage between population growth, resource scarcity, social effects (i.e., migration, decreased agricultural, or economic output), and conflict. Clearly, population growth is not solely or directly responsible for resource scarcity. Likewise, resource scarcity is not the only factor contributing to violence, but both become underlying causes that cannot be discounted.

The not-so-trivial question is whether the world can support *and* sustain a population of six billion, along with an acceptable standard of living, let alone a future population of seven to ten billion. It is unclear, for example, whether there is sufficient capacity to continue to feed the world's population. While some commentators have recently proclaimed that the crisis of feeding the world's population has passed, others point to declining agricultural production, loss of cropland, increasing demand, and a decreased likelihood of new crop strains that will significantly increase yield as indications that just the opposite is true—that sufficient food supplies are not yet ensured. The situation becomes more problematic if the goal of increasing the average standard of living for the world's population is targeted, which is a laudable and just goal. Doing so increases consumption by moving people "up the food chain" and increasing the consumption (both quantity and variety) of food. The same logic must also be extended to economic growth. Can a growing population that increasingly demands more resources be sustained in the future? Again, the emerging consensus indicates that population growth reduces economic growth by increasing poverty and underemployment, weakens investment in human and physical assets such as education or other institutions, decreases ingenuity, and degrades resources. Worse, rapid population growth and poor economic growth appear to be self-reinforcing, making it exceedingly difficult for countries to pull themselves out of this spiral given the lack of well-developed institutions in many of the poorest countries.

The effects of population growth will be clearly visible in urban areas as rural to urban migration and natural increase in the developing world fuels the growth of large urban areas. Megacities of ten million or more will not be uncommon. While there is, as of yet, no apparent limit to the size of cities before they produce more negative externalities and costs than benefits, and we can point to the ability of cities such as New York, London, or Tokyo to function, these cities are in the developed world. The majority of the new megacities will be in the developing world, and it is unknown whether the cities themselves or the states will be able to provide sufficient infrastructure and employment opportunities for the burgeoning urban population. More likely, the new megacities will be characterized by high levels of poverty, poor living conditions, poor health, and few employment opportunities: the very type of conditions that can easily breed resentment and insurrection.

In the developing world, population growth and increasing consumption of resources will create scarcities through degradation or depletion of resources. Even renewable resources are now recognized as being finite in situations where population growth exceeds the ability of the resource to regenerate or where the resource has been degraded through pollution or other means. Caused by resource scarcities, social effects, including decreased agricultural output, decreased economic output, migration, social segmentation, and the disruption of social institutions, will create an environment that promotes conflict. Complicating matters is that conflict related to resource scarcity will occur with greater severity, speed, and scale in the future, meaning that effects will not be confined to a spatially small area. Conflict will not be felt within the developing world alone. Instead, the consequences of resource scarcity and population growth will ripple across the globe, promoting (among other things) international migration and the displacement of populations, the destabilization of governments, threaten trade relations, or economic development, and induce further environmental degradation. The effects of global warming, which are not yet fully understood, remain a wild card but are likely to exacerbate resource scarcities.

Globalization of the world's economy may be touted as a new economic order that can lift nations out of poverty. Yet, it is more likely that large regions of the world will be left out of the new international arrangement. Africa, the Indian subcontinent, and parts of Asia will become marginalized, characterized by lack of international investment, poor leadership, and few resources. Unless the developed world is prepared to extend aid and investment, reversing the declines in international aid noted over the past few years, these regions are likely to be pulled into a reinforcing cycle of violence and poverty. Conflict will not take the traditional form of state versus state for control of territory. Instead, conflict will be sub-national and defined by local resource scarcities, with group identity conflicts focusing upon ideology or ethnic differences—a "we" versus "them" mentality—or local insurgencies and civil strife. Like Somalia, Angola, and Sierra Leone, countries may, for all intents and purposes, cease to exist, defined only by the traditional Western notion of maps and boundaries but torn apart by local conflicts. National governments will cease to operate, replaced by warlords and private armies controlling shifting territories.

Preventing or decreasing the likelihood of resource scarcity and conflict is a challenge. Education, better employment opportunities, and gender equity for women will go a long way toward reducing fertility levels and the risk of HIV infection. To meet these needs, however, there is a need for increased investment in the developing world, something that the developed world has backed away from in recent years. Economic optimists would simply point to the need for functioning institutions and free markets to encourage investment, innovation, and substitution. Yet, the value or applicability of such concepts is frequently limited. Globalization offers little hope for the least developed countries. If anything, countries may only hope to be suppliers of inexpensive labor, earning income from remitted funds. Input substitution does not necessarily offer alternatives, and ingenuity itself is not a costless or ubiquitous good. Instead, it is fostered where resources such as time and capital are abundant, a tangible concept that may be missing from many poor developing countries and that cannot simply be provided through free markets or democracy. Likewise, markets and other institutions including the government may be poorly developed and/or corrupt, short-circuiting any attempt to invest in a society. If the ability to generate ingenuity is missing, countries may be faced with an ingenuity gap, and their ability to respond to resource limits or other threats will be diminished.

Surely, the world of child six billion is jeopardized.

Glossary of Key Terms and Acronyms

age pyramid Representation of a population distributed by age and sex.

aging An increase in the proportion of population in older age groups.

AIDS Acquired immune deficiency syndrome.

alien A person resident in a country who has not acquired citizenship by naturalization.

anti-natalist Positions or policies that discourages fertility and childbearing. Disincentives may include reduced child benefits or other, more repressive options.

antiretroviral drugs The class of drugs that are used to suppress the HIV virus, inhibiting the development of HIV into AIDS. Also know as the triple cocktail.

assimilation The economic, social, cultural, and political processes of adjustment undergone by immigrants, transforming them to citizens of the host country.

asylees Individuals forced out of their country of origin who are seeking refuge in the new country in which they are living.

asylum The act of seeking refuge and protection within a country.

baby boom The rise in birthrates in many Western countries between 1946 and 1964.

boomsters *See* economic optimists.

Border Safety Initiative (BSI) Run by the Border Patrol to educate would-be illegal entrants of the dangers of crossing the border and to provide medical assistance if needed.

Bracero Mexicans who were admitted legally into the United States for labor between 1942 and 1964.

carrying capacity The maximum number of organisms that can be theoretically supported in a habitat for an indefinite period of time, dependent upon the social, economic, political, and natural systems, as well as upon the level of consumption.

cohort A group of individuals born in the same calendar year or group of years.

demographic transition (DTT) Process whereby a country moves from high to low mortality and fertility rates, accompanied by rapid population growth.

dependency ratio The ratio of people of dependent rate (0–14, 65 +) to the economically active population (15–64). The young dependency ratio is the ratio of those aged 0–14 to those in the labor force and is usually associated with rapid population growth.

developed world Following UN classification, the developed world includes Europe, North America, Australia, Japan, and New Zealand.

197

developing world   All countries and regions outside the developed world.

doomsters   *See* neo-Malthusian.

doubling time   The number of years it will take the population to double assuming a constant annual rate of natural increase.

ecological marginalization   The forced movement of individuals or groups into ecologically marginal areas.

economic optimists   Individuals who believe that population growth stimulates economic development.

emigrant   A person who leaves one country to settle in another.

epidemiological transition   Shifts in health and disease patterns as mortality moves from high to low rates.

FAO   United Nations Food and Agricultural Organization.

fecundity   The physiological ability of individuals to have children.

fertility   The ability to reproduce.

fertility transition   The shift from high to low fertility.

green revolution   The improvement in agricultural productivity in the 1940s and 1950s associated with new high-yield crop strains, fertilizer, irrigation, and pesticide use.

gross domestic product (GDP)   The total value of goods and services produced by a country, not including international trade.

HIV   Human immunodeficiency virus, the virus that causes AIDS.

illegal immigrants   Individuals entering a country without proper documentation or approval.

immigrant   A person who moves into a country where she or he is not a native to take up residence.

immigration gap   The differential between states immigration policy and their outcomes.

infant mortality rate (IMR)   Annual number of deaths of infants under one year of age per 1,000 live births.

INS   U.S. Immigration and Naturalization Service.

interdiction   The policy of stopping would-be refugee or asylee claimants before they enter a country and initiate the refugee claim process.

internally displaced persons (IDPs)   Individuals or groups forced to flee homes to escape armed conflict, violence, human rights abuses, or disaster. Unlike refugees, they are not residing outside their country of nationality.

IRB   Immigration Review Board (Canada).

IRCA   Immigration Reform and Control Act (1986).

least-developed countries   Defined by the United Nations, those countries where per capita income is less than $900(U.S.) per year.

life expectancy   The average number of years beyond age *x* an individual can expect to live under current mortality levels. Usually expressed as life expectancy at birth.

life span   The longest period over which a person may live.

Malthusian   References the writings of Malthus, who believed that population grows geometrically but food supplies grow linearly, resulting in an inadequate food supply and population decline through famine, disease, or war (positive checks).

maquiladoras   Assembly plants employing Mexicans where parts are shipped to Mexico, assembled, and then reexported for sale, allowing companies to benefit from the cheaper labor.

Marxist   Adherents to the theories of Karl Marx.

megacity   A city with a population over ten million.

morbidity   Sickness.

mortality (death) rate   The annual number of deaths per 1,000 people. This rate is not age-standardized to account for differential death rates across age groups.

natural increase   The birthrate minus the death rate, indicating the annual rate of population growth (without migration) expressed as a percentage.

neo-Malthusian   An individual who accepts Malthusian principles, but who believes birth control methods can be used to reduce population growth.

non-refoulement   The basic tenant of the United Nations Convention that prohibits states from returning a refugee against their will to their origin.

nonrenewable resources   Finite resources such as oil or minerals.

population explosion   The rapid growth of the world's population.

population momentum   The potential for population growth that is present within the age/sex structure of a population, even if fertility rates were to drop to replacement level.

prevalence   The number of people in a population sick with a disease at a particular time, regardless of when the illness began.

pro-natalist   Policies that favor a high birthrate. May include tax incentives, cash bonuses for number of children born in excess of the first, day care provision, or parental leaves.

Proposition 187   Legislation in California meant to limit access to education and health services among illegal immigrants, passed by a majority in 1994 but ruled unconstitutional by a federal judge.

quota system   U.S. immigration policies that imposed quotas on the number of immigrants based on a defined base (northern European) population.

refugees   Individuals or groups who, owing to well-founded fear of being persecuted for reasons of race, religion, nationality, or membership in a particular group or political opinion, is outside the country of nationality and is unable or unwilling to return.

renewable resources   Resources such as water, cropland, or forests that can be used indefinitely provided a threshold of sustainability is not exceeded.

replacement fertility   The fertility rate (2.1) that is required to exactly replace a generation, accounting for death before completion of childbearing years.

resource capture   Control of a scarce resource through the use of legislation or other means.

rivalrous resources   Resources that are used by one or more actors, which reduces its availability for others.

social segmentation   The division of society, typically along class, ethnic, or religious lines.

STDs   Sexually transmitted diseases, including syphilis, gonorrhea, or HIV.

sustainable development   The level of human activity that meets the needs of the present without compromising the ability of future generations to meet their own needs, subject to constraints.

total fertility rate (TFR)   The average number of children a woman would have assuming that current age-specific birthrates remain constant through the childbearing years (ages 15–49).

transmigrant   Refers to the relocation of individuals from one area to another. Typically refers to the relocation of Indonesians out of Java to other regions, or Russians to other republics or satellite states.

UNAIDS   United Nations program on HIV/AIDS.

UNHCR   United Nations High Commission on Refugees.

UNICEF   United Nations Children's Fund.

urban   Describes a concentration of people in space whose livelihoods are organized around nonagricultural activities. Different countries will define the urban threshold differently.

USAID   United States Agency for International Development.

USCR   United States Committee for Refugees.

WHO   World Health Organization.

xenophobia   The fear of strangers.

Selected Bibliography

Amery, Hussein, and Aaron T. Wolf, eds. *Water in the Middle East: A Geography of Conflict.* Austin: University of Texas Press, 2000.

Beaujot, Roderic. *Population Change in Canada.* Toronto: McClelland Stewart, 1991.

Bender, William, and Margaret Smith. "Population, Food, and Nutrition." *Population Bulletin* 51, no. 4 (February 1997).

Brockerhoff, Martin P. "An Urbanizing World." *Population Bulletin* 55, no. 3 (September 2000).

Brown, Lester R. *Who Will Feed China? Wake-up Call for a Small Planet.* New York: W. W. Norton, 1995.

Cincotta, Richard P., and Robert Engelman. *Economies and Rapid Change: The Influence of Population Growth.* Washington, D.C.: Population Action International, 1997.

Clark, William A. V. *The California Cauldron.* New York: Guilford Press, 1998.

Cornelius, Wayne A., Philip L. Martin, and James F. Hollifield, eds. *Controlling Immigration: A Global Perspective.* Stanford, Calif.: Stanford University Press, 1994.

Ehrlich, Paul. *The Population Bomb.* New York: Ballantine Books, 1968.

Ehrlich, Paul, Anne Ehrlich, and Gretchen Daily. "Food Security, Population, and Environment." *Population and Development Review,* 19, no. 1 (1993): 1–32.

Espenshade, Thomas J., ed. *Keys to Successful Immigration.* Washington, D.C.: Urban Institute Press, 1997.

Ferrie, Joseph P. *Yankeys Now: Immigrants in the Antebellum U.S., 1840–1860.* New York: Oxford University Press, 1999.

Foot, David. *Boom, Bust and Echo.* Toronto: McFarlane, Walters & Ross, 1996.

Gelbard, Alene, Carl Haub, and Mary M. Kent. "World Population Beyond Six Billion." *Population Bulletin* 54, no. 1 (March 1999).

Gimpel, James. *Separate Destinations.* Ann Arbor: University of Michigan Press, 1999.

Goliber, Thomas J. "Population and Reproductive Health in Sub-Saharan Africa." *Population Bulletin* 52, no. 4 (December 1997).

Gould, Peter. *The Slow Plague: A Geography of the AIDS Pandemic.* Oxford: Blackwell, 1993.

Hirschman, Charles, Philip Kasinitz, and Josh DeWind, eds. *The Handbook of International Migration.* New York: Russell Sage Foundation, 1999.

Homer-Dixon, Thomas F. *Environment, Scarcity, and Violence.* Princeton, N.J.: Princeton University Press, 1999.

Homer-Dixon, Thomas F. *The Ingenuity Gap.* Toronto: Alfred Knopf, 2000.

Isbister, John. *The Immigrant Debate: Remaking America.* West Hartford, Conn.: Kumarian Press, 1996.

Kaplan, Robert D. "The Coming Anarchy." *Atlantic Monthly* (February 1994): 44–76.

Livernash, Robert, and Eric Rodenburg. "Population Change, Resources, and the Environment." *Population Bulletin* 53, no. 1 (March 1998).

Lutz, Wolfgang, ed. *The Future World Population.* London: Earthscan, 1996.

Malthus, Thomas Robert. *An Essay on the Principle of Population.* Reprinted in Scott W. Menard and Elizabeth W. Moen, eds. *Perspectives on Population.* New York: Oxford University Press, 1987.

Massey, Douglas, Joaquin Arango, Graeme Hugo, Ali Kouaouci, Adela Pellegrino, and J. Edward Taylor. "An Evaluation of International Migration Theory: The North American Case." *Population and Development Review* 20, no. 4 (1994): 699–752.

Massey, Douglas, Joaquin Arango, Graeme Hugo, Ali Kouaouci, Adela Pellegrino, and J. Edward Taylor. "Theories of International Migration: A Review and Appraisal." *Population and Development Review* 19, no. 3 (1993): 431–466.

McFalls, Joseph A., Jr. "Population: A Lively Introduction." *Population Bulletin* 53, no. 3 (September 1998).

Menard, Scott W., and Elizabeth W. Moen, eds. *Perspectives on Population.* New York: Oxford University Press, 1987.

Moore, Eric G., and Mark W. Rosenberg. *Growing Old in Canada.* Ottawa: Statistics Canada Cat. No. 96-321-MPE, 1997.

Olshansky, S. Jay, Bruce Carnes, Richard G. Rogers, and Len Smith. "Infectious Diseases—New and Ancient Threats to World Health." *Population Bulletin* 52, no. 2 (July 1997).

Owram, Doug. *Born at the Right Time: A History of the Baby Boom Generation.* Toronto: University of Toronto Press, 1996.

Plane, David, and Peter Rogerson. *The Geographical Analysis of Population.* New York: Wiley, 1994.

Polunin, Nicholas, ed. *Population and Global Security.* Cambridge: Cambridge University Press, 1998.

Portes, Alejendro, ed. *The Economic Sociology of Immigration.* New York: Russell Sage, 1995.

Portes, Alejendro, and Reuben Rumbaut. *Immigrant America: A Portrait.* Berkeley: University of California Press, 1996.

Simmons, Alan B., ed. *International Migration, Refugee Flows and Human Rights in North America.* New York: Center for Migration Studies, 1996.

Simon, Julian L. *Population and Development in Poor Countries.* Princeton, N.J.: Princeton University Press, 1992.

Simon, Julian L. *The Ultimate Resource.* Princeton, N.J.: Princeton University Press, 1981.

Smith, James P., and Barry Edmonston. *The New Americans.* Washington, D.C.: National Academy Press, 1997.

Watts, Julie R. *An Unconventional Brotherhood: Union Support for Liberalized Immigration in Europe.* La Jolla, Calif.: Center for Comparative Immigration Studies, 2000.

Weeks, John R. *Population: An Introduction to Concepts and Issues,* 7th edition. Belmont, Calif.: Wadsworth, 1999.

Zelinsky, Wilbur. *A Prologue to Population Geography.* Englewood Cliffs, N.J.: Prentice Hall, 1966.

Population Web Sites

Web sites are current as of May 2001. Note that Web sites are not necessarily permanent, so the correct address cannot be guaranteed.

GENERAL

http://www.iom.int
The International Organization for Migration is an intergovernmental organization that promotes migration for economic development, understanding migration issues, and humanitarian programs to assist refugees and displaced persons. Among its publications, IOM publishes *International Migration*, a quarterly peer-reviewed journal.

http://www.demographics.com
American Demographics is a monthly journal that presents demographic issues in an easy to digest manner.

http://www.cis.org
The Center for Immigration Studies (CIS) is a nonprofit organization devoted to research and policy analysis of immigration. Site includes recent numbers, background reports, and news, reflecting a diversity of issues and opinions.

http://www.popnet.org
This is a comprehensive directory of population related Web sites, including governments, international organizations, NGOs, and universities.

http://www.populationinstitute.org
The Population Institute provides information about population issues and promotes programs to reduce population growth.

http://www.zpg.org
Zero Population Growth (ZPG) is an organization that has actively promoted a reduction in population growth. Web site includes many topical links and information as well.

http://www.npg.org
The Negative Population Growth Council (NPG) is an organization that educates the American public on the dangers of population growth. The Web site provides alternate perspectives to population issues, advocating a smaller U.S. population and reduced immigration levels in order to create a sustainable future. The site provides links to like-minded organizations, such as Californians for a Sustainable Population, along with mainstream agencies or groups such as the INS.

http://www.refugees.org
The United States Committee for Refugees is a private organization that helps refugees. The site includes information on refugees and asylees throughout the world.

http://www.acf.dhhs.gov/programs/orr
This is the Web site of the U.S. Office of Refugee Resettlement (ORR), providing information on refugee legislation and resettlement within the United States.

http://www.popcouncil.org
The Population Council is an international, nonprofit organization devoted to bio-medical, social science, and public health research related to population issues.

SOURCES OF DEMOGRAPHIC STATISTICS

http://www.aecf.org
The Annie E. Casey Foundation has worked to promote the opportunities and environments of children and families in the United States. The Web site includes demographic data on children within the United States.

http://www.prb.org
This is the Web site for the Population Reference Bureau (PRF). It is a very useful site for both lay and academic interests in population issues, including data, information, publications, and other services relating to the United States and the world.

http://www.ciesin.org
The Center for International Earth Science Information Network (CIESIN) at Columbia University is a nonprofit, nongovernmental organization. The Web site includes detailed demographic information, including interactive mapping from the

U.S. Census Bureau, census data, and other data sources including environmental information and social indicators of development.

http://www.census.gov
The Web site for the U.S. Census Bureau. It includes information on the 2000 census, and downloadable information and data on the United States at a variety of spatial scales. It also contains links to international statistical agencies, such as Mexico or Germany.

http://www.census.gov/ipc/www/idbsum.html
The International Data Base (IDB) section of the U.S. Census Bureau is particularly useful for demographic and socioeconomic data on other countries.

http://www.statcan.ca/start.html
This is Statistics Canada Web site. Language is available in both French and English, with information and data that are downloadable.

http://www.cic.gc.ca
Citizenship and Immigration Canada (CIC) maintains information on immigrant and refugee arrivals in Canada, along with current policy information and some historical records.

http://www.ins.usdoj.gov/graphics/index.htm
The U.S. Immigration and Naturalization Service (INS) Web site includes links to Border Patrol and Management, recent statistics on the origin of immigrants, immigrant class, and the settlement of arrivals.

http://www.usaid.gov/
The U.S. Agency for International Development (USAID) Web site includes information on current programs, missions, and statistics.

http://www.cdc.gov
The Centers for Disease Control and Prevention (CDC) is the lead federal agency for prevention and promotion of health. The site includes information on health topics and statistics for the United States and the world.

http://www.cdc.gov/nchs
The CDC provides links to the National Center for Health Statistics (NCHS), which includes vital statistics, including data on births, deaths, and marriages. Links to state health units are provided.

http://www.cihi.com
The Center for International Health (CIHI) provides a database funded by USAID. The data focus on the developing world and includes health profiles of countries.

http://www.ameristat.org
Ameristat is developed with the Population Reference Bureau and the Social Science Data Analysis Network, providing summaries of the U.S. population.

http://www.worldbank.org
The World Bank has a large amount of comparative world data, including population.

UNITED NATIONS

http://www.unaids.org
This Web site is operated by the United Nations and other health groups. It contains up-to-date information on the HIV/AIDS epidemic and links to other sources.

http://www.who.int
The Web site for the World Health Organization (WHO), which monitors world health. Includes updates on world health and health initiatives, and the Statistical Information Systems provides access to the latest world health data.

http://www.unhcr.ch
Web site for the United Nations High Commission on Refugees. Includes publications and up-to-date statistics.

http://www.un.org/unrwa/
This is the Web site of the UN Relief and Works Agency for Palestine Refugees in the Near East.

http://www.unicef.org
United Nations Children's Fund Web site. Includes resources and statistics related to children's health.

http://www.undp.org/popin
The United Nations Population Information Network coordinates population information activities at a variety of scales. Resources include links to other sites as well as an electronic library.

http://www.un.org/esa/population/
The United Nations runs its own population division, responsible for providing current data on population and development.

http://www.unfpa.org
The United Nations Population Fund helps developing countries with population issues. The UNFPA Web site includes information on recent programs.

http://www.fao.org
The Food and Agricultural Organization of the United Nations Web site includes information and statistics relating to nutrition, food, forestry, fisheries, and agriculture.

BIBLIOGRAPHIC DATABASES

http://www.popindex.princeton.edu
Organized through the Population Association of America (PAA), the Population Index is an important reference tool for all literature relating to population studies, providing citations and abstracts from four hundred journals in population and related fields.

http://canada.metropolis.net
This is the Web site for the Canadian Metropolis project, linking researchers at institutions across Canada and throughout the world that focus on immigration issues. The site has a digital library of papers produced by its associates, many of which are downloadable free of charge.

http://www.jhuccp.org/popline
Billed as the world's largest online bibliographic database on population issues, POPLINE is based at Johns Hopkins University.

ACADEMIC SITES

http://www.ccis-ucsd.org
Center for Comparative Immigration Studies at the University of California, San Diego, includes information on programs, research areas, and links to other sites.

http://wwww.ercomer.org
The European Research Center on Migration and Ethnic Relations (ERCOMER) is a European research center that focuses upon comparative migration analysis, ethnic relations, and ethnic conflict, based at Utrecht University in the Netherlands.

http://opr.princeton.edu/resources
The Office of Population Research Web site offers links to demographic centers throughout the world, as well as links to other statistical resources and organizations.

Index

About the Author

K. Bruce Newbold is an associate professor of geography at McMaster University, where he received his Ph.D. in 1994. He taught at the University of Illinois Urbana–Champaign between 1994 and 2000. His research interests include internal migration, immigration, and population health. With over twenty-five refereed journal articles or book chapters published, he has received funding from the Canadian Institutes of Health Research, Social Science and Humanities Research Council of Canada, the National Science Foundation, and the Social Science Research Council.